Fair and Equitable Treatment and the Fabric of General Principles

Fulvio Maria Palombino

Fair and Equitable Treatment and the Fabric of General Principles

ASSER PRESS

Springer

Fulvio Maria Palombino
Department of Law
University of Naples Federico II
Naples
Italy

ISBN 978-94-6265-209-5 ISBN 978-94-6265-210-1 (eBook)
https://doi.org/10.1007/978-94-6265-210-1

Library of Congress Control Number: 2017947459

Published by T.M.C. ASSER PRESS, The Hague, The Netherlands www.asserpress.nl
Produced and distributed for T.M.C. ASSER PRESS by Springer-Verlag Berlin Heidelberg

Translation of the Italian edition 'Il tratttamento giusto ed equo degli investimenti stranieri' by Fulvio Maria Palombino, © Il Mulino, Bologna, 2012

Printed on acid-free paper

This T.M.C. ASSER PRESS imprint is published by Springer Nature
The registered company is Springer-Verlag GmbH Germany
The registered company address is: Heidelberger Platz 3, 14197 Berlin, Germany

To my mentor and friend
Massimo Iovane

Foreword

With the slow proliferation of disputes referring to arbitration pursuant to international investment agreements (IIAs), we have also witnessed a significant increase of reliance on the guarantee of 'fair and equitable treatment' (FET). Less than half a century ago, in 1970, the International Court of Justice, in delivering its judgment in *Barcelona Traction*, noted the surprisingly slow evolution of investment law.[1] Despite the increased use of FET by disputing parties, the very content of the protection remains unclear. The language used in IIAs is laconic and as a result Delphic.[2] Some excellent books have already been published on the topic.[3] IIAs refer to an—allegedly non-contingent—minimum standard of protection in accordance with international law and often refer expressly to FET in relation to full protection and security.

Arbitral tribunals under different IIAs have tried to identify the significance of FET and several categories have been created including denial of justice, as well as regulatory and administrative actions that may trigger FET protection (and that covers, *inter alia*, legitimate expectations and review of due process in administrative decision-making). In addition, tribunals have also looked at factors that may justify actions of the State.

It seems that in the early stages of investment arbitration FET has become a very elastic term, perhaps with the view to being able to 'accommodate' all cases of breach of IIAs that would not qualify as expropriation; yet the pendulum has swung the other way so that now it appears that in new multilateral agreements, such as CETA or indeed the drafts of TTIP, FET has become narrower. The UNCTAD Investment Policy Hub records that FET was invoked in 384 cases but it was found to exist in only 98 cases, i.e. only in one in four cases.[4]

---

[1] *Barcelona Traction* (*Belgium v. Spain*), Judgment of 5 February 1970, para 89.

[2] McLachlan, Shore and Weiniger 2017, para 7.02.

[3] *See*, for example, Paparinskis 2012; Kläger 2011.

[4] *See* http://investmentpolicyhub.unctad.org/ISDS/FilterByBreaches.

This new monograph by Prof. Fulvio Maria Palombino addresses FET from the perspective of the fabric of general principles of international law and as such it is insightful and highly original. In Chap. 1, he explores the origins of the obligation of States to accord FET and characterizes FET as an expression of 'normative equity'. Against this background, in Chap. 2 Palombino discusses FET as an autonomous and non-contingent custom or a self-standing treaty clause; he argues that FET has penetrated into the fabric of general international law by means of general principles of law. In Chap. 3, he addresses denial of justice and due process (procedural fairness in administrative proceedings) and how they have shaped FET. In Chap. 4, the focus is on the nature and scope of legitimate expectations as an embodiment of a general principle of international law and as an element of FET. Chapter 5 is dedicated to the contours of proportionality as an element of FET; it is powerfully argued that proportionality is a general principle of international law with its own foundation in the international legal order and at the same time it is a balancing process (as an FET element) which allows us to look into the circumstances and related business risks before a full assessment regarding FET can be made. In Chap. 6, the steering role of case law is appraised as undoubtedly case law has shaped the notion and content of FET. In the concluding chapter, the author draws the conclusions together to highlight the normative basis and minimum reach of FET and places the topic and the findings in the context of the broader debate about fragmentation of international law. The positive note is that FET as a non-contingent and autonomous standard may have a unique unifying effect.

I have very much enjoyed reading the book. Most certainly it has not been an easy task. The research is extensive and multi-faceted, but the writing is accessible and the structure and overall approach is innovative. Palombino takes a complex academic topic, presents it in its full academic dimension but also frames it in useful practical terms: the discussion and findings are useful for both the scholar and practitioner of international law. Palombino succeeds in his endeavour and has produced a concise but rich monograph. I would expect the book to become a classic on the important topic of FET.

London, UK
March 2017

Prof. Loukas Mistelis

References

Kläger R (2011) 'Fair and Equitable' Treatment in International Investment Law. Cambridge University Press, Cambridge

McLachlan C, Shore L, Weiniger M (2017) International Investment Arbitration, 2nd edn. Oxford University Press, Oxford

Paparinskis M (2012) The International Minimum Standard and Fair and Equitable Treatment. Oxford University Press, Oxford

Acknowledgements

This monograph is dedicated to my mentor Prof. Massimo Iovane, who has always supported me over the years, with the affection and patience of a true father; I will never be sufficiently grateful for that. Several people helped me finalize this work, both with their advice and strong moral assistance. In that respect, I am especially indebted to my friends and colleagues Daniele Amoroso and Giovanni Zarra, who read the whole book and provided their invaluable expertise on a daily basis; Tobia Cantelmo, Francesca Capone, Loris Marotti, Piefrancesco Rossi, Fulvia Staiano and Alessandro Stiano constantly supported me during the different stages of this research. I am thankful to my friend Tony Ryan for language editing the book. Prof. Loukas Mistelis gave me the honour of writing the foreword. I would also like to acknowledge the tremendous support received from the team at T.M.C. Asser Press, in particular Philip van Tongeren (the now retired publisher, who believed in this project from the very start), Frank Bakker (the current publisher), Kiki van Gurp (the production coordinator) and Antoinette Wessels (marketing coordinator). Last but not least, and as always, I thank my beloved parents and the three women of my life, my wife Lucia and my two daughters Laura and Chiara, without whose tacit but indispensable encouragement this book would not exist.

The present book is a largely revised version of my previous book, published in Italian, 'Il tratttamento giusto ed equo degli investimenti stranieri', Il Mulino, Bologna, 2012.

Contents

Abbreviations

BIT	Bilateral Investment Treaty
BRA	Boston Redevelopment Authority
CARICOM	Caribbean Community
CCJ	Caribbean Court of Justice
CETA	Comprehensive Economic and Trade Agreement between Canada and the European Union
CJEU	Court of Justice of the European Union
DSU	Dispute Settlement Understanding
ECHR	European Convention on Human Rights
ECtHR	European Court of Human Rights
EIB	Estonian Innovation Bank
EU	European Union
FDI	Foreign Direct Investment
FET	Fair and Equitable Treatment
FPS	Full Protection and Security
GATT	General Agreement on Tariffs and Trade
ICC	International Criminal Court
ICJ	International Court of Justice
ICSID	International Centre for the Settlement of Investment Disputes
ICTY	International Criminal Tribunal for the Former Yugoslavia
IIL	Institute of International Law
ILC	International Law Commission
ILO	International Labour Organization
ITO	International Trade Organization
LPA	Lafayette Place Associates
MAI	Multilateral Agreement on Investment
MFN	Most-Favoured-Nation
NAFTA	North America Free Trade Agreement
NDT	Non-Discrimination Treatment
NT	National Treatment

OECD	Organization for Economic Cooperation and Development
PCIJ	Permanent Court of International Justice
RTC	Revised Treaty of Chaguaramas
SJC	Supreme Judicial Court
TEU	Treaty on European Union
TFEU	Treaty on the Functioning of the European Union
UN	United Nations
UNCITRAL	United Nations Commission on International Trade Law
UNCTAD	United Nations Conference on Trade and Development
VCLT	Vienna Convention on the Law of Treaties
WTO	World Trade Organization

Chapter 1
Introduction

Contents

Abstract This chapter inquires into the origins of the obligation to accord fair and equitable treatment to foreign investments and traces it back to a manifestation of 'normative equity', i.e. a kind of equity which affects the substantive content of the law going so far as to be subsumed under specific treaty provisions. Moving on from the increasing importance of this obligation in investor-State arbitration, the second part of the chapter provides an outline of the book.

Keywords Fairness · Equity · Treaties · Arbitration · Investment · Sleeping Beauty

1.1 Introduction

Currently, the obligation to provide fair and equitable treatment (FET) to foreign investments occurs in the great majority of international investment agreements and proves to be the most invoked standards in investor-State arbitration. Hence, it is no overstatement to describe this standard as the *Grundnorm* of international investment law. Yet both its meaning and normative basis continue to be shrouded in ambiguity and to inspire, as a consequence, a considerable number of interpretations by legal writers. This author's intention is precisely to unravel such ambiguity as far as possible and offer the reader an interpretive key to moving through an

F.M. Palombino, *Fair and Equitable Treatment and the Fabric of General Principles*, https://doi.org/10.1007/978-94-6265-210-1_1

increasingly large and tricky judicial practice. On these premises, this chapter aims first to explore the FET origins. It is alleged that FET is nothing but a manifestation of 'normative equity', that is to say a kind of equity which affects the substantive content of the law going so far as to be subsumed under specific treaty provisions. Accordingly, the origins of the standard can be traced back to the various treaties (especially those of Friendship, Commerce and Navigation drawn up by the United States) and draft conventions (like the 1959 Draft Convention on Investment Abroad) adopted since the late 1940s and which—as the precursors to modern investment treaties—enclosed FET either as a general clause aimed at guaranteeing foreign capital with an equitable treatment or as a 'security valve' against any State actions disregarding international obligations. The second part of the chapter, as well as illustrating in brief why both current treaty practice and case law prevent the FET content from being identified once and for all, provides an outline of the book.

1.2 FET as a Manifestation of 'Normative Equity'

As a matter of law, the meaning of the term 'equity' radically changes depending on the national legal system to be evaluated.[1] In England, as well as in those common law countries following a closely comparable model,[2] equity is a veritable source of law which courts shall apply in the same vein as the law in the strict sense.[3] In civil law countries, inversely, the supposed unity of the legal order prevents a system of equity, seen as independent of one of *strictum jus*, from coming into force.[4] Nonetheless, equity remains a benchmark of substantive justice which is intended

[1] For an in-depth analysis of the concept of equity in a comparative law perspective, *see* Newman 1973; Falcon y Tella 2008.

[2] *See* Falcon y Tella 2008, pp. 70 et seq.

[3] In England, originally, the possibility for a court of law to apply both *strictum jus* and equity was foreclosed. Equity constituted a separate branch of law and a special kind of justice, administered by special courts, i.e. courts having jurisdiction only when the available remedy was incomplete or inadequate. *See* Story 1846, p. 32: 'Perhaps the most general, if not the most precise, description of a Court of Equity, in the English and American sense, is, that it has jurisdiction in cases of rights, recognised and protected by the municipal jurisprudence, where a plain, adequate, and complete remedy cannot be had in the Courts of Common Law'. Following the reform of the Judicature Acts of 1873–1875, the system of equity and that of strict law have been unified as well as the judge competent to apply them (the High Court of Justice). The separation between the two systems, however, continues to affect the structure of the English legal order; accordingly, the distinction among legal rights and equitable rights, as well as among their respective holders, is still of relevance. Cf. Sereni 1956.

[4] Razi 1963, p. 24, observes as follows: 'In Anglo-American jurisprudence, Equity, like almost everything else, has been the creation of the courts. In the civil law world the natural habitat of equity has been the Academy. It is in the universities that for more than two thousand years the word has been handled by philosophers and writers who, needless to say, have seldom defined it in identical terms.'

to influence the activity of both the judge, who relies on equitable considerations with a view to accommodating the specific circumstances of a given case (the so-called 'equity *infra legem*'),[5] and the legislator, who might make the same considerations explicit in a law provision (the so-called 'normative equity').[6]

A notion of equity fairly akin to the latter may be found in the international legal order,[7] where it both allows the judge to choose the interpretation of the law 'that appears [...] to be closest to the requirements of justice'[8] (i.e. a power which is inherent in the function of the judge and does not need any special consent of the

---

[5] One well-defined manifestation of this idea can be found in the case law of the Italian Supreme Court. *See*, for instance, the judgment of 11 November 1991, No. 12014 (United Sections). Of course, a different hypothesis arises where a specific norm vests the judge with the power to decide *ex aequo et bono*. That is the case of Articles 113 and 114 of the Italian Code of Civil Procedure. According to these Articles, when passing the decision, the judge is required to apply the rules of law, unless the applicable law gives him the power to decide *ex aequo et bono*.

[6] As far as the Italian Civil Code is concerned, suffice it to think about all those provisions resorting to equity as a criterion of judgment. One example is Article 1226, which states as follows: 'If the precise amount of the damage to the plaintiff resulting from a breach of the defendant's obligation cannot be proved, the judge shall fix the amount according to equitable principles'. For further examples of normative equity (or equity in legislation), *see* Razi 1963, pp. 27 et seq. This same author, also in light of what has been observed thus far, concludes by observing that 'as in many other confrontations, the civil law and the common-law systems, despite their different outlook, meet. Their organization is different and so are their techniques. But below the surface the two systems are nourished by the same sources and ideals. To think about it, it could not have been otherwise since, after all, both systems are but two aspects of the same civilization' (p. 44).

[7] A conclusion of this kind may be inferred from the resolution adopted in 1937 by the Institute of International Law (Annuaire de l'Institut de Droit International 38:271) and concerning 'La compétence du juge international en équité'; its Article 1 states that 'l'équité est normalement inhérente à une saine application du droit, et que le juge international, aussi bien que le juge interne, est, de par sa tâche même, appelé à tenir compte dans la mesure compatible avec le respect du droit'. In this matter, *see ex multis* Degan 1970; Franck 1995 and Higgins 1994, pp. 219 et seq.

[8] *Continental Shelf (Tunisia v. Libya)*, Judgment of 24 February 1982, para 71. Once again, we refer to equity *infra legem*, on the proviso that both equity *praeter legem* (i.e. aimed at filling lacunae) and equity *contra legem* (i.e. a mitigation of the applicable law for extra-legal reasons) are not allowed in the international legal order. This kind of equity is increasingly relied on in commercial arbitration. This on the assumption, rightly identified by Youssef 2012, that '[t]he classic regulation of arbitration, rooted in the requirements of consent and writing, is indifferent to economic realities (such as the factual or legal nexus among independent legal entities or among autonomous instruments) and insensitive to considerations of equity which *may arise in specific cases*. It is based on consent as a *per se* rule. The classic simple yes-no question, whether a written arbitration agreement exists, is often simplistic and fails to reflect the true complexity of the jurisdictional issues which arise in complex arbitrations' (p. 106); accordingly, 'when courts and tribunals exclude the normal application of arbitration law to accommodate economic realities or to take into account considerations that are deemed more *just*, the 'equities' of the case are not mere *dicta*. They constitute an integral part of the *legal* reasoning of courts and tribunals' (p. 109).

parties to the dispute)[9] and affects the substantive content of the law, going so far as to be subsumed under specific treaty or soft law provisions. This is a circumstance occurring in a large number of fields (such as the law of the sea[10] and environmental law),[11] but it is primarily within international economic law that equity fulfils a very specific task: recourse to equitable considerations for regulatory reasons served *different* purposes therein, which epitomised *different* ways of conceiving the economic relationships among States.

In detail, at least until the end of the Cold War, equity echoed a clear need for redistributive justice, acting as a tool by which to reconcile the conflicting economic interests between industrialized and developing countries. Following this logic, equity mainly represented the rationale behind the so-called 'New International Economic Order',[12] thereby coming into consideration in the three well-known declarations of principles, adopted by the General Assembly of the United Nations (the Declaration on the Establishment of a New International Economic Order, the Action Plan on Establishment of a New International Economic Order, and lastly

[9] Of course, a different hypothesis arises where the statute of a certain international tribunal expressly recognizes the judge's power to decide *ex aequo et bono*: 'the [judge] can take such a decision only on condition that Parties agree [...], and the [judge] is then free form the strict application of legal rules in order to bring about an appropriate settlement. The task of the [judge] in the present case is quite different: it is bound to apply equitable principles as part of international law, and to balance up the various considerations which it regards as relevant in order to produce an equitable result. While it is clear that no rigid rules exist as to the exact weight to be attached to each element in the case, this is very far from being an exercise of discretion or conciliation; nor it is an operation of distributive justice.' (*Continental Shelf (Tunisia v. Libya)*, Judgment of 24 February 1982, para 71). One example is Article 38 of the Statute of the International Court of Justice. Paragraph 2 of that Article states that, if the parties agree thereto, the Court may decide a case *ex aequo et bono*. A similar provision may be found in Article 42, para 3, of the 1965 Washington Convention, setting up the International Centre for the Settlement of Investment Disputes: 'The provisions of paras (1) and (2) shall not prejudice the power of the tribunal to decide a dispute *ex aequo et bono* if the parties so agree'. In this last regard, *see* Schreuer 1996. As to the power to decide *ex aequo et bono* in international commercial arbitration, *see* Mistelis 2011, p. 221.

[10] One example can be found in the preamble of the 1982 UN Convention on the Law of the Sea: 'Recognizing the desirability of establishing through this Convention, with due regard for the sovereignty of all States, a legal order for the seas and oceans which [...] will promote [...] the equitable and efficient utilization of their resources'.

[11] Article 5 of the 1997 Convention on the Law of the Non-Navigational Uses of International Watercourses, proves quite revealing. In line with this Article, '1. Watercourse States shall in their respective territories utilize an international watercourse in an equitable and reasonable manner. In particular, an international watercourse shall be used and developed by watercourse States with a view to attaining optimal and sustainable utilization thereof and benefits therefrom, taking into account the interests of the watercourse States concerned, consistent with adequate protection of the watercourse. 2. Watercourse States shall participate in the use, development and protection of an international watercourse in an equitable and reasonable manner. Such participation includes both the right to utilize the watercourse and the duty to cooperate in the protection and development thereof, as provided in the present Convention.'

[12] Giuliano 1978; Janis 1983; Francioni 2007; Sacerdoti 2011.

the Charter of Economic Rights and Duties of States).[13] Each of these declarations contains significant references to equity, hence manifesting the wish to establish and maintain a just and equitable economic order,[14] i.e. an order where: first, there is little room for the freedom of trade and private initiative; and second, States exercise without outer limits their 'permanent sovereignty over natural resources and economic activities', in such a way as to render foreign investments economically disadvantageous. Moreover, precisely on the basis of the principle of permanent sovereignty, developing countries have challenged the rule of 'prompt, adequate and effective' compensation (in case of large-scale expropriations of foreign goods)[15] and claimed the exclusive jurisdiction of their own domestic courts in foreign investment disputes.[16]

---

[13] GA Res. No. 3201, XXIX, 1974; GA Res. No. 3202, XXIX, 1974; GA Res. No. 3281, XXIX, 1974.

[14] *See*, for instance, the preamble of the Charter of Economic Rights and Duties of States: '*The General Assembly, Recalling* that the United Nations Conference on Trade and Development [UNCTAD], in its resolution 45 (III) of 18 May 1972, stressed the urgency to establish generally accepted norms to govern international economic relations systematically and recognized that it is not feasible to establish a just order and a stable world as long as a charter to protect the rights of all countries, and in particular the developing States, is not formulated [...] *Noting* that, in its resolution 3082 (XXVIII) of 6 December 1973, it reaffirmed its conviction of the urgent need to establish or improve norms of universal application for the development of international economic relations on a just and equitable basis and urged the Working Group on the Charter of Economic Rights and Duties of States to complete, as the first step in the codification and development of the matter, the elaboration of a final draft Charter of Economic Rights and Duties of States, to be considered and approved by the General Assembly at its twenty-ninth session; *Bearing in mind* the spirit and terms of its resolutions 3201 (S-VI) and 3202 (S-VI) of 1 May 1974, containing, respectively, the Declaration and the Programme of Action on the Establishment of a New International Economic Order, which underlined the vital importance of the Charter to be adopted by the General Assembly at its twenty-ninth session and stressed the fact that the Charter shall constitute an effective instrument towards the establishment of a new system of international economic relations based on equity, sovereign equality and interdependence of the interests of developed and developing countries'.

[15] On this point, *see infra* para 1.3.

[16] This is nothing but a manifestation of the well-known 'Calvo doctrine' (from the name of an Argentinian lawyer, who in the 20th Century developed a concept of domestic nationalism to be applied to foreign investments), i.e. the idea that foreign investors are, or ought to be, required to settle their foreign investment disputes exclusively in the courts of the host State, thereby limiting recourse to diplomatic protection. Accordingly, all disputes arising from an investment in a given State would be dealt with by the judicial system of that State. Notably, the doctrine was generally accepted by Latin American States, many constitutions of which contain an express reference to it. For example, under Article 27 of the Mexican Constitution, 'the State may grant the same right to foreigners, provided they agree before the Ministry of Foreign Relations to consider themselves as nationals in respect to such property, and bind themselves not to invoke the protection of their governments in matters relating thereto; under penalty, in case of non-compliance with this agreement, of forfeiture of the property acquired to the Nation.' In contrast to most other writers on the subject, who paid little attention to the Calvo doctrine partly due to its failure to enter the corpus of customary international law, Wanyama (2015, pp. 78 et seq.) has recently regarded this doctrine as an essential means by which to protect weaker States against developed nations.

The same notion of equity (as a criterion of distributive justice) also affected rules governing the most-favoured-nation (MFN) clause in the context of the 1947 General Agreement on Tariffs and Trade (GATT), i.e. the most important agreement relating to international trade in goods signed in the immediate aftermath of the Second World War. According to this clause, each State party undertakes to extend the benefits granted to a product from any country in a certain field (for example, in customs matters) to all other contracting parties. For reasons of distributive justice, however, this rule does not equally apply to all. This is due to the so-called 'Enabling clause', introduced by the GATT Contracting Parties' decision of 1979[17] and whose aim is to allow developed countries to accord more favourable and non-reciprocal treatment in favour of developing countries.

With the end of the Cold War, the aforementioned idea of equity exhausted much of its driving force. The prospect of a New International Economic Order was in fact completely replaced by a neo-liberal economic system, in respect of which the World Trade Organization (WTO) represented and still represents the natural embodiment. What underpins this system, therefore, is no longer the need to 'ensure […] to developing countries preferential treatment, reflecting the duality of the rules applicable, respectively, to the North-North and North-South trade, but the concern, at least in principle, to promote integration on the same level […] of both industrialized and developing countries.'[18]

The effects of the new system ended up being reflected also in the international protection of foreign investments, and particularly in the wording of the numerous bilateral investment treaties (BITs) concluded in its wake. This was also 'a reaction to the *Barcelona Traction* case, in which diplomatic protection by the country of shareholders was denied,'[19] and to the invitation by the International Court of Justice (ICJ) to make use, as far as possible, of treaties directly involving the private investor and the State hosting the investment.[20]

[17] Decision of 28 November 1979 (L/4903). Para 1 of this decision states that the Contracting Parties 'may accord differential and more favourable treatment to developing countries, without according such treatment to other contracting parties'. Cf. Yusuf 1980; Stamberger 2003; Bartels 2010; Choi and Won-Mog 2012.

[18] Picone and Ligustro 2002, p. 460 (author's translation).

[19] Sacerdoti 2008, p. 133.

[20] *Barcelona Traction (Belgium v. Spain)*, Judgment of 5 February 1970. Para 90 of the judgment, in particular, states as follows: '[T]he protection of shareholders requires that recourse be had to treaty stipulations and special agreements directly concluded between the private investor and the State in which the investment is placed. States ever more frequently provide for such protection, in both bilateral and multilateral relations, either by means of special instruments or within the framework of wider economic arrangements. Indeed, whether in the form of multilateral or bilateral treaties between States, or in that of agreements between States and companies, there has since the Second World War been considerable development in the protection of foreign investments. The instruments in question contain provisions as to jurisdiction and procedure in case of disputes concerning the treatment of investing companies by the States in which they invest capital. Sometimes companies are themselves vested with a direct right to defend their interests against States through prescribed procedures.'

Unsurprisingly, while the treaties under review are still far from altogether liberal regarding investments' admission and continue to enhance the host State's powers in this matter,[21] the same treaties have introduced general standards of protection which are both irrespective of national law and clearly aimed at fostering foreign capital's entry.[22] Reference is especially made to the general acceptance of the standard of FET and the contextual provision of several fora for solving disputes dealing with it. Of course, as Francesco Francioni rightly observes, by means of this standard equity 'has penetrated into the fabric of positive law governing the treatment of foreign investments.'[23]

This argumentation, in our view, proves persuasive, but some commentators seem to disagree. Assuming that FET is the best example of a standard about which 'many purport to know much, but without much basis for doing so' (*sic!*), Todd Weiler contends that, from a functional perspective, the roots of this standard are to be found in the 'justiciability clauses' that supported the work of a large number of mixed claims commissions during the 19th and early 20th Centuries, i.e. treaty provisions vesting the arbitrator 'with authority to decide matters in a way that would conform with international law but that would nonetheless also be just and equitable.'[24] To put it differently, for Weiler FET, in its original dimension, worked

---

[21] Mauro 2003, p. 143. *See* also Mauro 2011, pp. 638 et seq.

[22] Mauro 2003, p. 122. *See* also Atik 1995, p. 26, holding as follows: 'A universal right of establishment would be difficult for the multilateral community to swallow in the near term. FDI [Foreign Direct Investment] is visibly more intrusive on national sensitivities than is the presence of imported goods. Indeed, the fact that Open FDI was not realized within U.S./Canada FTA or NAFTA, particularly with respect to U.S.-sourced FDI in Canada and Mexico, demonstrates this. There is likely no nation so economically and physically secure that it could tolerate high levels of FDI without considerable discomfort. Yet Open FDI embodied in a right of establishment may be useful as an aspiration and a guide to interpretation, being the strongest expression of commitment to a liberal economic order.'

[23] Francioni 2007, p. 8. The same author observes that '[a]s a consequence of this movement it is safe to say that today the fair and equitable standards of treatment of foreign economic interest are part of the customary body of international law and play a fundamental role in the protection of foreign investors together with the traditional rules of non-discrimination [...], public interest justification for a taking of foreign property, and the requirement of just compensation in the event of expropriation.' Still, the normative basis of FET is far from being clear. On this point, *see infra* Chap. 2.

[24] Weiler 2013, p. 185. Reference is made, for example, to Article 7 of the Convention Relative to the Establishment of an International Prize Court (2 AJIL Spec. Supp. 179, 1989) states as follows: 'If a question of law to be decided is covered by a treaty in force between the belligerent captor and a power which is itself or whose subject or citizen is a party to the proceedings, the court is governed by the provisions of the said treaty. In the absence of such provisions, the court shall give judgment *in accordance with the general principles of justice and equity*' (emphasis added).

as a canon of adjudication, that is to say a parameter in the hands of the judge, by which a given dispute could be solved. Yet a claim of this kind might be questioned conceptually. Indeed, the idea whereby States are required to treat foreign investments fairly and equitably alludes first to a canon of conduct that is intended to inspire the State behaviour. From this angle, it is not implausible that the word 'equitable' as it appears in the FET standard is a manifestation of 'normative equity', at least as the latter has been understood in continental legal thinking.[25]

1.3 FET and Treaty Practice

Standards of investments protection have been only partially defined in their content and, to this end, the impact of customary law is far from being decisive. Of course, one of the fields putatively covered by this source of law refers to standards of compensation; and indeed, in case of expropriation of foreign owned property, there is little dispute about awarding compensation. Nonetheless, as to the modalities by which the latter must be given, judicial practice is anything but certain. A number of lawyers are in favour of a 'prompt, adequate and effective' compensation, the formula (mentioned earlier) used by the U.S. Secretary of State, Cordell Hull, on the occasion of the Mexican expropriations[26] and enshrined in an

---

[25] Even if articulated in different and more cautious terms, a similar opinion may be found in UNCTAD 1999, p. 213: '[S]ome guidance on the plain meaning of fair and equitable treatment may be derived from international law in general. Specifically, although international law has had opportunities to incorporate concepts of equity from particular national legal systems, this has not been done. By extension, while maxims of equity from specific legal systems could add certainty to the concept of fair and equitable treatment, this approach should be avoided. At the same time, however, it is possible to identify certain forms of behaviour that appear to be contrary to fairness and equity in most legal systems and to extrapolate from this the type of State action that may be inconsistent with fair and equitable treatment, using the plain meaning approach. Thus, for instance, if a State acts fraudulently or in bad faith, or capriciously and wilfully discriminates against a foreign investor, or deprives an investor of acquired rights in a manner that leads to the unjust enrichment of the State, then there is at least a *prima facie* case for arguing that the fair and equitable standard has been violated.' In quoting this report, Weiler 2013, p. 184, footnote 529, is fairly critical, by observing that it 'first suggested that 'equity' in the FET standard may have been an intended reference to English equity, only to caution against the desirability of such an approach thereinafter.' Still, as may be inferred from Sect. 1.2 above, such a criticism echoes a misunderstanding, since no reference to English equity had been made.

[26] Reference is made to the famous note drafted by Hull on 22 August 1938, which states as follows: 'No government is entitled to expropriate [foreign] private property, for whatever purpose, without provision for prompt, adequate and effective payment thereof' (text in AJIL (1938), Supll., p. 192).

increasing number of treaties.[27] However, while some tribunals rely on this formula and regard it as a manifestation of general international law,[28] others (also in the wake of its being challenged by several developing countries as well as some industrialized countries) contend that the 'appropriate' compensation should be determined in a flexible way, i.e. by an inquiry into all the circumstances relevant to the particular case.[29] The same doubts about the role of custom in matter of investments may be expressed even more strongly with regard to other rules, which, at the most, may be seen as 'candidates for customary status.'[30] The foregoing remarks have produced the twofold effect of preventing the adoption of a multilateral treaty ruling the matter in its entirety and, at the same time, of calling for the conclusion of several agreements on a bilateral or regional basis (such as the 1992 North American Free Trade Agreement—NAFTA).[31]

Now, one of the key issues which has emerged in arbitral practice regards the content of at least one of the general standards of treatment, i.e. the

[27] For example, Article 13 of the 1991 Energy Charter Treaty states as follows: '(1) Investments of Investors of a Contracting Party in the Area of any other Contracting Party shall not be nationalized, expropriated or subjected to a measure or measures having effect equivalent to nationalization or expropriation (hereinafter referred to as 'Expropriation') except where such Expropriation is: 1. (a) for a purpose which is in the public interest; 2. (b) not discriminatory; 3. (c) carried out under due process of law; and 4. (d) accompanied by the payment of *prompt, adequate and effective compensation*. Such compensation shall amount to the fair market value of the Investment expropriated at the time immediately before the Expropriation or impending Expropriation became known in such a way as to affect the value of the Investment (hereinafter referred to as the 'Valuation Date'). Such fair market value shall at the request of the Investor be expressed in a Freely Convertible Currency on the basis of the market rate of exchange existing for that currency on the Valuation Date. Compensation shall also include interest at a commercial rate established on a market basis from the date of Expropriation until the date of payment.' Emphasis added.

[28] For example, in *Amco I v. the Republic of Indonesia*, Award of 20 November 1984 (in «International Legal Materials», 24, 1985, pp. 1022 et seq., pp. 1036–1037), the tribunal held that 'the full compensation of prejudice, by awarding to the injured party, the *damnum emergens* and the *lucrum cessans* is a principle common to the main systems of municipal law, and therefore, a general principle of law which may be considered as a source of international law. Moreover, the same principle has been applied, in cases of breach of contract by a State (and in particular, in cases of breach of a concession contract which are closely comparable to an unjustified revocation of a licence to invest) by a number of authoritative international judicial decisions and awards.'

[29] A similar position was taken in 1994 by the Iran-US Claims Tribunal in *Shahin Shaine Ebrahimi et al.* (Final Award of 12 October 1994, Iran-US Claims Tribunal Reports, 30, 1994, pp. 174 et seq.). According to this decision, indeed, customary international law would limit itself to favouring an 'appropriate compensation' standard, whose aim is to ensure that 'the amount of compensation is determined in a flexible manner, that is, taking into account the specific circumstances of each case. The prevalence of the 'appropriate' compensation standard does not imply [hence] that the compensation *quantum* should be always 'less than full' or always 'partial'. Cf. Levy 1995; Cassese 2005.

[30] This expression is to be credited to D'Aspremont 2012, p. 34.

[31] On international customary investment law, *see* more generally D'Aspremont 2012.

above-mentioned FET standard,[32] a legal term of art (in the words of Judge Rosalyn Higgins) well known in the field of overseas investment protection.[33] At first blush, FET is the principle[34] according to which a State hosting foreign investments is required to treat them fairly and equitably, with due regard to all the surrounding circumstances. This is a principle widely provided for in treaties related to foreign investments, but whose precise normative content is far from clear and still difficult to predict, above all if one wishes to grasp its maximum scope; not only do relevant agreements in the matter usually contain rules which are both general and vague in nature, but also arbitral decisions on the application and interpretation of the principle only partially lend themselves to one single interpretation.

The first reference to FET can be traced back to the 1948 Havana Charter, establishing the International Trade Organization (ITO). Article 11, para 2, of the Charter provided in fact that foreign investments should be ensured 'just and equitable treatment.' Likewise at the regional level, Article 22 of 1948 Economic Agreement of Bogotá (adopted at the end of the Ninth International Conference of American States) bound the contracting parties to guarantee foreign capital with an equitable treatment. Still, because of a number of unresolved issues, neither of these two agreements came into force. In the same period, FET began to be included in bilateral agreements. We refer to the various treaties of Friendship, Commerce and Navigation—the precursors to modern investment treaties—drawn up by the United States since the early 1950s and which, sometimes, enclosed FET as a 'security valve' against any State actions that violated internationally accepted norms.[35] Against the same background, but with a view to adopting a multilateral agreement on investment, one must consider two draft conventions that, while never being

[32] Just to mention the monographs on this subject matter, *see* Tudor 2008; Kläger 2011; Diehl 2012; Weiler 2013; Dumberry 2013; Paparinskis 2013; Schernbeck 2013.

[33] Separate opinion of Judge Higgins, *Oil Platforms case* (*Iran v. US*), ICJ Reports 1996, pp. 803 et seq., p. 853.

[34] The word 'principle', at the moment, is not used in technical terms. For the debate concerning the legal nature of FET, see *infra* Chap. 2.

[35] One example may be found in the Treaty of Amity and Economic Relations (Ethiopia–U.S.), 7 September 1951. Article VIII(1) of that treaty states as follows: 'Each High Contracting Party shall at all times accord fair and equitable treatment to nationals and companies of the other Contracting Party, and to their property and enterprises; shall refrain from applying unreasonable or discriminatory measures that would impair their legally acquired rights and interests; and shall assure that their lawful contractual rights are afforded effective means of enforcement, in conformity with the applicable laws.' The Friendship, Commerce and Navigation Treaty between Ireland and the U.S., 21 January 1950, is equally revealing. Article V provides: 'Each Party shall at all times accord equitable treatment to the capital of nationals and companies of the other Party. Neither Party shall take unreasonable or discriminatory measures that would impair the legally acquired rights and interests of nationals and companies of the other Party in the enterprises which they established or in the capital, skills, arts or technology which they have supplied. Neither Party shall deny appropriate opportunities and facilities for the investment of capital by nationals and companies of the other Party; nor shall either Party unreasonably impede nationals and companies of the other Party from obtaining on equitable terms the capital, skills and technology it needs for its economic development.' Regarding these agreements, *see* Vandevelde 1988.

opened for signature, had a wide impact on subsequent treaty practice. The first one is the 1959 Draft Convention on Investment Abroad, developed under the leadership of Herman Abs (Director-General of the Deutsche Bank) and Lord Shawcross (UK Attorney General): in the terms of its Article 1 'each Party shall at all times ensure fair and equitable treatment to the property of the nationals of the other Parties […]'.[36] Later on, in the wake of the foregoing initiative, the Organization for Economic Cooperation and Development (OECD) produced its own Draft Convention on the Protection of Foreign Property, which included an FET clause (1967).[37]

In a nutshell, the first references to FET are fairly lacking, since all the treaties and draft conventions analysed thus far do not define the content of the standard, but limit themselves to recommending or prescribing its observance. In this regard, the opinion has been offered by Todd Weiler, whereby the malleable nature of the term 'equitable', rather than being a mere coincidence, was intended in principle to cover both *sovereign equality of host States* and *substantive fairness for the alien*:

> '[E]quitable' had the special quality of meaning different things to different people. On the [one] hand, the term could be construed as a manifestation of the principle of sovereign equality, as in the equitable treatment of nations. In this sense, 'equity' fostered a generous construction of the freedom required for the State to exercise its police powers in the (allegedly) best interests of its people. On the other hand, 'equity' could be construed as being a manifestation of the principles of good faith and/or equality of treatment – from the perspective of the alien.[38]

Such a remark might explain why FET encompasses a principle like proportionality (i.e. the principle by means of which a balance between the interests of the host State and those of the investor is required),[39] but does not actually contribute to shedding light on the FET content. On the other hand, modern investment treaties (the overwhelming majority of which are bilateral) do not prove of much more assistance.

First, FET clauses continue to be both vague and general in content, so much so that one commentator, besides Weiler, regards also current FET provisions as *intentionally vague*, but for a different reason: they would be 'designed to give

---

[36] Abs and Shawcross 1960. In the words of Schwarzerberger 1960, p. 152, the language used in Article 1 of the Draft Convention embodies 'an imaginative attempt to combine the minimum standard with standard of equitable treatment.' *See* also Shawcross 1961.

[37] In more detail, Article 1(a) states that: 'Each Party shall at all times ensure fair and equitable treatment to the property of national of the other Parties'. Notably, the idea of a multilateral agreement providing a general protection of FET was not abandoned in the decades later, but all the efforts in this sense ended up collapsing. Reference is made to the Draft United Nations Code of Conduct on Transnational Corporations, the last negotiating text of which dates back to 1983, (the text may be found in UNCTC, The United Nations Code of Conduct on Transnational Corporations, Current Studies, Series A (1986), UN Doc ST/CTC/SER A/4, Annex 1) and to the Multilateral Agreement on Investment (MAI), proposed by the OECD in 1995.

[38] Weiler 2013, p. 200.

[39] In this regard, *see* Chap. 5.

adjudicators a quasi-legislative authority to articulate a variety of rules necessary to achieve the treaty's object and purpose in particular disputes'.[40] Notably, a comparable vagueness may also be found in the 2016 Comprehensive Economic and Trade Agreement (CETA) between Canada and the European Union (EU) (not yet in force): its Section D, Article 8.10 (entitled 'Treatment of Investors and Covered Investments), as well as containing an FET clause, indicates an exhaustive list of instances that may entail a violation of the said clause;[41] however, not only does one of these instances refer to 'manifest arbitrariness', a concept intrinsically vague,[42] but according to the same Article (para 3), the parties 'shall regularly or upon request of a Party, review the content of the obligation to provide fair and equitable treatment', which means preserving FET's status as a 'catch-all' provision.[43] Perhaps the main exceptions from this point of view may be found in the 2015 Indian Model Bilateral Investment Treaty, Article 3, ('Each Party shall not subject Investments of Investors of the other Party to measures which constitute (i) Denial of Justice under customary international law; (ii) Un-remedied and egregious violations of due process; or (iii) Manifestly abusive treatment involving continuous, unjustified and outrageous coercion or harassment') and the 2009 ASEAN (Association of Southeast Asian Nations) Comprehensive Investment Agreement, Article 11, para 2, ('fair and equitable' treatment requires each Member State to not deny justice in any legal or administrative proceedings in accordance with the principle of due process), which move away from the traditional 'fair and equitable' terminology, as they avoid references to 'arbitrariness' or 'legitimate expectations'.[44]

Second, the manner in which FET clauses are drafted vary significantly. In effect, three main forms of drafting may be identified: (1) FET as a freestanding obligation;[45] (2) FET as an obligation included in a clause referring to a number of

---

[40] Brower 2003, p. 63. In the same vein, *see* Bernasconi-Osterwalder 2016.

[41] In detail, this Article states as follows: '1. Each Party shall accord in its territory to covered investments of the other Party and to investors with respect to their covered investments fair and equitable treatment and full protection and security in accordance with paras 2 through 6. 2. A Party breaches the obligation of fair and equitable treatment referenced in para 1 if a measure or series of measures constitutes: (a) denial of justice in criminal, civil or administrative proceedings; (b) fundamental breach of due process, including a fundamental breach of transparency, in judicial and administrative proceedings; (c) manifest arbitrariness; d) targeted discrimination on manifestly wrongful grounds, such as gender, race or religious belief; (e) abusive treatment of investors, such as coercion, duress and harassment; or (f) a breach of any further elements of the fair and equitable treatment obligation adopted by the Parties in accordance with para 3 of this Article'.

[42] Bernasconi-Osterwalder 2016, pp. 336 et seq.

[43] This expression is credited to Collins 2016, p. 127.

[44] In this regard, *see* Hanessian and Duggal 2015.

[45] One example may be found in Article 2, para 2, of the BIT Argentina-Great Britain (1993): 'Investments of investors of each Contracting Party shall at all times be accorded fair and equitable treatment and shall enjoy protection and constant protection in the territory of the other Contracting Party.'

standards of treatment;[46] (3) FET as an obligation that is required by international law.[47]

In summary, it is clear that 'the text of investment treaties does not provide a great deal of guidance about what distinguishes fair and equitable treatment from unfair and inequitable treatment.'[48]

1.4 The Role of Case Law and Scholarship in the Interpretation of FET

The failure of treaty practice to define the FET content has been only partially remedied by arbitral case law. In detail, several fora serve the purpose of solving disputes dealing with FET as well as with investment disputes more generally. Of course, at international law level, the International Centre for the Settlement of Investment Disputes (ICSID) (which was established in 1965 as a tool of the World Bank 'to provide facilities for conciliation and arbitration of other Contracting States')[49] is the most renowned, but not the only one available to investors. Additional fora are represented by (1) *ad hoc* tribunals working under the United Nations Commission on International Trade Law (UNCITRAL) Arbitration Rules (initially

[46] *See*, e.g., Article 10, para 1, of the 1991 Energy Charter Treaty: 'Each Contracting Party shall, in accordance with the provision of this Treaty, encourage and create stable, equitable and transparent conditions for Investors of other Contracting Parties to make Investments in its Area. Such conditions shall include a commitment to accord all times to Investments of Investors of other Contracting Parties fair and equitable treatment. Such Investments shall also enjoy the most constant protection and security and no Contracting Party shall in any way impair by unreasonable or discriminatory measures their management, maintenance, use, enjoyment or disposal.'

[47] Reference is especially made to Article 1105, para 1, of the NAFTA: 'Each Party shall accord to investments of investors of another Party treatment *in accordance with international law*, including fair and equitable treatment and full protection and security' (emphasis added). Along the same logic, one may consider the already quoted MAI. On the one side, its Preamble states that 'fair, transparent and predictable regimes complement and benefit the world trading system'; on the other side, the clause concerning the *General Treatment* provides that 'each contracting Party shall accord fair and equitable treatment and full and constant protection and security to foreign investments in their territories. In no case shall a contracting Party accord treatment less favourable than that required *by international law*' (emphasis added).

[48] Bonnitcha 2015, p. 145.

[49] Article 1(2) of the ICSID Convention. Part of ICSID is also the arbitration under the 1978 Additional Facility Rules, which was created by the World Bank with the aim of offering arbitration for certain disputes that fall outside the scope of the ICSID Convention such as: i) arbitration of investment disputes between a State and a foreign national, one of which is not an ICSID member State or a national of an ICSID member State; and ii) arbitration of disputes that do not arise directly out of an investment between a State and a foreign national, at least one of which is an ICSID member State or a national of an ICSID member State.

adopted by UNCITRAL on 28 April 1976 and updated for the first time in 2010);[50] (2) arbitration under the auspices of the International Chamber of Commerce Rules of Arbitration; (3) the London Court of International Arbitration and (4) the Arbitration Institute of the Stockholm Chamber of Commerce. It goes without saying that also national jurisdictions, albeit in a somewhat ambiguous manner, are increasingly asked to deal with disputes concerning FET.[51] Such a plethora of tribunals, however, is not necessarily of assistance, because, first, their jurisprudence 'is generally limited to a list of examples of conduct breaching the standard';[52] and second, most of them usually investigate in depth single elements of the principle, that is to say, those elements which are useful to the resolution of a given dispute only.

At least in part as a consequence of this fragmentation, also in academic debate the scope of FET is open to divergent interpretations. Hence, while some authors tend to link it to other standards of investment (like the MFN), most scholars see FET as an autonomous concept and identify its content by resorting (i) to general international law (including both customary law and principles common to domestic systems), (ii) to the interpretation criteria laid down in the 1969 Vienna Convention on the Law of Treaties (VCLT) or (iii) regarding the standard under consideration as an embodiment of the Rule of Law principles.

1.5 Outline of the Book

To quote the words of Cristopher Schreuer, FET has existed as a 'sleeping beauty' in bilateral treaties since the end of World War II.[53] But, in the last few years, the growing number of petitions brought before arbitral tribunals on the basis of such a clause highlights how relevant the question concerning its normative content has become within international investment law.[54] Not by coincidence, such a relevance has been

---

[50] It is worth mentioning that the use of UNCITRAL Arbitration Rules in investment cases is often established by an arbitration clause contained in a BIT or in a contract. These clauses, in particular, may either exclusively provide for *ad hoc* arbitration under the UNCITRAL rules (*see* the 1991 Netherlands-Czech Republic BIT) or vest the parties (the host State and the investor) with the power of referring their dispute either to ICSID or UNCITRAL arbitration (*see* the 1990 United Kingdom-Argentina BIT). Generally, in this latter case, should the parties be unable to agree on the competent arbitrator after a certain period, they are bound to submit their dispute to UNCITRAL arbitration.

[51] *See*, for instance, the Italian Supreme Court, Judgment of 19 October 2015, No. 21085, and the German Constitutional Court, *Vattenfall*, 1 BvR 2821/11, Judgment of 6 December 2016.

[52] Hirsch 2011, pp. 783 et seq.

[53] Schreuer 2007, p. 92.

[54] *See*, e.g., Schreuer 2005, p. 357 (stating that FET 'is currently the most important standard in investment disputes.'); Muchlinski 2008, p. 24 (observing that 'currently the most important standard, from the perspective of investor protection, is the fair and equitable treatment standard.'); Subedi 2008, p. 63 (noting that FET 'is a major, if not the most important, principle of foreign investment law.'); Montt 2009, p. 294 (according to whom FET 'has become the most relevant cause of action in international investment arbitration. It has superseded in prominence the

expressly recognized by both the International Law Commission (ILC) (which included the subject at issue in its long-term work plan)[55] and the Institute of International law (IIL) (which in 2013—Rapporteur: A. Giardina—adopted a resolution regarding the 'Legal Aspects of Recourse to Arbitration by an Investor Against the Authorities of the Host State under Inter-State Treaties', devoting its Article 13 to FET).[56]

The main focus of this book is precisely to pinpoint the content of FET in terms of its minimal and essential elements, arguing from a perspective that is intended to read the pertinent case law as a whole or, put differently, to perceive it as a single corpus of law. To this end, the inquiry will be divided into three parts. The first part (Chap. 2) will review the main academic opinions on the FET content, showing that none of them is capable of providing a satisfactory solution to the issue. Accordingly, the view will be put forth whereby FET has been progressively shaped by arbitral tribunals, going so far as to embody a (composite) general principle specific to international investment law. This is unsurprising; as has been observed in *Enron* more generally

> The evolution that has taken place [in international investment law] is for the most part the outcome of a case by case determination by courts and tribunals [...] This explains that [...] there is a fragmentary and gradual development. Such development however partly hinges on the gradual formulation – both in cases and legal writings – of 'general principles of law' [...] able to guide and 'discipline' the evaluation of State conduct under investment treaty standards.[57]

(Footnote 54 continued)

expropriation clause, which was traditionally regarded as the most important provision of investment treaties. The FET standard has thus become the 'alpha and omega' of the BIT generation'). In the case law, *see Suez et al.* and *Awg Group v. Argentina*, ICSID Case No. ARB/03/19, Decision on Liability, 30 July 2010, para 181: 'Indeed, to borrow the terminology of Hans Kelsen, it is no exaggeration to say that the obligation of a host State to accord fair and equitable treatment to foreign investors is the *Grundnorm* or basic norm of international investment law.'

[55] Rep. of Int'l Law Comm'n, 63d Sess., Apr. 26–June 3, July 4–Aug. 12, 2011, para 365, U.N. Doc. A/66/10; GAOR, 66th Sess., Supp. No. 10 (2011). In detail, Annex D (moving from the assumption that the concept of fair and equitable treatment has assumed considerable prominence in the practice of States and that this prominence is owed in large part to the emergence of bilateral investment treaties as the main sources of law in the field of investment) raises a number of questions relating to the standard, including: (1) whether the FET is synonymous with the International Minimum Standard; (2) whether the FET is an independent standard; (3) whether the FET does represent customary international law; (4) whether the FET is a principle of international law; (5) what are the elements of the FET in practice; (6) in what ways the FET has affected other provisions of bilateral investment treaties.

[56] This Article states as follows: 'Fair and equitable treatment, which is a key standard of investment protection, must accord investors and investments, in particular: (i) due process, (ii) non-discrimination and non-arbitrary treatment, (iii) due diligence, and (iv) respect of legitimate expectations. The notion of legitimate expectations, as applied to the investor, shall not be construed to include mere expectations of profit, in the absence of specific engagements undertaken towards them by competent State organs. Compensation due to an investor for violation of the FET standard shall be assessed without regard to compensation that could be allocated in case of an expropriation, in accordance with the damage suffered by the investor.'

[57] *Enron v. Argentina*, ICSID Case No. ARB/01/3, Award of 21 May 2007, para 257.

In the second part of the book (Chaps. 3, 4 and 5), the suitability of this contention will be tested with regard to the main FET components, viz. due process of law, legitimate expectations, and proportionality. In detail, Chap. 3 will expound on the scope of due process in investment disputes, making it clear that the latter is conceivable both in terms of (i) denial of justice (resembling the German model of *Justizverweigerung*), and (ii) procedural fairness in administrative proceedings. Chapter 4 will investigate the contours of legitimate expectations and particularly the different forms this principle may assume, depending on whether such expectations are generated by (i) contractual commitment, (ii) unilateral promise or (iii) legislation. Chapter 5 will inquire into the principle of proportionality, having regard to its function and scope as an FET element.

The third and final part (Chap. 6) will shed some light on the driving role of case law for the FET content to be pinpointed. It will be argued that the approach followed in investor-State arbitration to this end, as well as more generally, transcends the traditional dichotomy between binding and persuasive precedent. Rather, it echoes the so-called 'taking into account' approach, which means that the arbitrator is obliged to consider previous decisions, but may disregard them where there are sound reasons to suggest doing so. Notably, an approach of this kind, while being fairly well-established in both national and international practice, proves to be particularly fitting with regard to an open-texture standard such as FET.

References

Abs H, Shawcross H (1960) The Proposed Convention to Protect Foreign Investment: A Round Table: Comment on the Draft Convention by its Authors. Journal of Public Law 9: 115–118

Atik J (1994–1995) Fairness and Managed Foreign Direct Investment. Columbia Journal of Transnational Law 32: 1–42

Bartels LL (2010) The WTO Enabling Clause. In: Remiche B, Fabri HR (eds) Le commerce international entre bi- et multilatéralisme. Larcier, Paris, pp. 261–277

Bernasconi-Osterwalder N (2016) Giving Arbitrators Carte Blanche - Fair and Equitable Treatment in Investment Treaties. In: Lim CL (ed) Alternative Visions of the International Law on Foreign Investment. Essays in Honour of Muthucumaraswamy Sornarajah. Cambridge University Press, Cambridge, pp. 324–346

Bonnichta J (2015) Substantive Protection under Investments Treaties. A Legal and Economic Analysis. Cambridge University Press, Cambridge

Brower CH (2003) Structure, Legitimacy and NAFTA's Investment Chapter. Vanderbildt Journal of Transnational Law 36: 37–94

Cassese A (2005) International Law, 2nd edn. Oxford University Press, Oxford

Choi WM, Won-Mog YS (2012) Facilitating Preferential Trade Agreements Between Developed and Developing Countries: A Case for 'Enabling' the Enabling Clause. In: Minnesota Journal of International Law 21: 1–20

Collins D (2016) An Introduction to International Investment Law. Cambridge University Press, Cambridge

D'Aspremont J (2012) International Customary Law: Story of a Paradox. In: Gazzini T, De Brabandere E (eds) International Investment Law: the Sources of Rights and Obligations. Nijhoff, Leiden

Degan VD (1970) L'équité e le droit international. Nijhoff, The Hague

Diehl A (2012) The Core Standard of International Investment Protection. Fair and Equitable Treatment. Kluwer Law International, Alphen aan den Rijn
Dumberry P (2013) The Fair and Equitable Treatment Standard: A Guide to NAFTA Case Law on Article 1105. Kluwer Law International, Alphen aan den Rijn
Falcón y Tella MJ (2008) Equity and Law. Nijhoff, Leiden
Francioni F (2007) Equity in International Law. Max Planck Encyclopedia of Public International Law. Online Edition. Available at http://opil.ouplaw.com
Franck TM (1995) Fairness in International Law and Institutions. Oxford University Press, Oxford
Giuliano M (1978) La cooperazione degli Stati e il commercio internazionale. Giuffrè, Milan
Hanessian G, Duggal K (2015) The Final 2015 Indian Model BIT: Is This the Change the World Wishes to See? ICSID Review 32:216–226
Higgins R (1994) Problems and Process. International Law and How to Use It. Clarendon Press, Oxford
Hirsch M (2011) Between Fair and Equitable Treatment and Stabilization Clause: Stable Legal Environment and Regulatory Change in International Investment Law. The Journal of World Investment & Trade 12:783–806
Janis MW (1983) The Ambiguity of Equity in International Law. Brooklyn Journal of International Law, 9: 7–34
Kläger R (2011) 'Fair and Equitable' Treatment in International Investment Law. Cambridge University Press, Cambridge
Levy T (1995) NAFTA's Provision for Compensation in the Event of Expropriation: A Reassessment of the "«Prompt, Adequate and Effective»" Standard. Stanford Journal of International Law 31: 423–453
Mauro MR (2003) Gli accordi bilaterali sulla promozione e la protezione degli investimenti. Giappichelli, Turin
Mauro MR (2011) Investimenti stranieri. Enciclopedia del diritto, Annali 4:628–665
Mistelis L (2011) General Principles of Law and Transnational Rules in International Arbitration: An English Perspective. World Arbitration and Mediation Review 5:201–229
Montt S (2009) State Liability in Investment Treaty Arbitration. Global Constitutional and Administrative Law in the BIT Generation. Hart, Oxford
Muchlinski P (2008) Policy Issues. In: Muchlinski P et al (eds) The Oxford Handbook of International Investment Law. Oxford University Press, Oxford
Newman RA (ed) (1973) Equity in the World's Legal System. A Comparative Study. Bruylant, Bruxelles
Paparinskis M (2013) The International Minimum Standard and Fair and Equitable Treatment. Oxford University Press, Oxford
Picone P, Ligustro A (2002) Diritto dell'Organizzazione mondiale del commercio. Cedam, Padua
Razi GM (1963) Reflections on Equity in the Civil Law Systems. American University Law Review 13:24–44
Sacerdoti G (2008) The Proliferation of BITs: Conflicts of Treaties, Proceedings and Awards. In: Sauvant KP (ed) Appeals Mechanism in International Investment Disputes. Oxford University Press, Oxford, pp. 127–136
Sacerdoti G (2011) Nascita, affermazione e scomparsa del Nuovo Ordine Economico Internazionale: Un bilancio trent'anni dopo. In: Ligustro A, Sacerdoti G (eds) Problemi e tendenze del diritto internazionale dell'economia. Liber amicorum in onore di Paolo Picone. Editoriale Scientifica, Naples, pp. 127–152
Schernbeck A (2013) Der Fair and Equitable Treatment Standard in Internationalen Investitionsschutzabkommen. Nomos, Baden-Baden
Schreuer C (1996) Decisions Ex Aequo et Bono Under the ICSID Convention. ICSID Review 11: 3–63
Schreuer C (2005) Fair and Equitable Treatment in Arbitral Practice. Journal of World Investment and Trade 6:357–386

Schreuer C (2007) Fair and Equitable Treatment in Investment Treaty Law. In: Ortino F, Liberty L, Sheppard A, Warner H (eds) Investment Treaty Law - Current Issues II. British Institute of International and Comparative Law, London, pp. 92–96

Schwarzenberger G (1960) The Abs-Shawcross Draft Convention on Investment Abroad: A Critical Commentary. Journal of Public Law 9:147–171

Sereni AP (1956) Studi di diritto comparato. Giuffrè, Milan

Shawcross HW (1961) Le problème de investissements à l'étranger en droit international. Recueil des Cours 102:365–393

Stamberger JL (2003) The Legality of Conditional Preferences to Developing Countries under the GATT Enabling Clause. Chicago Journal of International Law 4: 607–618

Story J (1846) Commentaries on Equity Jurisprudence as Administered in England and America, Vol. I, 4th edn. Maxwell, Edinburgh/Dublin

Subedi SP (2008) International Investment Law. Reconciling Policy and Principle. Hart, Oxford

Tudor I (2008) The Fair and Equitable Treatment Standard in the International Law of Foreign Investment. Oxford University Press, Oxford

UNCTAD (1999) Fair and Equitable Treatment. Series on Issues in International Investment Agreements, United Nations, New York/Geneva

Vandevelde KJ (1988) The Bilateral Investment Treaty Program of the United States. Cornell International Law Journal 21: 201–276

Wanyama E (2015) The Impact of the Calvo Doctrine on the Principles of Protection of Foreign Nationals in the Area of Investment. Nalsar International Law Journal 1: 78–96

Weiler T (2013) The Interpretation of International Investment Law. Equality, Discrimination and Minimum Standards of Treatment in Historical Context. Nijhoff, Leiden

Youssef K (2012) The Present – Commercial Arbitration as a Transnational System of Justice: Universal Arbitration Between Freedom and Constraint: The Challenges of Jurisdiction in Multiparty, Multi-Contract Arbitration. In: Van den Berg AJ (ed) The Next Fifty Years, Vol. 16. Kluwer Law International, Alphen aan den Rijn

Yusuf AA (1980) Differential and More Favourable Treatment: The GATT Enabling Clause. World Trade Law 14: 488–508

Chapter 2
FET and the Ongoing Debate on Its Normative Basis

Contents

Abstract This chapter investigates the main academic opinions on the FET normative basis, pinpointing how none of them is able to give a completely suitable solution to the question. It is argued that FET has penetrated into the fabric of general international law by means of the category of principles peculiar to a certain field of international law, i.e. those principles having their own foundations in the international legal order itself, but which, through the mediation of the judge, end up being shaped according to the features typical of a specific normative field.

Keywords Legal writings · Custom · Treaties · Rule of law · Custom · Judicial practice

F.M. Palombino, *Fair and Equitable Treatment and the Fabric of General Principles*, https://doi.org/10.1007/978-94-6265-210-1_2

2.1 Introduction

Although the State obligation to treat foreign investments fairly and equitably is common to most investment treaties, clauses containing this provision are somewhat vague going so far as to have inspired a large number of interpretations by legal writers. To date, doctrinal discussion rests on five main alternatives, whose terms may be summarized as follows: FET has been described as (i) an 'evaluation rule' establishing a goal that is expressed at some level of generality; (ii) a term of art for a reference to other standards of treatment; (iii) part of the corpus of customary law; (iv) a self-standing treaty clause to be understood in accordance with the interpretation criteria laid down in the VCLT; or (v) an embodiment of the principles behind the rule of law as it may be understood in the major domestic legal systems of liberal democracies. While each of these views will be assessed in depth hereinafter, this book's argument is that FET has penetrated into the fabric of general international law, but by means of a source somewhat neglected in legal doctrine. We refer to the category of *general principles peculiar to a certain field of international law*, i.e. those principles having their own foundations in the international legal order itself, but which, through the mediation of the judge, end up being shaped according to the features typical of a specific normative field. An argument of this kind is convenient from more than one angle. First, it makes it possible to overcome any difficulties closely related to the alleged existence of a custom or a general principle common to domestic systems, and which mainly depend on the lack of the traditional requirements necessary to this end. Second, it is the argument which provides most insight into the current FET content. Third, it may be applied with regard to all the FET core elements, viz. due process of law, legitimate expectations, and proportionality.

2.2 FET as an 'Evaluation Rule'

Despite being very recent, the first opinion to be considered is that advanced by Michael Reisman in 2015.[1] This is because he assumes *a priori* the futility of pinpointing the FET content. In detail, the underlying argument moves from the distinction between what Reisman calls 'verification rules' and 'evaluation rules'. *Verification rules*, in his words, are intended to 'authorize those charged with applying them to do nothing more than verify compliance with an explicit metric.'[2] A sound example would be that 'an intercontinental ballistic missile is to be fired by the officer in the silo only upon receiving a coded signal from the President of the United States.'[3] *Evaluation rules*, contrariwise, indicate a goal to be accomplished

[1] Reisman 2015.

[2] Idem, p. 617.

[3] Idem.

and that is expressed at some level of generality. Article 39 of the Charter of the United Nations (UN) would embody a rule of this kind, insofar as it vests the Security Council with the duty to determine the existence of any threat to the peace, breach of the peace, or act of aggression, and to make recommendations, or decide what measures shall be taken (in accordance with Articles 41 and 42 of the same Charter) to maintain or restore international peace and security; indeed, those who are called on to apply the said provision, viz. permanent representatives in the UN Security Council, should consider a range of variables, including general evaluative concepts such as fairness, equity and justice. To sum up, while verification rules basically exclude (or reduce to a minimum) any discretion by those applying them, evaluation rules do the opposite, meaning that the way these rules are applied is very flexible and should echo in principle any values existing at the time of their application.

> The point is that it is in the nature of the linguistic structure of an evaluation rule that it retains the potential for re-evaluation. Even if the rule seems to have morphed in successive applications, into what is then taken as a verification rule, it always remains open to reconsideration in terms of other variables, including popular morality and ethics.[4]

Following the above perspective, FET would represent a typical example of evaluation rule, since it requires arbitral tribunals dealing with it to take account of all the changing cultural values. As a consequence, despite the importance of judicial practice in the identification of the standard content, any efforts 'to contain and roll back the democratic evolution of the international community's expectations of, and demand for, FET [...] have, until now, proved futile.'[5]

The opinion under consideration is not altogether convincing. As to its premises, the impression one gets is that the distinction between verification rules and evaluation rules is nothing but a different way to express the distinction between 'rules' and 'principles' as rooted in legal theory, i.e. a distinction relying on the extent to which they work differently. While *rules* impose a specific course of conduct, *principles* have a restricted regulatory range, since they essentially aim to prescribe a direction that must be followed. Hence, they would work like *directives*, guidance criteria which the judge is expected to take into account in the exercise of his duties (*Richtungsbegriffe*, according to the expression used by German scholars of procedural law). Such a distinction, introduced by Ronald Dworkin[6] and followed by many other legal theorists later on,[7] while raising some criticism over the years, remains a useful conceptual tool to discuss the role of principles in the international legal order as well as in international investment law.[8]

---

[4] Idem, p. 618.

[5] Idem, p. 633.

[6] Dworkin 1977, pp. 24–26.

[7] *See*, e.g., Iovane 2008.

[8] An appropriate use of this distinction within international investment law may be found in Di Benedetto 2013, pp. 220 et seq.

Still, this remains a terminological question which does not entail any particular problems. Rather, what is hardly acceptable is the conclusion of Reisman's proposition, that is to say, the idea whereby the nature of FET as an evaluation rule/general principle would make pointless any efforts towards the identification of its elements. No doubt FET is an evolving concept, capable of changing as State practice changes, but this does not impede its content from being grasped, at least with regard to the minimum reach. All the opinions that will be assessed in the next paragraphs move from this premise.

2.3 FET as a Term of Art for a Reference to All Other Standards of Investment Protection

Due to the vagueness surrounding the FET content, one issue is whether this content could be determined in combination with a reference to other standards of protection of foreign investments.[9] A distinguished scholar like Francis A. Mann, in a note appearing in the *British Yearbook of International Law* in 1981, answered in the affirmative, regarding FET as an overarching obligation which embraces all the other standards and is distinct, as such, from any existing international law; hence, in line with his approach, should one of these standards be infringed, an FET violation would occur as well.[10] On the other hand, following this approach, the question concerning the FET legal nature should not arise at all, since this nature would be the same as the standard it refers to.

Apparently, several elements of both treaty and judicial practice support this allegation. One element can be found in Article 10, para 1, of the 1991 Energy Charter Treaty, which is a composite provision that refers not only to FET, but also to constant protection and security, to a prohibition of unreasonable or discriminatory measures, to treatment required by international law and to the observance of obligations entered into.[11] Unsurprisingly, in *Petrobart*, this provision was regarded

---

[9] Schreuer 2007.

[10] Mann 1981, p. 243. More in detail, this author, who based his analysis on the 1980 UK treaty with the Philippines, observes as follows: 'It is submitted that the right to fair and equitable treatment goes much further than the right to most-favoured nation and to national treatment [...] So general a provision is likely to be almost sufficient to cover all conceivable cases, and it may be that other provisions of the Agreement affording substantive protection are no more than examples or specific instances of this overriding duty.' Shihata 1993, p. 78, also refers to FET as an 'overarching principle'.

[11] In detail, the text of this provision states as follows: 'Each Contracting Party shall, in accordance with the provisions of this Treaty, encourage and create stable, equitable, favourable and transparent conditions for Investors of other Contracting Parties to make Investments in its Area. Such conditions shall include a commitment to accord at all times to Investments of Investors of other Contracting Parties fair and equitable treatment. Such Investments shall also enjoy the most constant protection and security and no Contracting Party shall in any way impair by unreasonable or discriminatory measures their management, maintenance, use, enjoyment or disposal. In no case

as a clear indication of the overarching nature of FET.[12] Likewise, the *Noble Ventures* tribunal advanced the opinion whereby FET would cover all potential standards:

> Considering the place of the fair and equitable standard at the very beginning of Art. II (2) [of the Romania-United States BIT],[13] one can consider this to be a more general standard which finds its specific application in *inter alia* the duty to provide full protection and security, the prohibition of arbitrary and discriminatory measures and the obligation to observe contractual obligations toward the investor.'[14]

Further, the *SD Myers*[15] and *Pope and Talbot*[16] tribunals approvingly quoted the opinion here discussed.

Now, on closer inspection, Mann's argument, as well as arbitral decisions falling in the same line of thought, is questionable. Of course, as appropriately observed, in 1981 (that is, at the time this argument was spelled out) 'BITs were a minor and still uncertain legal phenomenon [and] the wave of BIT was just starting to sweep the world'.[17] In other words, Mann basically spoke in a *de lege ferenda* perspective, so much so that his book *The Legal Aspects of Money* (published one year after the note of 1981) advanced a much narrower idea of FET, which was regarded as a clause amounting to no more 'than a confirmation of the obligation to act in good faith, or to refrain from abuse or arbitrariness.'[18] With this caveat in mind, the following remarks should be drawn.

Having specific regard to the interaction between FET and other standards of legal protection, it is firstly noticeable that several BITs tend to combine FET with the national treatment (NT) and MFN clauses, i.e. those two traditional standards that serve to ensure legal equality between foreign and domestic investors on the one hand and between foreign investors and investors of a third State on the other hand. Article 4 of the 1991 Norway-Peru BIT is quite revealing. According to this Article each contracting party

---

(Footnote 11 continued)

shall such Investments be accorded treatment less favourable than that required by international law, including treaty obligations. Each Contracting Party shall observe any obligations it has entered into with an Investor or an Investment of an Investor of any other Contracting Party.'

[12] *Petrobart v. The Kyrgystan*, Arbitration Institute of the Stockholm Chamber of Commerce, Award of 29 March 2005, p. 76.

[13] According to this article '[i]nvestment shall at all times be accorded fair and equitable treatment, shall enjoy full protection and security and shall in no case be accorded treatment less than that required by international law.'

[14] *Noble Ventures. Inc. v. Romania*, ICSID Case No. ARB/01/11, Award of 29 March 2005, para 182.

[15] *S.D. Myers Inc v. Canada*, UNCITRAL (NAFTA), Partial Award of 13 November 2000, para 265.

[16] *Pope and Talbot v. Canada*, UNCITRAL (NAFTA), Award on the Merits on Phase 2 of 10 April 2001, para 111, note 105.

[17] Reisman 2015, p. 629, note 49.

[18] Mann 1982, p. 510. For a critical assessment of Mann's theory, *see* Thomas 2002, pp. 51 et seq.; Weiler 2013, pp. 195–196.

> 1[...] will accord in its territory for the investments made by investors of the other Contracting Party fair and equitable treatment. 2. The treatment referred to in paragraph 1 of this Article shall as a minimum not be less favourable than that which is granted with regard to investments by investors of any third State.

A circumstance of this kind, however, fails to answer the issue debated here. First, the content of these standards is shrouded in ambiguity as well. The NT clause, for instance, while having the *apparent* advantage of referring to the host State's internal law, only rarely specifies which national provisions should be taken into account for it to be applied.[19] Similar problems arise with reference to the actual scope of protection offered by an MFN provision, the interpretation of which ranges from a relatively expansive approach to a more restrictive one.[20] Second, also provided that a violation of one of such standards would be able to entail an FET violation, the opposite is not always true. Indeed, the right to FET goes much further than the right to NT and MFN: the FET obligation can be violated even where the foreign investor is treated the same as investors from the host State or benefits from an MFN clause.[21]

Equal conclusions are applicable to the relationship between FET and the standard of non-discrimination treatment (NDT). To a certain extent, the latter standard resembles those mentioned above (NT and MFN), but it differs insofar as it limits itself to imposing a 'negative duty' on the host State: the duty to refrain from taking discriminatory measures against foreign investments.[22] Several courts regard this standard as a mere example of FET; and this even where the investment treaty in question governs the two principles separately. For example, the *CMS Gas Transmission Company* tribunal stated that

> the standard of protection against arbitrariness and discrimination is related to that of fair and equitable treatment. Any measure that might involve arbitrariness or discrimination is in itself contrary to fair and equitable treatment.[23]

Along the same logic, one may mention *Rumeli Telekom A.S. et al.*:[24]

> The Arbitral Tribunal notes that the violations alleged by Claimants and allegedly constituting unreasonable, arbitrary or discriminatory measures, have also been invoked by Claimants as constituting a violation of the fair and equitable treatment principle. The Arbitral Tribunal considers that these violations are better qualified and dealt with as issues falling under *the fair and equitable treatment standard, which also includes in its generality the principle of no-unreasonable, arbitrary or discriminatory measures.*[25]

---

19 Mauro 2003, p. 174.

20 In this regard, *see* Fietta 2005; Savarese 2011.

21 *See* Collins 2016, p. 128. The same circumstance is recognized by Mann himself, 1981, p. 243.

22 Cf. Charpentier 1963; Heiskanen 2008.

23 *CMS Gas Transmission Company v. Argentina*, Award of 12 May 2005, para 290.

24 *Rumeli Telekom A.S. et al. v. Kazakistan*, Award of 29 July 2008.

25 Emphasis added.

Contrariwise, other tribunals examine the two standards separately, arguing that the violation of one of them would not automatically imply the violation of the other. The decision in *LG&E Energy Corporation* is to be mentioned:

> [C]haracterising the measures as not arbitrary does not mean that such measures are characterized as fair and equitable or regarded as not having affected the stability of the legal framework under which gas transportation companies in Argentina operated.[26]

Now, in this author's view, a number of reasons suggest regarding the last-mentioned trend as the most fitting. First, while the rationale behind NDT seems to be straightforward, the application of the different legal elements which constitute a non-discrimination obligation has proven challenging.[27] Second, unlike NDT, FET imposes not only a 'negative duty' of avoiding acting in a certain way, but also and above all a 'positive duty' to take specific actions in order to enhance the investments' protection: the obligation to guarantee due process of law clearly exemplifies this.[28] In other words, should a BIT link the two standards to each other, the FET normative content would end up being identified only partially.

Full protection and security (FPS) is an additional standard in respect of which FET has been put into connection. This standard entails an obligation of due diligence by the host State, namely the obligation to take any measures which are necessary to protect the investor and his investments from injurious acts by government agents or third parties.[29] Still, as to the possibility of defining FET in combination with a reference to this standard, the arbitral case law is far from clear. In detail, some courts treat the two standards together, in the sense that a breach of FET would amount to an absence of FPS (and *vice versa*).[30] This depends on the tendency of these courts to follow an expansive approach in the interpretation of FPS, going so far as to include certain elements (like legal and economic stability) which are also part of FET.[31] On the other hand, several tribunals come to the

---

[26] *LG&E Energy Corporation v. Argentina*, Award of 3 October 2006.

[27] Diebold 2011.

[28] In this regard, *see* Chap. 3.

[29] Cordero Moss 2008; Schreuer 2010.

[30] One may mention *Wena Hotels LTD v. Egypt*, ICSID Case No. ARB/98/4, Award of 8 December 2000, paras 84–95. In the same vein, *see Occidental Exploration and Protection Company v. Ecuador*, UNCITRAL, Award of 1 July 2004, para 187 ('The tribunal accordingly holds that the Respondent has breached its obligations to accord fair and equitable treatment under Article II(3)(a) of the Treaty. In the context of this finding the question of whether in addition there has been a breach of full protection and security under this Article becomes moot as a treatment that is not fair and equitable automatically entails and absence of full protection and security of the investment').

[31] One example is *Azurix v. Argentina*, ICSID Case No. ARB/01/12, Award of 14 July 2006, para 408: 'The tribunal is persuaded of the interrelationship of fair and equitable treatment and the obligation to afford the investor full protection and security. The cases referred to above show that full protection and security was understood to go beyond protection and security ensured by the police. It is only a matter of physical security; the stability afforded by a secure investment environment is as important from an investor's point of view. The tribunal is aware that in recent free trade agreements signed by the United States, for instance, with Uruguay, full protection and

opposite solution, especially because, almost always, BITs set out these two standards separately;[32] assuming this, for example, the *Eureko* Tribunal highlighted that the stability of the investment climate is part of FET only, and may not be included in FPS accordingly.[33]

The need to differentiate the two standards under consideration has been highlighted also by a part of scholarship; it has been argued that while FET would entail essentially a 'negative obligation' to refrain from conduct that is unfair and unjust, FPS would require a positive act, i.e. the commitment to create a factual and legal framework that guarantees and protects investors from adverse circumstances, including the provision of national means of recourse.[34] Indeed, the positive or negative nature of the obligation (to which one may refer in order to distinguish FET from the NDT) does not solve the question at issue here. As has been claimed, FET is a complex criterion which entails both positive and negative obligations. Regardless of this, also as a result of its scarce application in most recent practice, the meaning of the term of art 'full protection and security' is open to widely varying interpretations. Hence, should one accept the idea according to which FPS is no more than a specific instance of FET, the content of the latter would nevertheless remain vague and unclear.

Last but not least, the relationship between FET and expropriation must be considered. In *PSEG* such a relationship was described in the following terms:

(Footnote 31 continued)

security is understood to be limited to the level of police protection required under customary international law. However, when the terms 'protection and security' are qualified by 'full' and no other adjective or explanation, they extend, in their ordinary meaning, the content of this standard beyond physical security. To conclude, the tribunal, having held that the Respondent failed to provide fair and equitable treatment to the investment, finds that the Respondent also breached the standard of full protection and security under the BIT'.

[32] *Jan de Nul v. Egypt*, ICSID Case No. ARB/03/13, Award of 6 November 2008, para 269: 'The notion of continuous protection and security is to be distinguished here from the fair and equitable standard since *they are placed in two different provisions of the BIT*, even if the two guarantees can overlap. As put forward by the Claimants, this concept relates to the exercise of due diligence by the State' (emphasis added). The decision in *Houben v. Burundi*, ICSID Case No. ARB/13/7, Award of 2 January 2016, must be cited to the same effect. Its paras 155–156 state as follows: 'Le Tribunal est conscient qu'une ligne de jurisprudence s'est développée en matière CIRDI qui génère certaines confusions et un certain chevauchement entre ces différentes normes de protection trouvées dans la plupart des TBI, en particulier en ce qui concerne le standard du traitement juste et équitable et le standard de la sécurité et protection constante. Le défendeur lui-même, bien qu'ayant proposé une définition autonome du standard de sécurité et protection constante comme couvrant l'obligation pour l'Etat d'accueil de «*protéger les investissements étrangers de dommages physiques causés par des tierces parties*», n'a pas été à l'abri de certaines approximations concernant le contenu de ces deux standards. Le Tribunal considère, pour sa part, que si le TBI a pris soin de prévoir deux standards de protection, c'est que chacun recouvre une protection différente, par application du principe général de l'effet utile dans l'interprétation des traités internationaux.'

[33] *Eureko v. Poland*, Ad Hoc Arbitration, Partial Award of 19 August 2005, paras 248–253.

[34] Schreuer 2010, pp. 13–14.

> The standard of fair and equitable treatment has acquired prominence in investment arbitration as a consequence of the fact that other standards traditionally provided by international law might not in the circumstances of each case be entirely appropriate. This is particularly the case when the facts of the dispute do not clearly support the claim for direct expropriation, but there are notwithstanding events that need to be assessed under a different standard to provide redress in the event that the rights of the investor have been breached.[35]

Put simply, a tribunal might deny the existence of an expropriation, but still find a violation of FET. The opposite, however, is not equally true, in the sense that an uncompensated expropriation almost always ends up involving an FET violation. Bearing this in mind, the two standards, while necessarily connected with each other, remain separate. This is to say that FET may be part of the requirements for a legal expropriation,[36] but without any implications on its autonomous relevance. Neither is it possible to affirm that the connection between such standards answers the question concerning the FET content. In the words of Christoph Schreuer,

> protection against expropriation has by no means become superfluous through the introduction of FET. At times, reliance on FET may not be possible. Most but not all treaties provide protection against unfair and inequitable treatment. Investment insurance typically covers expropriation but not the violation of FET. Under some treaties, jurisdiction for investor-State arbitration exists only with respect to expropriation, sometimes only for the amount of compensation due, but not for violation of FET. In order to establish the tribunal's jurisdiction the claimant will have to base its claim on expropriation.[37]

2.4 FET and Custom. FET as a Specific Instance of the International Minimum Standard

Also moving from the difficulty of identifying the FET content by means of a combination with other standards of treatment,[38] several authors make reference to customary international law and regard FET either (i) as an embodiment in matter

---

[35] *PSEG v. Turkey*, ICSID Case No. ARB/02/04, Award of 19 January 2009, para 238.

[36] One may mention all those provisions on expropriation, like Article 1110(1) of NAFTA or Article IV(1) of the 1991 Argentina-US BIT, which contain a reference to FET.

[37] Schreuer 2008, p. 3.

[38] Such a circumstance has been highlighted in *PSEG v. Turkey*, ICSID Case No. ARB/02/04, Award of 19 January 2009. Its para 239 states as follows: 'Because the role of fair and equitable treatment changes from case to case, it is sometimes not as precise as would be desirable. Yet, it clearly does allow for justice to be done in the absence of the more traditional breaches of international law standards. This role has resulted in the concept of fair and equitable treatment acquiring a standing on its own, separate and distinct from that of other standards, albeit many times closely related to them, and thus ensuring that the protection granted to the investment is fully safeguarded'. A normative confirmation of the same circumstance may be found in some recent investment agreements, such as the 2012 China-Japan-Korea Trilateral Investment

of foreign investments of the 'international minimum standard' (IMS) or (ii) as an autonomous custom. With regard to the first opinion, it is worth recalling that IMS is the traditional rule whereby any State, when dealing with foreign nationals and their property, must respect a minimum set of principles. Hence, this standard owns an *absolute* (rather than a *relative*) character, since it would be completely independent of the host State's legal system. Along with a significant diplomatic[39] and treaty practice,[40] the customary nature of the rule may be inferred from a copious arbitral case law. The long-standing decisions in *Neer* and *Roberts* passed by the United States-Mexico General Claims Commission in 1926 are fairly informative.[41] In similar terms, they recognize that the *ultimate test* to evaluate the merits of a complaint for mistreatment of an alien is whether he is treated in accordance with ordinary standards of civilization in light of international law.[42] These same decisions, on the other hand, are significant insofar as they contribute to clarify the IMS content. In detail, the *Neer* tribunal stated as follows:

> The treatment of an alien, in order to constitute an international delinquency, should amount to an outrage, to bad faith, to wilful neglect of duty, or to an insufficiency of governmental action so far short of international standards that every reasonable and impartial man would readily recognize its insufficiency. Whether the insufficiency proceeds from the deficient execution of a reasonable law or from the fact that the laws of the countries do not empower the authorities to measure up to international standards is immaterial.[43]

(Footnote 38 continued)

Agreement. According to its Article 5, a determination that there has been a breach of a standard different from FET does not *ipso facto* entail a violation of the latter.

[39] One example is the opinion expressed by the American State Department with regard to the existence of an International Minimum Standard. *See* 77 *American Journal of International Law* 1, 1983, pp. 135 et seq. The view that FET is part of the customary MST was also put forward by the Swiss Foreign Office in 1979 ('On se réfère ainsi au principe classique du droit des gens selon lequel les Etats doivent mettre les étrangers se trouvant sur leur territoire et leurs biens au bénéfice du 'standard minimum' international, c'est-à-dire leur accorder un minimum de droits personnels, procéduraux et économiques'; Annuaire Suisse de Droit International 1980, p. 178.)

[40] One may mention the Treaty of Amity, Economic Relations, and Consular Rights between the U.S. and Italy (February 2, 1948). Its Article 5, para 2, states as follows: 'The nationals of each High Contracting Party shall receive, within the territories of the other High Contracting Party, the most constant protection and security for their persons and property, and shall enjoy in this respect the full protection and security required by international law'. In legal doctrine, *see* Lanfranchi 1968.

[41] *Neer v. Mexico*, Award of 15 October 1926, in *Reports of International Arbitral Awards*, vol. IV, p. 60; *Roberts v. Mexico*, Award of 2 November 1926, idem, p. 77.

[42] *Roberts*, p. 80: '[F]acts with respect to equality of treatment of aliens and nationals may be important in determining the merits of a complaint of mistreatment of an alien. But such equality is not the ultimate test of the propriety of the acts of the authorities in the light of international law. That test is, broadly speaking, whether aliens are treated in accordance with ordinary standards of civilization.'

[43] *Neer*, pp. 61–62.

On these assumptions, FET would plausibly do nothing but extend IMS, as it has evolved in current international law, to the treatment of foreign investments.[44] A number of significant circumstances seem to support such a conclusion. A first circumstance lies in Article 1105(1) of NAFTA (entitled 'Minimum Standard of Treatment')[45] and its binding interpretation issued by the NAFTA Free Trade Commission on July 21, 2001. According to this interpretation:

> Article 1105 (1) prescribes the customary international law minimum standard of treatment of aliens as the minimum standard of treatment to be afforded to investments of investors of another Party. The concepts of 'fair and equitable treatment' and 'full protection and security' do not require treatment in addition to or beyond that which is required by the customary international law minimum standard of treatment of aliens.[46]

The same wording may be found in Articles 5 of the 2004 Canada's Model Foreign Investment Protection Agreement,[47] Article 5 of the 2012 United States Model Bilateral Investment Treaty[48] and, more recently, in Article 9.6 of the 2015 Trans-Pacific Partnership Treaty (not yet in force).[49] Further, some arbitral

---

[44] Cf. e.g. Fatouros 1962, pp. 135–141, 214–215; Kohona 1987, p. 91; Mo 1991, p. 52; Juillard 1994, pp. 131–135; Sacerdoti 1997, p. 341; Leben 1999, p. 13; OECD 2004; Orakhelashvili 2008; Montt 2009, p. 69.

[45] In particular, the Article states that '[e]ach Party shall accord to investments of investors of another Party treatment in accordance with international law, including fair and equitable treatment and full protection and security.'

[46] On the history of Article 1105 of NAFTA, *see* Thomas 2002.

[47] In detail, Article 5 ('Minimum Standard of Treatment') states as follows: '1. Each Party shall accord to covered investments treatment in accordance with the customary international law minimum standard of treatment of aliens, including fair and equitable treatment and full protection and security. 2. The concepts of 'fair and equitable treatment' and 'full protection and security' in para 1 do not require treatment in addition to or beyond that which is required by the customary international law minimum standard of treatment of aliens.'

[48] In detail, Article 5 ('Minimum Standard of Treatment') states as follows: '1. Each Party shall accord to covered investments treatment in accordance with customary international law, including fair and equitable treatment and full protection and security. 2. For greater certainty, para 1 prescribes the customary international law minimum standard of treatment of aliens as the minimum standard of treatment to be afforded to covered investments. The concepts of 'fair and equitable treatment' and 'full protection and security' do not require treatment in addition to or beyond that which is required by that standard, and do not create additional substantive rights. The obligation in para 1 to provide: (a) 'fair and equitable treatment' includes the obligation not to deny justice in criminal, civil, or administrative adjudicatory proceedings in accordance with the principle of due process embodied in the principal legal systems of the world; and (b) 'full protection and security' requires each Party to provide the level of police protection required under customary international law.'

[49] In detail, this Article ('Minimum Standard of Treatment') states as follows: '1. Each Party shall accord to covered investments treatment in accordance with applicable customary international law principles, including fair and equitable treatment and full protection and security. 2. For greater certainty, para 1 prescribes the customary international law minimum standard of treatment of aliens as the standard of treatment to be afforded to covered investments. The concepts of 'fair and equitable treatment' and 'full protection and security' do not require treatment in addition to or beyond that which is required by that standard, and do not create additional substantive rights. The

decisions come to a closely comparable result. In *Deutsche Bank v. Sri Lanka*,[50] for example, the tribunal argued that 'the actual content of the treaty standard of fair and equitable treatment is not materially different from the content of the minimum standard of treatment in customary international law, as recognized by numerous arbitral tribunals and commentators.'[51] Last but not least, one may consider all those treaty provisions which do not *expressly* put FET and IMS on an equal footing, but do so *implicitly* by evoking international law. Arguably, should a treaty provision accord FET to investors and their investments *in accordance with principles of international law*, a reference to the IMS rule would be supposed.[52]

Now, besides the fact that some decisions expressly reject any possible equation between the two standards,[53] one difficulty with an approach like this, which remains 'rather dogmatic and conceptual',[54] lies in the absence of a general consensus on what constitutes IMS under customary international law. Indeed, this standard is itself ambiguous and lacks a precise content. Suffice it to mention the variety of interpretations of the standard given by several NAFTA tribunals shortly after the Free Trade Commission's clarification. Three lines of thought may be

(Footnote 49 continued)

obligations in para 1 to provide: (a) 'Fair and Equitable Treatment' includes the obligation not to deny justice in criminal, civil or administrative adjudicatory proceedings in accordance with the principle of due process embodied in the principal legal systems of the world.'

[50] *Deutsche Bank AG v. Democratic Socialist Republic of Sri Lanka*, ICSID Case No. ARB/09/2, Award of 31 October 2012.

[51] Paras 418–419.

[52] Article 3 of the 1991 BIT Argentina-France is a good example: 'Each Contracting Party shall undertake to accord in its territory and maritime zone just and equitable treatment, *in accordance with principles of international law*, to the investments of investors of the other Party and to ensure that the existence of the rights so granted is not impeded either *de jure* or *de facto*' (emphasis added). As to the case law, one may mention, among others, the decision in *OI European Group B. V. v. Venezuela*, ICSID Case No. ARB/11/25, Award, 10 March 2015, para 481: '[T]he Treaty [...] only offers protected investors FET 'in accordance with international law.' The Treaty therefore does not guarantee FET in abstract, but rather only as recognized by international law. And the level of protection that international law offers and ensures to foreign nationals is precisely what is known as the minimum customary standard.' The same decision, para 489, adds that '[w]hat is relevant is not the standard as it was defined in the 20th century, but rather the standard as it exists and is accepted today—since both Customary International Law and the standard itself are constantly evolving. And it is quite possible that the minimum customary standard and the FET envisaged in the treaties have converged, according the investor with substantially equivalent levels of protection.'

[53] *See*, for example, *Crystallex International Corporation v. Venezuela*, ICSID Case No. ARB (AF)/11/2, Award, 4 April 2016, para 530: 'the tribunal is of the opinion that the FET standard embodied in the Treaty cannot [...] be equated to the 'international minimum standard' under customary international law, but rather constitute an autonomous treaty standard.'

[54] *SAUR International S.A. v. Argentina*, ICSID Case No. ARB/04/4, Decision on Jurisdiction and Liability of 6 June 2012, para 491. By the same token, *see Rusoro v. Venezuela*, ICSID Case No. ARB(AF)/12/5, Award of 22 August 2016, para 520.

identified in this connection: first, IMS is equated to the *Neer* standard;[55] second, IMS goes beyond the *Neer* standard;[56] third, IMS is in fact no different from an obligation to provide FET.[57] Seen from this perspective, also the opinion advanced by Patrick Dumberry is not of much more assistance. According to this author, while 'there are *in general*, good reasons to interpret the term 'fair and equitable treatment' found in most BITs, as a reference to something *other than* the minimum standard of treatment under custom [...] any possible ambiguities disappear when [as in the case under NAFTA Article 1105] there is clear and undeniable evidence that the intention of the State parties was in fact that the FET standard be considered as a reference to the minimum standard of treatment under custom.'[58] This opinion reflects the more general idea that the question concerning the status of FET in international law would only be relevant in situations where there is no treaty 'that governs the relationship between a foreign investor and the host country of the investment' or a treaty '*does* govern the relationship between a foreign investor and the host country [without containing] any FET clause'.[59] Yet, as will be further

---

[55] *Glamis Gold, Ltd. v. United States*, UNCITRAL (NAFTA), Award of 8 June 2009, para 22: '[A] lthough situations presented to tribunals are more varied and complicated today than in the 1920s, the level of scrutiny required under *Neer* is the same. Given the absence of sufficient evidence to establish a change in the custom, the fundamentals of the *Neer* standard thus still apply today: to violate the customary international law minimum standard of treatment codified in Article 1105 of the NAFTA, an act must be sufficiently egregious and shocking—a gross denial of justice, manifest arbitrariness, blatant unfairness, a complete lack of due process, evident discrimination, or a manifest lack of reasons—so as to fall below accepted international standards and constitute a breach of Article 1105(1)'.

[56] *Waste Management v. Mexico*, ICSID Case No. ARB (AF)/00/3, Award of 30 April 2004. According to this decision, in particular, '[b]oth the Mondev and ADF tribunals rejected any suggestion that the standard of treatment of a foreign investment set by NAFTA is confined to the kind of outrageous treatment referred to in the Neer case' (para 93). Indeed, 'despite certain differences of emphasis a general standard for Article 1105 is emerging. Taken together, the S.D. Myers, Mondev, ADF and Loewen cases suggest that the minimum standard of treatment of fair and equitable treatment is infringed by conduct attributable to the State and harmful to the claimant if the conduct is arbitrary, grossly unfair, unjust or idiosyncratic, is discriminatory and exposes the claimant to sectional or racial prejudice, or involves a lack of due process leading to an outcome which offends judicial propriety—as might be the case with a manifest failure of natural justice in judicial proceedings or a complete lack of transparency and candour in an administrative process'(para 98). More recently, the same view has been advanced by an UNCITRAL Tribunal in *Grand River Enterprises Six Nations, Ltd. et al. v. United States*, Award of 12 January 2011, para 166: 'Article II(2) of the BIT refers to the "principles of international law" in accordance with which fair and equitable treatment is to be bestowed. To determine these principles the tribunal must consider the present status of development of public international law in the field of investment protection. It is the tribunal's view that public international law principles have evolved since the *Neer* case and that the standard today is broader than that defined in the *Neer* case on which Respondent relies.'

[57] *Merril & Ring v. Canada*, UNCITRAL Rules, Award of 31 March 2010, paras 182 et seq.

[58] Dumberry 2013, p. 44; in other words, in this author's view, 'the debate as to whether the FET is an autonomous standard or linked to the minimum standard of treatment under international law is simply *not relevant* in the context of Article 1105' (p. 45).

[59] Dumberry 2016, pp. 4–5.

clarified here shortly, also in these cases, and thus regardless of whether FET is or is not ruled in a treaty provision, the question concerning its content remains unanswered in any event. And, indeed, the wording of treaty clauses existing in the matter is too vague for the FET content to be identified.

On the other hand, even where a conventional provision requires FET to be understood by reference to general principles of international law, this includes 'a reference to the whole of international law and not to a specific part of it [which would be the case with IMS].'[60]

2.4.1 FET as an Autonomous Custom

Unlike the views mentioned in the previous section, some authors argue that FET, as a result of a plentiful and consistent State practice, would eventually pass into the corpus of customary international law, giving rise to a new and autonomous rule.[61] It is an opinion which rests on the classical dualistic conception of this source of law, conceived as a set of two elements: an objective element (*diuturnitas*), understood as the existence of a uniform State practice, and a subjective element (*opinio juris sive necessitatis*), i.e. the opinion whereby that practice is mandatory.[62]

More squarely, the two-element approach is widely adopted in national and international judicial practice. Suffice it to mention Article 38, para 1(b) of the ICJ Statute (whereby the Court shall apply 'international custom, as evidence of a general practice accepted as law'),[63] and the current work on the identification of customary international law carried out by the UN ILC, which during its sixty-eighth session (held in Geneva from 2 May to 10 June, and from 4 July to 12

[60] *Urbaser S.A. et al. v. Argentina*, ICSID Case No. ARB/07/26, Award of 8 December 2016.

[61] One may mention the case of *Sempra Energy International v. Argentina*, ICSID Case No. ARB/02/16, Award of 18 September 2007, para 296: 'the tribunal finds the Respondent to be right in arguing that fair and equitable treatment is a standard that is none too clear and precise. This is because international law is itself not too clear or precise as concerns the treatment due to foreign citizens, traders and investors. This is the case because the pertinent standards have gradually evolved over the centuries. Customary international law, treaties of friendship, commerce and navigation, and more recently bilateral investment treaties have all contributed to this development.'

[62] Conforti and Labella 2012, p. 31; Treves 2012.

[63] One recent example may be found in *Jurisdictional Immunities of the State*, (Germany v. Italy: Greece intervening), Judgment of 3 February 2012, para 55: '[T]he Court must determine, in accordance with Article 38(1)*(b)* of its Statute, the existence of 'international custom, as evidence of a general practice accepted as law' conferring immunity on States and, if so, what is the scope and extent of that immunity. To do so, it must apply the criteria which it has repeatedly laid down for identifying a rule of customary international law. In particular [...], the existence of a rule of customary international law requires that there be 'a settled practice' together with *opinio juris*.'

August, 2016) adopted a set of sixteen draft conclusions on first reading.[64] Remarkably, draft conclusion 2 states that

> [t]o determine the existence and content of a rule of customary international law, it is necessary to ascertain whether there is a general practice that is accepted as law (*opinio juris*).

Draft conclusion 3 further specifies as follows:

> 1. In assessing evidence for the purpose of ascertaining whether there is general practice and whether the practice is accepted as law (*opinio juris*), regard must be had to the overall context, the nature of the rule, and the particular circumstances in which the evidence in question is to be found. 2. Each element is to be separately ascertained. This requires an assessment of evidence for each element.

Of course, the need to identify customary rules is also peculiar to the law of foreign investments, where the underlying approach remains always the same: both elements (objective and subjective) are required, and the wording of some bilateral[65] and multilateral[66] investment treaties is a clear indication of this.

Now, having specific regard to the topic under consideration here, it is worth noting that, in respect of *diuturnitas*, the growing number of international agreements providing for an FET clause may in and of themselves serve as evidence of State practice,[67] but—as in part described earlier—at least in appearance these

[64] *See* Report of the International Law Commission on the Work of its Sixty-Eighth Sess., Supp. No 10, 74, at 76, UN Doc. A/71/10 (2016).

[65] For example, according to Annex A to the treaty between the government of the United States of America and the government of the Republic of Rwanda concerning the encouragement and reciprocal protection of investment (2008), parties 'confirm their shared understanding that 'customary international law' generally and as specifically referenced in Article 5 and Annex B results from a general and consistent practice of States that they follow from a sense of legal obligation.'

[66] For example, Annex 9-A of the 2016 Trans-Pacific Partnership Treaty ('Customary International Law') states as follows: 'The Parties confirm their shared understanding that 'customary international law' generally and as specifically referenced in Article II.6 (Minimum Standard of Treatment) results from a general and consistent practice of States that they follow from a sense of legal obligation. The customary international law minimum standard of treatment of aliens refers to all customary international law principles that protect the investments of aliens.'

[67] Once again, the idea whereby treaties represent a manifestation of practice for the purpose of customary international law may be inferred from the ILC's Report (*supra* note 64), p. 24, para 41 (h) (*Practice in connection with treaties*): 'Negotiating, concluding and entering into, ratifying and implementing bilateral or multilateral treaties (and putting forward objections and reservations to them) are another form of practice. Such practice does not concern the law of treaties alone; it may also relate to the obligations assumed through the relevant international legal instrument.' *See* also D'Amato 1988, p. 462: 'What makes the content of a treaty count as an element of custom is the fact that the parties to the treaty have entered into a binding commitment to act in accordance with its terms. Whether or not they subsequently act in conformity with the treaty, the fact remains that they have so committed to act. The commitment itself, then, is the 'State practice' component of custom'.

clauses lack uniformity; indeed, while sometimes they mention FET alone[68] or in combination with a reference to international law,[69] more often they combine FET with other standards of treatment (like MFN,[70] NT,[71] NDT,[72] or FPS).[73] In brief, the question remains whether the existence of different categories of treaty FET clauses implies the absence of a uniform practice. For this question to be solved, the 2016 ILC Report is once again of guidance. In its terms, what is required is not a complete uniformity of practice, but rather a core of meaning that does not change.[74] The same indications may be found both in some arbitral decisions and in legal doctrine. As to case law, a passage of the *Mondev* decision is very significant.[75] In the view of the tribunal, the vast number of bilateral and regional investment treaties that *almost* (*but not always*) uniformly provide for fair and equitable treatment of foreign investments reveals 'a remarkably widespread basis [on which] States have repeatedly obliged themselves to accord foreign investment such treatment'.[76] In the same vein, authors in favour of the customary nature of FET argue that practice uniformity should be assessed in a flexible way:

---

[68] This minimal approach can be found in a number of investment agreements such as the already mentioned Article 2, para 2, of the 1993 Argentina-Great Britain BIT: 'Investments of investors of each Contracting Party shall at all times be accorded fair and equitable treatment and shall enjoy protection and constant security in the territory of the other Contracting Party.' The 1998 Australia-China BIT is relevant in the same vein. Its Article 3 states as follows: 'A contracting party shall at all times ensure fair and equitable treatment in its own territory to investments and activities associated with such investments.'

[69] As has been frequently observed, Article 1105, para 1, of the NAFTA, is a good example in that respect.

[70] *See supra* para 2.3.

[71] Idem.

[72] Idem.

[73] Idem.

[74] Draft conclusion 8 states as follows: '1. The relevant practice must be general, meaning that it must be sufficiently widespread and representative, as well as consistent. 2. Provided that the practice is general, no particular duration is required.' The same approach has been followed by the ICJ: 'It is not to be expected that in the practice of States the application of the rules in question should have been perfect [...] The Court does not consider that, for a rule to be established as customary, the corresponding practice must be in absolutely rigorous conformity with the rule. In order to deduce the existence of customary rules, the Court deems it sufficient that the conduct of States should, in general, be consistent with such rules, and that instances of State conduct inconsistent with a given rule should generally have been treated as breaches of that rule, not as indications of the recognition of a new rule'; (*Military and Paramilitary Activities in and against Nicaragua (Nicaragua v. United States)*, Judgment of 27 June 1986, para 186.

[75] *Mondev International Ltd v. United States*, ICSID Case No. ARB(AF)/99/2, Award of 11 October 2002.

[76] Paragraph 117. Albeit in more general terms, the decision in *Merrill & Ring Forestry L. P. v. Canada*, NAFTA (UNCITRAL), Award of 31 March 2010, para 210, seems to express the same line of thought: '[A] requirement that aliens be treated fairly and equitably in relation to business, trade and investment [...] has become *sufficiently* part of widespread and consistent practice so as to demonstrate that it is reflected today in customary international law as *opinio juris*' (emphasis added).

> [T]he differences mainly concern the relationship of FET to principles of international law and to other standards. This relationship cannot and should not be clarified in a uniform and ever-congruent way and thus cannot stand in the way of the formation of custom because it is the very nature of a standard not to be uniform and specific but to be broad and open for fact-specific analysis. […] What truly counts is […] whether there is a uniform practice insofar as a high number of the BITs existing today provide for FET for investments and/or investors. As this is the case, *the first element of custom is fulfilled* – despite the fact that several categories of FET clauses exist.[77]

Let us turn now to the second constituent element of custom, viz. *opinio juris sive necessitatis*. In line with a typical feature of international law, a voluntary limitation of State sovereignty may never be merely supposed; hence, while implicitly rejecting the idea whereby the extensive BIT practice would in itself be a manifestation of *opinio juris*,[78] the same authors mentioned above bring this element back to an interest of States in a rule of customary international law providing for FET.[79]

> States have a real interest in a set of basic principles on foreign investment in customary international law. Since FET is the core standard in the law of foreign investment, States especially have a real interest in a customary FET standard. Hence, the element of *opinio juris* is present. In light of the over-arching interest in a healthy investment climate […], a reliable legal framework, fostered by a set of principles in customary international law and de-escalating potential conflicts in an area of overlapping treaties and sovereignties is in the interest of the community of States. It is even in the interests of developing States, as they would be able to present themselves as more reliable partners: in the absence of treaty protection, the FET of investments would be guaranteed pursuant to customary international law.[80]

---

[77] Diehl 2012, pp. 135–136 (emphasis added.). For a similar opinion, *see* also Tudor 2008, pp. 74 et seq. *Contra* Kishoiyian 1993, p. 372, according to whom 'there is not sufficient consistency in the terms of the investment treaties to find in them support for any definite principles of customary international law [T]he foregoing analysis of BITs has manifested so much uncertainty and contradiction, so much fluctuation and discrepancy in the rapid conclusion of BITs, and the practice has been so much influenced by considerations of political expediency in the various cases, that it is not easy to discern in all the treaties any constant and uniform usage, accepted as law regulating foreign investment.'

[78] Once again, this idea may be found in *Mondev* (note 53), paras 110–111: '[NAFTA Parties] appear to question whether the parties to the very large numbers of bilateral investment treaties have acted out of a sense of legal obligation when they include provisions in those treaties such as that for 'fair and equitable' treatment of foreign investment […] The question is entirely legitimate. It is often difficult in international practice to establish at what point obligations accepted in treaties, multilateral or bilateral, come to condition the content of a rule of customary international law binding on States not party to those treaties. Yet the United States itself provides an answer to this question, in contending that, when adopting provisions for fair and equitable treatment and full protection and security in NAFTA (as well as in other BITs), the intention was to incorporate principles of customary international law.'

[79] The idea whereby *opinio juris* should reflect an interest of the community of States to establish a rule of customary international law is to be traced back to Doehring 2004, margin no. 317.

[80] Diehl 2012, p. 145.

For a number of reasons, an approach of this kind is not altogether persuasive. First, the frequency with which States conclude investment treaties would indeed tacitly reveal the absence of customary principles in the matter, 'inasmuch as it could be assumed that such clauses were adopted precisely because they set a standard other than that required by custom.'[81] Second, 'only through the presence of *opinio juris sive necessitatis* can a customary rule be inferred from treaty practice';[82] this is widely supported in State practice[83] as well as in the above-mentioned ILC Report.[84] Accordingly, it is hardly acceptable that such an *opinio* stems from a general and undefined interest of the international community as a whole nor, *a fortiori*, from the mere existence of a copious treaty practice, which does not generate *per se* a presumption of *opinio*.[85] As clearly stated by the ICJ in the renowned *Diallo* case:

---

[81] *Cargill v. Mexico*, ICSID Case No. ARB(AF)/05/2, Award of 18 September 2009, para 276. In the same vein, *see* Sornarajah 2010, p. 232: 'The view is stated that the large number of bilateral investment treaties that have been signed in recent years has led or will lead to the creation of customary principles of international law on the protection of foreign investments. The frequency with which this view is stated is puzzling in view of the fact that the evidence and the theory are against the possibility of investment treaties creating customary international law [...] Had the rules on investment protection been clear, there would have been no reason for such treaties.'

[82] Conforti and Labella 2012, p. 33. More in detail, according to the same authors, '[d]omestic courts often resort to treaties in their decisions as evidence of a customary international rule. However, treaties can be construed as either confirming pre-existing customary principles or as creating new rules applicable only to contracting States. Only an assessment of *opinio juris sive necessitatis* can determine which of these two effects was intended by the contracting States, and thereby establish whether the treaty supports or contradicts the existence of a customary rule' (pp. 33–34).

[83] One may mention *Camuzzi International S.A. v. Argentina*, ICSID Case No. ARB/03/2, Decision on Objections to Jurisdiction, 11 May 2005, para 144: 'There is no obstacle in international law to the expression of the will of States through treaties being at the same time an expression of practice and of the *opinio juris* necessary for the birth of a customary rule if the conditions for it are met.'

[84] Draft Conclusion 11 states as follows: '1. A rule set forth in a treaty may reflect a rule of customary international law if it is established that the treaty rule: (a) codified a rule of customary international law existing at the time when the treaty was concluded; (b) has led to the crystallization of a rule of customary international law that started to emerge prior to the conclusion of the treaty; or (c) has given rise to a general practice that is accepted as law (*opinion juris*), thus generating a new rule of customary international law. 2. The fact that a rule is set forth in a number of treaties may, but does not necessarily, indicate that the treaty rule reflects a rule of customary international law.'

[85] For the suggestion of the existence of such a presumption in similar cases, *see* Crawford 2013, paras 167–174.

> The fact […] that various agreements, such as agreements for the promotion and protection of foreign investments and the Washington Convention, have established special legal regimes governing investment protection, or that provisions in this regard are commonly included in contracts entered into directly between States and foreign investors, is not sufficient to show that there has been a change in customary rules of diplomatic protection; it could equally show the contrary.[86]

Likewise, already in 1986, Oscar Schachter observed that 'the repetition of common clauses in bilateral treaties does not create or support an inference that those clauses express customary law [because to] sustain such claim of custom one would have to show that apart from the treaty itself, the rules in the clauses *are considered obligatory*.'[87]

Third, and most importantly, the classification of FET as an autonomous custom does not answer the question concerning its normative content. As already said, most treaty norms providing for an FET clause do not pinpoint its elements, but

[86] *Guinea v. Congo* (*Preliminary Objections*), Judgment of 24 May 2007, para 90. In the same vein one may mention the more ancient decision in *North Sea Continental Shelf* (*Germany v. Denmark*; *Germany v. Netherlands*) Judgment of 20 February 1969, para 76: 'Over half the States concerned, whether acting unilaterally or conjointly, were or shortly became parties to the Geneva Convention, and were therefore presumably so far as they were concerned, acting actually or potentially in the application of the Convention. From their action no inference could legitimately be drawn as to the existence of a rule of customary law.'

[87] Schachter 1984, p. 126 (emphasis added). The same remark in relation to FET clauses may be found in Kläger 2011, p. 269 ('[E]ven if the overwhelming State practice—which is indeed represented by the sheer number of BITs incorporating fair and equitable treatment—may ease the requisition of an *opinio iuris*, demonstrating that evidence of the latter is still a matter of great difficulty. This is also because the rise of arbitral decisions in recent years has created some new controversies which also contributed to an increased textual diversity in relation to fair and equitable treatment clauses.') and, more recently, in Dumberry 2016, p. 1, 23 ('There is indeed no indication in treaty text (or in the *travaux preparatoires* or anywhere else) showing that States include FET clauses in their BITs out of a sense of conviction that this is the type of protection they *have* to provide to foreign investors *under international law*. While the present author has found a number of clear examples of such existing *opinio juris* in BITs in other contexts, none was found regarding the FET clause. States sign BITs to protect their own interests, not out of sense of obligation'). A less pessimistic opinion may be credited to Valenti 2014, p. 26, 32 ('[O]ne must acknowledge that [the] insertion of [FET] into BITs is a widespread practice of States. However, it is not easily proven that such a practice is backed by a sense of legal obligation (opinio juris), which must also be found before concluding by stating the customary status of the rule. Given the uncertainty surrounding the subjective element of custom with reference to the FET, we do not believe that it has already attained the customary status. In our opinion, however, the evolution that the standard has undergone, especially the progressive definition of its content by the arbitral practice and scholarly conceptualization, reveals that it would be ready to take this qualitative step.'

limit themselves to imposing its observance.[88] From this point of view, the opinion of Carlo Santulli whereby FET provisions would be rules of 'renvoi mobile' to customary law, i.e. as this law changes so does the content of the provision, is not of much more assistance.[89]

2.5 FET as a Self-Standing Treaty Clause

According to a further and more formalistic proposal, also supported by some judicial decisions,[90] FET would embody a self-standing treaty clause, the content of which should be determined on a case-by-case basis, that is to say in light of the particular circumstances in which any given BIT is concluded. To this end, one

---

[88] Not by chance, in order to answer this objection, the same authors claiming the customary nature of FET resort to the different category of general principles common to domestic systems. For example, Tudor 2008, p. 54, argues as follows: 'Establishing that FET is part of customary law does not exclude it from being a general principle of law. This duality is recognized by the very structure of Article 38, which considers custom and general principles in two separate paragraphs. The relevance of recognizing a dual nature—custom/general principle—to the FET is, first, that the function and nature of these two sources are different and second, that this duality testifies to the FET's importance and almost unavoidable presence in international law. As a custom, the FET standard has to comply with [two] requirements […], i.e., State practice and *opinio juris*. As a general principle of law, it enjoys an independent status and its opposability to States does no longer depend on its effective acceptance at the international level but on its place at the domestic level. Therefore, it remains relevant to examine the FET as a general principle of law even once its roots in both conventional and customary law are established. 'Likewise, Diehl 2012, pp. 178–179, observes that 'the FET standard is a 'twofold sources-standard', that is, a standard based on two sources of public International law: The fact that customary International law is largely shaped by the *outward* behaviour of States as it is reflected in their practice on the international plane, whereas general principles of law find their pivotal underpinning in the *internal* structure of the States' own legal orders, is not merely of terminological importance. If a standard is customary international law only, States are largely free to change or to destroy it by modifying their behaviour in inter-State relations. A general principle of law, by contrast, can only be overcome if a sufficiently relevant number of States change their internal legal orders in order to do away with it. Furthermore, the classification of the FET standard as a general principle of law enables arbitral tribunals to not only draw on the case law of other international courts and tribunals, but to look to domestic jurisprudence for guidance on how to interpret this broad standard.' In any case, on the possibility of referring to general principles common to domestic systems in matter of FET, *see infra*.

[89] Santulli 2015, p. 84: 'Le renvoi effectué par la clause de traitement juste équitable est mobile en ce sens qu'il permet de tenir compte des évolutions postérieures (de la pratique comme de la perception des valeurs protégées) à la conclusion de l'accord—*a fortiori* ne se réfère-t-il pas à des conceptions plus anciennes.'

[90] *See*, for instance, *The Rompetrol Group N.V. v. Romania*, ICSID Case No. ARB/06/3, Award of 6 May 2013, para 197: '[The tribunal] sees no benefit in engaging in an abstract debate as to whether Article 3(1) [of the Netherlands-Romania BIT], and in particular its reference to 'fair and equitable treatment', was or was not intended by the Parties simply to incorporate the 'minimum standard' under customary international law, still less to engage in any debate as to what that 'minimum standard' should now be understood to be. It prefers instead (in keeping with the

must resort to the interpretation criteria set out in the VCLT,[91] especially to its Article 31, which defines a single rule of interpretation comprising various elements.[92]

In line with the first of these elements, the terms 'fair' and 'equitable' demand to be defined in their ordinary meaning;[93] still, such a meaning is anything but capable of providing assistance. As noted by the *Saluka* tribunal:

> [t]he 'ordinary meaning' of the 'fair and equitable treatment' standard can only be defined by terms of almost equal vagueness. In *MTD*, the tribunal stated that: 'in the ordinary meaning, the terms 'fair' and 'equitable' [...] mean 'just', 'even handed', 'unbiased', 'legitimate'. On the basis of such and similar definitions, one cannot say more than the tribunal did in *S.D. Meyers* by stating that an infringement of the standard requires 'treatment in such an unjust or arbitrary manner that the treatment rises to a level that is unacceptable from an international perspective.'[94]

In other words, albeit at the risk of using a tautology, the question pertaining to the FET content is not susceptible to be solved on a purely semantic level. And the

(Footnote 90 continued)

approach adopted by other arbitral tribunals) to follow the ordinary meaning of the word used, in their context, and in the light of the object and purpose of the BIT.'

[91] This opinion has been clearly maintained by Bronfman 2006. To his mind, the FET clause should be understood 'according to the real intention of the parties. In other words, it grants the best protection to the investor, which implies the fairest and most equitable conduct by the host State in regard to the specific facts of the case' (p. 678). More recently the same opinion has been shared by Kläger 2011, p. 280: '[F]air and equitable treatment represents a conventional norm which, due to its general texture, serves as a gateway for the integration of principled arguments that guide its application. The fact that fair and equitable treatment is systematically interlinked to arguments derived from legal principles, based on other conventional agreements, custom or general principles of law, does not change the position of fair and equitable treatment in the system of international law sources. Taking into account also the principles of fair and equitable treatment and their normative status helps to avoid the difficulties in the classification of fair and equitable treatment and provides a more comprehensive picture of fair and equitable treatment and the international law sources.' With regard to the case law, *Petrobart v. The Kyrgystan*, Arbitration Institute of the Stockholm Chamber of Commerce, Award of 29 March 2005, p. 26, seems to be quite revealing: '[T]here is no specific definition of this obligation under international law. Its meaning therefore should be determined by applying the applicable rules of interpretation in light of the circumstances of the present case.'

[92] In general, on treaty interpretation in investment arbitration, *see* Weeramantry 2012.

[93] Article 31, para 1, VCLT, states as follows: 'A treaty shall be interpreted in good faith in accordance with the ordinary meaning to be given to the terms of the treaty in their context and in the light of its object and purpose.'

[94] *Saluka v. Czech Republic*, UNCITRAL, Partial Award of 17 March 2006, para 297.

fact that several scholars of legal theory have dealt with the concept of fairness is of little guidance, considering the high degree of abstraction of their contributions.[95]

That being said, and turning again to Article 31 VCLT, FET should also be understood in light of both the object and purpose of the given BIT, as they are reflected in the preamble.[96] In detail, recourse to preambles for interpretive reasons is very frequent in international case law,[97] and investment arbitral jurisprudence is no exception, especially where the FET content comes under consideration.[98] One may mention, for example, the cases *Lauder*[99] and *CME*.[100] Yet, on closer

---

[95] *See*, e.g., Rawls 2001; Franck 1995. Both these authors were quoted by an ICSID Tribunal, but precisely with the view to highlighting the limited relevance of their volumes for the FET scope to be established. Reference is made to *Suez et al. v. Argentina*, ICSID Case No. ARB/03/19, Decision on Liability of 30 July 2010, para 221: 'What, then, is the meaning of 'fair and equitable treatment' with respect to the investments undertaken by the Claimants? Philosophers and scholars have devoted tomes to the subject of fairness. While their work is helpful in understanding the abstract concept and its implications, it does not answer a fundamental and practical question that every arbitral tribunal must answer: By what criteria, standard, or test is an arbitral tribunal to determine whether the specific treatment accorded to the investments of a particular foreign investor in a given context is or is not "fair and equitable"? To say that "fair and equitable" means "just", "even-handed", "unbiased", or "legitimate", as some tribunals have done, is quite frankly to state a tautology. Such formulations are not judicially operational in the sense that they lend themselves to being readily applied to complex, concrete investment fact situations, like those found in the present cases.'

[96] Article 31, para 2, VCLT, states as follows: 'The context for the purpose of the interpretation of a treaty shall comprise, in addition to the text, including its preamble and annexes: (a) any agreement relating to the treaty which was made between all the parties in connexion with the conclusion of the treaty; (b) any instrument which was made by one or more parties in connexion with the conclusion of the treaty and accepted by the other parties as an instrument related to the treaty.' For a comment on this Article, *see* Dörr and Schmalebach 2012, pp. 62 et seq.

[97] The ICJ Judgment in *Nationals of the Unites States of America in Morocco* (*France v. United States*), Judgment of 27 August 1952, p. 196, is quite revealing: 'The purposes and objects of this Convention were stated in its Preamble [...] In these circumstances, the Court cannot adopt a construction by implication of the provisions [...] of the Convention which would go beyond the scope of its declared purposes and object.'

[98] In this regard, *see* Ciurtin 2015, pp. 64, 74. As far as international contracts are concerned, and despite the absence in the matter of a provision akin to that set forth in the VCLT, Crivellaro 2001 argues that preambles should serve the same interpretive purpose.

[99] *Lauder v. Czech Republic*, UNCITRAL, Final Award of 3 September 2001, para 292: 'Article II (2)(a) of the Treaty sets forth that '[*i*]*nvestments shall at all times be accorded fair and equitable treatments* [...]'. As with any treaty, the Treaty shall be interpreted by reference to its object and purpose, as well as by the circumstances of its conclusion (Vienna Convention on the Law of Treaties, Articles 31 and 32). The preamble of the Treaty states that the Parties agree '*that fair and equitable treatment of investment is desirable in order to maintain a stable framework for investment and maximum effective utilization of economic resources*'.

[100] *CME Czech Republic B.V. v. Czech Republic*, UNCITRAL, Partial Award of 13 September 2001, para 155: 'The Treaty further provides that investments are to be ensured 'fair and equitable treatment.' Treaty at Article 3(I). The Treaty's Preamble underscores the importance of this obligation, acknowledging that 'fair and equitable treatment' of investments plays a major role in realizing the Treaty's goal of encouraging foreign investment.'

inspection, the terms of the question do not change. Such preambles appear equally vague,[101] limiting themselves to identifying with the economic cooperation and the need to foster the exchange of capital and technologies the main reasons underpinning the adoption of an investment treaty.[102] Of course, the above circumstance does not reduce the relevance of the treaty's object and purpose in the matter at issue, but their function seems to be a more limited one, i.e. to guarantee a FET interpretation which is compatible with them. One example is the decision in *Lemire*, where the words used in the preamble of the 1994 Ukraine-United States BIT ('fair and equitable treatment of investment is desirable in order to maintain stable framework for investment') were regarded as symptomatic of the tie existing between FET and the notion of legitimate expectations.[103]

In some respects at least (i.e. insofar as the VCLT's interpretation criteria are relied on), close to the opinion now scrutinized is that recently put forward by Martins Paparinskis,[104] and which assumes that FET, in its ordinary meaning under Article 31, para 1, VCLT, would be a term of art for a reference to customary minimum standard:

> If one takes together the pre- and post-Second World War materials pre-dating investment arbitrations, it seems permissible to conclude [so], in particular regarding administration of justice. More recent practice confirms this view by necessary implication. The considerable number of arbitral decisions that read in the elements of customary law of denial of justice (particularly regarding the exhaustion of remedies) in the treaty rules on fair and equitable

---

[101] One may mention the Preamble of the 1993 Argentina-France BIT: 'Desiring to develop economic cooperation between the two States and to create favourable conditions for French investments in Argentina and Argentinian investments in France, Convinced that the promotion and protection of such investments are likely to stimulate transfers of capital and technology between the two countries in the interest of their economic development [...].'

[102] Such a sceptical view has been advanced, for instance, in *Suez* and *AWG*, ICSID Case No. ARB/03/19, Award of 30 July 2010, para 218: 'When one examines the stated purposes of the three BITs, one sees that they all have broader goals than merely granting specific levels of protection to individual investors. In the case of the Argentina-France BIT and the Argentina-Spain BIT, the Contracting States are seeking to further economic cooperation between them. The protection and promotion of foreign investment, while important to attaining that goal, are only a means to that end. Similarly, the Argentina-U.K. BIT is seeking to increase the prosperity of the two States. Through these treaties, the Contracting States pursue the broader goals of heightened economic cooperation between the two States concerned with a view toward achieving increased economic prosperity or development.'

[103] *Joseph Charles Lemire v. Argentina*, ICSID Case No. ARB/06/18, Decision on Jurisdiction and Liability of 14 January 2010, para 264: 'Words used in treaties must be interpreted through their context. The context of Article II.3 is to be found in the Preamble of the BIT, in which the contracting parties state '*that fair and equitable treatment of investment is desirable in order to maintain a stable framework for investment...*'. The FET standard is thus closely tied to the notion of legitimate expectations—actions or omissions by Ukraine are contrary to the FET standard if they frustrate legitimate and reasonable expectations on which the investor relied at the time when he made the investment.'

[104] Paparinskis 2013.

treatment necessarily engage in a reference to custom. It would be *prima facie* impossible to derive different standards of exhaustion merely from the neutral expression of treaty language.[105]

On the other hand, the same author underlines that, should an argument of this kind be rejected, customary international law (in the interpretation of FET clauses) could be 'taken into account' in any event; which would be merely a consequence related to the systemic interpretation rule enshrined in Article 31(3)(c) of the VCLT.[106] According to this rule, when interpreting a treaty provision, any relevant rules of international law applicable in the relations between the parties shall be taken into account. Indeed, the term 'relevant rules of international law' has been understood more broadly or narrowly by legal writers, but there is no doubt that its minimum reach refers to general international law (including both customary international law and general principles of law).[107] Moving from these premises, Paparinskis concludes that, whatever approach one adopts, the content of FET is likely to be always the same; the vagueness of the standard 'makes the argument about perceptible differences between the ordinary meaning and (context-level) customary law complicated to demonstrate'.[108]

Nonetheless, also the opinion under consideration proves unconvincing. While being supported by a sophisticated and rigorous argumentation, it ends up sharing the traditional trend of several legal writers (as well as of a number of arbitral tribunals) to regard FET as the transposition of IMS in international investment law; therefore, the same criticism applies.[109]

2.6 FET and the 'Rule of Law' Argument

In more pragmatic terms, some scholars, like Stephan Schill, tend to enhance the increasing arbitral case law effort to identify the constituent elements of FET, like due process of law (understood in a broad sense), legitimate expectations and proportionality, namely some of the most fundamental pillars underpinning the rule of law as it may be understood in the major domestic legal systems of liberal democracies. By doing so, their central argument is that all these canons are transposable to the international level, *going so far as to be subsumed under FET,*

[105] Idem, p. 163.

[106] Idem, p. 166. In detail, Article 31, para 3, VCLT, states as follows: 'There shall be taken into account, together with the context: (a) any subsequent agreement between the parties regarding the interpretation of the treaty or the application of its provisions; (b) any subsequent practice in the application of the treaty which establishes the agreement of the parties regarding its interpretation; (c) any relevant rules of international law applicable in the relations between the parties.' For a comment on this Article, *see* Dörr and Schmalebach 2012, pp. 70 et seq.

[107] Focarelli 2015, p. 407.

[108] Paparinskis 2013, p. 167.

[109] *See* Sect. 2.3.

and that this would be possible thanks to the bridge offered by general principles common to domestic systems under Article 38, para 1(c), of the ICJ Statute.[110]

More in detail, a comparative approach to the rule of law standard would influence the FET interpretation in two main respects:

> First, it may enable investment tribunals to positively deduce institutional and procedural requirements from the domestic rule of law standards for a context-specific interpretation of fair and equitable treatment. [...] Second, a comparative analysis of the implications of the rule of law under domestic law may be used to justify the conduct of a State vis-à-vis a foreign investor under the fair and equitable treatment standard. If similar conduct [...] is generally accepted by domestic legal systems as being in conformity with their understanding of the (national) concept of the rule of law, investment tribunals can transpose such findings to the level of investment treaties as an expression of a general principle of law.[111]

An argument of this kind has the advantage of grasping a circumstance which is increasingly evident in the practice of arbitral tribunals. Nonetheless, with a view to establishing whether it is appropriate, one should prove the existence of a twofold condition: (a) a commonly accepted notion of rule of law at national level, and (b) the possibility of regarding the principles behind it as operative at international level as well.

As far as the first question is concerned, attention must primarily be paid to the trend (common to both European and non-European countries) of using the terms 'legal State' and 'rule of law' in a quite controversial and ambiguous way. This terminological difference, indeed, is not accidental and refers to two political and legal traditions which significantly differ from each other: the German experience of the second half of the 19th century and that rooted in the political and constitutional history of Great Britain. Accordingly, the question arises as to whether the two notions debated here, that in turn were reflected in the national legal experience of other countries, may be compounded into a single, shared notion of the rule of law, at least in terms of reference values.

The German concept of *Rechtsstaat*, whose spiritual father is undoubtedly Immanuel Kant and his 'Theory of the State', mainly developed in the aftermath of the Restoration which followed the 1848 revolts and was conceived as both a response to the absolute State, and a reworking of the classical liberal thought and the principles behind it, namely the public protection of fundamental rights and the separation of powers. These two principles, in particular, resulted in two additional axioms. The first one relates to Jellinek's theory of 'subjective public rights', and rests on the circumstance that sovereignty, as well as the power to establish individual rights and ensure their protection, belongs to Parliament only. The second

[110] Schill 2010, pp. 151 et seq. With regard to FET as the perfect prism trough which evaluating the relevance of general principles within international investment law, *see* also Gazzini 2009, pp. 116 et seq.; Battini 2008, p. 12; McLachlan 2008, pp. 395 et seq.; Schill 2012, pp. 162 et seq.; Jacob and Schill 2015, pp. 700 et seq. More generally on the contribution of international investment law to the rule of law, *see* Happ 2016, pp. 279 et seq.

[111] Schill 2010, pp. 151, 175.

axiom is reflected in the principle of legality (*Gesetzmässigkeit*), whereby the Executive and the Judiciary are required to rigorously comply with the acts of Parliament, this being a legitimacy condition of their acts.[112] The term *Rechtsstaat*, which was exported from Germany to the rest of continental Europe (giving birth for example to the Italian *Stato di diritto*), is expressly mentioned in Article 28, para 1, of the current German Constitution, which states as follows:

> The constitutional order in the *Länder* must conform to the principles of a republican, democratic, and social State governed by the rule of law, within the meaning of this Basic Law.

The English variant of the rule of law is different from the German legal State, since it shares the idea according to which sovereignty belongs to Parliament, but claims the normative supremacy of the latter over the Executive alone: given the common law countries' features and, in particular, the absence of a written Constitution, courts are the main bodies entrusted with the normative function and the protection of individual rights. This is also the reason why, according to a widespread opinion, the difference between the German and Anglo-American doctrine of rule of law lies in the fact that where the former is contained in the codified legislation, the latter may be found in the courts' decisions.[113]

Despite the polysemy of traditions which flow into the notion of the rule of law, the opinion has been put forth whereby these traditions would be based on the same philosophical and political assumptions and stand for the same grounding values.

> Under such a perspective, the rule of law is a normative and institutional structure of the European modern State, within which […] the legal system is entrusted with the task of protecting individual rights, by constraining the inclination of political power to expand, to act arbitrarily and to abuse its prerogatives.[114]

More squarely, *two* principles underlie the rule of law so conceived: 'differentiation of power' and 'diffusion of power'. In particular, the principle of differentiation plays a dual role, being aimed at separating both the legal-political system from other social sub-systems (like the economic or religious one) and the State function consisting in enacting legislation (*legis latio*) from that of enforcing it

[112] As observed by Gosalbo-Bono 2010, p. 242, an obligation like this 'was the most effective defence against political misuse of powers and constituted the supreme guarantee for the protection of individual rights. However, the nineteenth century A.D. theory of the *Rechtsstaat* failed to take into account the potential arbitrary use of legislative power […] and was too optimistic in taking for granted the trust of the citizens since it assumed a perfect correspondence between the will of the State, legality, and moral legitimacy'.

[113] On this point, *see* Dedov 2014, p. 63.

[114] Zolo 2007, p. 19. In the same vein one may consider Dedov 2014, p. 62, once again: 'It is not a mistake to say that the legal State doctrine almost has the same meaning. As it usually happens, two different legal systems (the common law system and the civil law system) give different names to a doctrine in question while they move in the same direction purporting to prevent abuse of power and arbitrariness and to impose limits on politics in accordance with short-term interests.'

(*legis executio*). The principle of diffusion of power serves, on the other hand, to limit State powers (by means of explicit restraints), and to expand consistently the scope of individual freedoms, making them more and more independent of political interference.

The last-mentioned principle entails in turn a number of further principles which include, *inter alia*, due process of law, reasonable expectations and proportionality, that is to say those same principles referred to above. Nonetheless, this circumstance is not enough to suggest that similar guarantees should be granted at the international level. Going more into detail, the ideal of the rule of law is also relevant within the international legal order; both the United Nations[115] and the European Union,[116] for example, make the promotion of this ideal one of their priorities. Yet, in order to transpose the guarantees in question to the international level, it must be proved that they belong to general international law, and in particular to the category of general principles. No doubt, especially where the latter are understood in terms of principles common to domestic systems, such a task is anything but easy. As appropriately observed by Martins Paparinskis,

> [t]o the extent that the argument is made in legal terms, it has to fulfil the requirements of the traditional methodology: examine diverse approaches in different legal systems (not limited to the few convenient accessible traditional claimant States); identify whether sufficient similarities exist for generalization; extrapolate the principle; consider the possibility and manner of expressing it in the very different international legal context, demonstrate its relevance and role for the interpretation of treaty law. While there is no reason why such a legal argument could not be successfully made, the not entirely unfounded criticism of the traditional standard as a crude restatement on the international level of constitutional law of certain claimant States would require each methodological step to be made with particular diligence. It is not obvious that this can be done or has been done in existing practice.[117]

On the other hand, the possibility of relying on sources of this kind cannot, generally speaking, be rejected. The very fact that several FET clauses refer to international law is meaningful, since such an indication—it is worth restating —'must be understood as a reference to the sources of [the international legal order]

[115] *See* UN General Assembly, 'The Rule of Law at the National and International Levels', A/RES/68/116, 16 December 2013.

[116] By the celebrated judgment of 23 April 1986 known as *Les Verts* (Case 294/83 *Les Verts v. Parliament*, para 23), the European Court of Justice referred to the European Community as a 'Community based on the rule of law, inasmuch as neither its Member States nor its institutions can avoid a review of the question whether the measures adopted by them are in conformity with the basic constitutional charter, the Treaty.' From that moment on, much water has flowed under the bridge and several references to the rule of law may be found within the EU's realm. This is recalled by Article 2 of the Treaty on European Union (TEU), as well as by the Preambles to the same Treaty and to the Charter of Fundamental Rights of the EU. This is also why, under Article 49 TEU, respect for the rule of law is a precondition for EU membership. Last but not least, the 2014 European Commission Communication, COM(2014)158, to the EU Parliament and the Council ('A new EU Framework to Strengthen the Rule of Law') is of relevance. On the whole matter, *see* Pech 2009.

[117] Paparinskis 2013, p. 20.

as a whole',[118] therefore including all sources set out in Article 38(1) of the Statute of the International Court of Justice, among them general principles of law.

2.6.1 Rule of Law and General Principles Common to Domestic Systems

Scholars of international law have long argued that the expression 'general principles of law' may be relied on to identify a twofold category of law sources: (a) general principles common to domestic systems and (b) general principles of international law, with their own foundations in the international legal order itself.[119]

The inquiry into the legal basis and function of the first variant of principles began in 1920, on occasion of the adoption of the Permanent Court of International Justice (PCIJ) Statute. As is well known, in fact, its Article 38, para 1(c), which has been retained in the ICJ Statute as well, refers to 'general principles of law recognized by civilized nations', placing them among the sources to which the Court may refer in order to resolve any disputes of which it is seized. Not surprisingly, with a view to limiting judicial discretion in this respect, these principles were expected to be inferred from the internal law of international society members, and thus by adopting a 'domestic analogy'.

From that moment on, legal doctrine began to show a significant interest in the subject matter, suggesting two main systematic models. Some authors consider these principles as mere *material* sources of international law that like other factors, such as the need for justice and necessity, consist of those means from which the substance of a rule of international law is derived.[120] Contrariwise, other authors tend by and large to bring them back to formal sources of international law.[121] In detail, the first mentioned opinion is clearly anchored in the drafting history of Article 38, para 1(c), i.e. the idea whereby the source it provides for does not stand on the same footing as customary and conventional international law.[122] Indeed, general principles would mainly serve the purpose of filling any normative gaps of international law—because of the absence of customary or conventional rules

[118] *Merrill & Ring Forestry L. P. v. The Government of Canada*, NAFTA (UNCITRAL), Award of 31 March 2010, para 184.

[119] Several writers in the legal doctrine have highlighted such a circumstance. We refer, *inter alia*, to Gaja 2008 and Crawford 2012, p. 37.

[120] As to the distinction between formal and material sources, *see* Salmond 1924, p. 164.

[121] For an overall overview of the debate existing in the matter cf., *inter alia*, Vitanyi 1982; Focarelli 2015, pp. 296 et seq.

[122] We refer to the work carried out by the Advisory Committee of Jurists appointed by the Council of the League of Nations to draft the PCIJ Statute and which engaged in a discussion on what to do, should a rule of customary or conventional law to be applied to a given dispute be lacking. On this point, *see* recently Vos 2013, pp. 111–113.

applicable in a given case—and to avoid a *non liquet* on the part of international judges. Accordingly, decisions resorting to principles would be *dispositive* in nature, insofar as they create a norm which may be applied to a given case only.[123] A similar reductive approach to the matter is also typical of those authors who, inspired by opinions maintained less recently at the time of the PCIJ, limit its application to cases where a treaty provision, such as that set forth in Article 38, expressly allows it.[124]

Turning to the argument that most enhances the role of principles, one may firstly recall the view whereby the international legal system would be provided with a Constitution, understood in formal terms. Hence, general principles common to domestic systems would enter into the international legal order by means of a provision of this Constitution.[125] In the opinion of other authors, instead, general principles would be no more than a *sui generis* category of international customary rules:

> State practice in this case consists exclusively of the existence and consistent application of these rules within the national legal systems. *Opinio juris sive necessitatis* clearly exists with respect to [...] the old rules of legal logic and justice [such as *nemo judex in res sua*, *in claris non fit interpretation*, *ne bis in idem*, etc.]. These are rules viewed as universal by all State organs and applied in any legal system, including the international system. With respect to other consistent domestic rules, evidence of *opinio juris sive necessitatis* at the international level will be required on a case-by-case basis.[126]

Until quite recently, the question relating to the legal nature of principles common to domestic systems has played little practical significance. Two reasons explain this. First, the use of such principles by international tribunals has proved anything but easy. Indeed, the polysemy of meanings that principles are able to take on within the different national legal systems makes their identification particularly arduous. Second, even when principles were used, they primarily served interpretive purposes, that is to say 'to bolster a proposition that could already be formulated on the basis of other rules or principles.'[127]

The issue has been revitalized by the emergence of new areas of international law and the awareness that, in order to fill a large number of gaps, custom and treaties in force are inadequate. In this context, general principles clearly work as a subsidiary means of law-creation, which resorts to principles common to domestic systems (of both civil and common law) and, through the custom, transpose them to the international legal order. This applies to various areas.

International criminal law, a field which has proved particularly deficient from the very start, is one of the areas to be considered. International criminal tribunals have frequently resorted to general principles of criminal law recognized in the

[123] Anzilotti 1964, p. 107. In the same vein, *see* Morelli 1967, p. 46.

[124] Treves 2005, p. 249.

[125] Balladore Pallieri 1962, p. 24.

[126] Conforti and Labella 2012, p. 40.

[127] Cassese 2005, p. 192.

main legal systems of the world. Not by chance, Article 21, para 1(c) of the Statute of the International Criminal Court (ICC), also in the wake of Article 38 of the ICJ Statute, refers to this category of source, stating that the Court shall apply:

> general principles of law derived [...] from national laws of legal systems of the world including, as appropriate, the national laws of States that would normally exercise jurisdiction over the crime, provided that those principles are not inconsistent with this Statute and with international law and internationally recognized norms and standards.

In the same vein, one may consider international investment law. Also within this context, in fact, there is significant room for the use of general principles common to domestic systems. In the terms of Article 42, para 1, of the ICSID Convention,

> the tribunal shall decide a dispute in accordance with such rules of law as may be agreed by the parties. In the absence of such agreement, the tribunal shall apply the law of the Contracting State party to the dispute (including its rules on the conflict of laws) and such rules of international law as may be applicable.[128]

Arguably, the expression 'rules of international law' refers, *inter alia,* to principles common to domestic systems. Evidence of it can firstly be found in the Report of the Executive Directors of the World Bank on the ICSID Convention.[129] This Report, in effect, interprets Article 42, para 1,

> in the sense given to it by Article 38 (1) of the Statute of the International Court of Justice, allowance being made for the fact that Article 38 was designated to apply to inter-State disputes.

From this point of view, general principles common to domestic systems would come into consideration, assuming that reference to Article 38 covers all sources of international law as set forth in this Article.[130] The same conclusion, moreover, can be inferred from a copious arbitral case law which on the one hand is in line with the World Bank Report, and on the other hand shares the idea whereby a general principle is applicable insofar as it is provided for in most national legal systems of the world. *Amco* is the first (and for some authors[131] also the most relevant) arbitral

---

[128] On this point, *see*, e.g., Kahn 1968, p. 27; Schreuer et al. 2009, pp. 545 et seq. and 603 et seq.

[129] Report of the Executive Directors of the International Bank for Reconstruction and Development on the Convention on the Settlement of Investment Disputes between States and Nationals of other States, para 41, available at http://icsid.worldbank.org/ICSID/StaticFiles/basicdoc/CRR_English-final.pdf.

[130] Schreuer et al. 2009, p. 604: 'The reference to the enumeration of sources of international law as contained in Article 38(1) of the ICJ Statute by no means resolves the problem of establishing the rules of international law relevant to the particular dispute. It is debatable whether the list provided there paints a complete picture of contemporary international law and whether the neat categories suggested there conform to the complex realities of international legal practice. Nevertheless, this reference demonstrates that an ICSID tribunal is directed to look at the full range of sources of international law in a similar way as the International Court of Justice.'

[131] *See*, e.g., Tudor 2008, pp. 91 et seq.

decision that clearly illustrates the traditional manner in which general principles of this kind work.[132] In its terms, these principles are expected to be common to the main national legal orders and their existence should be ascertained by relying on comparative methods. Hence, the tribunal concluded that 'the full compensation of prejudice, by awarding to the injured party the *damnum emergens* and *lucrum cessans* is a principle common to the main systems of municipal law, and therefore, a general principle of law which may be considered as a source of international law.'[133] The ICSID award in *Inceysa* is equally revealing, insofar as it states that general principles of law should be regarded

> as general rules on which there is international consensus to consider them as universal standards and rules of conduct that must always be applied and which [...] are important rules of law on which the legal systems of the States are based.[134]

Now, the opinion claiming the existence of an international rule of law which would be relevant also within the field of foreign investments usually relies on the 'domestic analogy' argument, in the sense of viewing FET through the lens of the rule of law domestic standards and regarding the latter as principles common to most legal systems of the world. This opinion, however, is far from convincing. Indeed, as has been rightly observed,

> the more specific requirements of the rule of law often reflect a State's particular historical and constitutional evolution, and differ from State to State. The international rule of law cannot be identified with any one national meaning of the concept, and in this, as in other areas of public international law, principles, concepts and rules of national legal systems are at best an approximate guide to the content of the international analogue.[135]

---

[132] *Amco Asia Corp, Pan American Development Ltd and PT Amco Indonesia v. Indonesia*, ICSID, Award of 31 May 1990.

[133] On this point, see what has been observed in the introduction.

[134] *Inceysa v. El Salvador*, ICSID Case No. ARB/03/26, Award of 2 August 2006, para 227. For a case where the existence of a general principle has been rejected, given the absence of a general consensus within national legal systems, *see Klöckner v. Cameron*, Decision on Annulment of 31 May 1985, para 72: 'In the latter case, is it possible to hold that the Award has 'applied the law of the Contracting State' as required in Article 42(1)? It is true that the principle of good faith is 'at the basis' of French civil law, as of other legal systems, but this elementary proposition does not by itself answer the question. In Cameroonian or Franco-Cameroonian law does the 'principle' affirmed or postulated by the Award, the "duty of full disclosure", exist? If it does, no doubt flowing from the general principle of good faith, from the obligation of frankness and loyalty, then *how*, by what *rules* and under what *conditions* is it implemented and within what *limits?* Can a duty to make a "*full* disclosure" even to one's own prejudice, be accepted, especially without limits? Is there a single legal system which contains such a broad obligation? These are a few of the questions that naturally come to mind and that the Award provides no basis for answering.'

[135] Watts 1994, p. 16. A similar opinion has been recently advanced by Hachez 2013, pp. 307 et seq. In this author's view, indeed, 'one must recognize that the international legal order is profoundly different from the domestic legal orders in the context of which the ideal of rule of law was first expressed, then theorized.' Of course, the term 'international rule of law' may refer also to other questions, as that to establish whether the law is actually ruling at the international level. In this regard, *see* recently Krieger and Nolte 2016.

For example, the scope of principles like that of reasonable expectations proves to be very wide in some national legal systems and very narrow in others.[136]

In light of the above, the question remains as to whether one may rely on the different category of general principles of international law.

2.6.2 Rule of Law and General Principles of International Law

General principles of international law, unlike principles common to domestic systems, are identified on the basis of the normative dynamics peculiar to the international legal order itself, and epitomize, as such, an autonomous source of general international law (that is, independent of custom).[137] Bearing in mind the already mentioned distinction between rules and principles[138] and following the opinion advanced by Antonio Cassese, there are two classes of general principles.[139]

The *first variant* includes *general principles of international law*, namely those principles that can be inferred by way of induction and generalization from conventional and customary rules and which inform the international legal order as a whole. One example is the ICJ Judgment in *Corfu Channel*.[140] In this case, in order to assert the Albanian authorities' obligation of notifying the existence of a minefield in their own territorial waters and warning the approaching British warships of the imminent danger to which the minefield exposed them, the ICJ: (i) took the moves from a treaty provision applicable only in war times (the Hague Convention of 1907, No. VIII); (ii) identified the general principles underlying this provision (i.e. 'elementary considerations of humanity, even more exacting in peace than in war; the principle of the freedom of maritime communication; and every State's obligation not to knowingly allow its territory to be used for acts contrary to the rights of other States');[141] and finally (iii) extracted from these principles the rule to be applied in the case in hand. It is a line of argument that increasingly occurs in international jurisprudence, and which may be split into two stages: in the first stage, *by way of induction*, the judge infers the principle from pre-existing rules; in the second stage, *by way of deduction* and therefore on the basis of the

---

[136] *See infra* Chap. 4, Sect. 4.1.

[137] Among the authors supporting the existence of this category of general principles, *see* Quadri 1968, pp. 119 et seq. *See* also Strozzi 1992.

[138] *See supra* Sect. 2.2

[139] Cassese 2005, p. 189. *See* also Cassese 1995, pp. 126 et seq.

[140] *Corfu Channel (United Kingdom v. Albania)*, Judgment of 9 April 1949, p. 22.

[141] Idem.

principle which has been identified, he lays down the rule applicable to a given case.[142] This is anything but surprising. As already mentioned, if one assumes that general principles may be regarded as guiding criteria, it follows that applying a principle means giving to it a concrete content.[143] This particular approach adopted by the international judge, as well as ensuring the completeness of the legal order, serves to stimulate the emergence of new rules, especially in those areas of law where the law-ascertainment role is played by specialized tribunals. It is a very meaningful circumstance that allows the introduction of the *second variant* of general principles.

We refer to the hypothesis where the *regula iuris*, deduced from a general principle of international law and aimed at governing a certain case within a given area of law, becomes *stable* by way of a constant and uniform case law and ends up embodying a *general principle peculiar to that area of law only* (e.g. the law of international responsibility, humanitarian law and so on).[144] It is a fairly graspable phenomenon which, as far as principles are concerned, reflects the 'relative' nature of the concept of 'general'. As is known, indeed, the same rule can be 'regarded as a general principle in relation to more specific rules, and as a special rule with respect to a more general rule'.[145] One example in this connection is once again Article 21 of the Statute of the ICC, which vests the latter with the power to apply general principles of international humanitarian law. A decision of the International Labour Organization Administrative Tribunal of 1989 is equally instructive; its para 4 refers to 'the general principles of law that govern the international civil service'.[146]

[142] Such an opinion has been widely developed by Iovane 2008. In the same line of thought, *see* also Cannizzaro 2016, pp. 136 et seq.

[143] Guastini 2011, p. 693. A similar opinion may bc found in Cassese 1995, pp. 128–129: 'Principles do not differ from treaty or customary rules simply in that they are more general and less precise [...] Rather, principles differ from legal rules in that they are the expression and result of conflicting views of States on matters of crucial importance. When States cannot agree upon definite and specific standards of behaviour because of their principles, opposing attitudes, but need, however, some sort of basic guideline for their conduct, their actions and discussions eventually lead to the formulation of principles [P]rinciples have great normative potential and dynamic force: among other things, one can deduce from them specific rules, to the extent that these rules are not at variance with State practice.'

[144] In this regard, what Cassese 2005, p. 189, highlights, is quite revealing: 'Normally principles are spelled out by courts, when adjudicating cases that are not entirely regulated by treaty or customary rules. In this respect courts have played and are increasingly playing an essential role: they identify and set out principles 'hidden' in the interstices of the normative network, thus considerably contributing to the enrichment and development of the whole body of international law. It cannot be denied that by so acting courts fulfil a meritorious function very close to, and almost verging on, the creation of law.'

[145] Bobbio 1994, p. 275. (own translation)

[146] Judgment of 27 June 1989, No. 962.

2.6.2.1 FET as a General Principle Specific to International Investment Law

In this author's view, FET is undoubtedly part of the category of general principles specific to a certain field of international law. For its content to be identified, the judge has firstly taken into account the rule of law principles and regarded them as an embodiment of the values underpinning the normative framework of the current international legal order. These values, which apply to the relations between States as well as between States and individuals, include *inter alia* due process of law, legitimate expectations and proportionality. Secondly, on the basis of these principles, that same judge has formulated a number of rules peculiar to the matter of foreign investments. Lastly, by way of a constant and uniform case law, these rules have become stable and have been subsumed, as such, under FET, i.e. a composite principle peculiar to international investment law or, to put it differently, its *Grundnorm*. Remarkably, also authors (like Stephan Schill) mainly relying on general principles common to domestic systems in order to identify the FET content, do not exclude the relevance of 'a cross-regime comparison with other international law regimes that incorporate rule of law standards';[147] the jurisprudence of the European Court of Human Rights (ECtHR) concerning Article 6 of the European Convention on Human Rights (ECHR) would be relevant in this connection.[148] Moreover, insofar as the same authors deem it necessary 'to keep in mind the specific context of investment treaties',[149] they are unwittingly admitting the existence of general principles of international law, the concretization of which cannot but change as the normative field where they are applied changes.

A final remark seems appropriate. It may be contended that our argument demands a careful demonstration. This will be done hereinafter, but with a caveat. Even where the 'reasoning by principles' is not *expressly* articulated in all the aforementioned steps, its relevance for our purposes does not diminish. A reasoning of this kind must be considered in its entirety, above all having regard to its final capacity of enhancing the normative force of these principles and, accordingly, of finding a rule pertinent to the particular case. In such pragmatic terms, it is difficult to reject the idea whereby the FET content has been progressively shaped by arbitral tribunals by means of a reasoning which is both inductive and deductive.

---

[147] Schill 2010, p. 176.

[148] Idem: 'This provision can be viewed as an expression of a more general standard of an institutional and procedural understanding of the rule of law. The rich jurisprudence of the ECtHR could thus be used to further concretize fair and equitable treatment, for example with respect to the timely administration of justice or the right to a fair trial. Similarly, comparative recourse could be had to the emerging principles of European administrative law or the jurisprudence of the WTO Appellate Body in order to further develop the rule of law requirements with respect to the exercise of public power.'

[149] Schill 2010, p. 176.

2.7 Conclusion

The analysis conducted in this chapter has tried to dispel any doubts concerning the FET normative basis. Plausibly, what is required to this end is to accept the close link existing between FET and general principles of international law, in the sense that the latter, through the medium of the judge, seems to have been refashioned in order to operate under the former. In these terms, all the shortcomings generally associated with the main academic views may be overcome, and the very content of FET, at least in its minimum reach, is in the end straightforward.

References

Anzilotti D (1964) Corso di diritto internazionale, vol. I, 4th edn. Cedam, Padua

Balladore Pallieri G (1962) Diritto internazionale pubblico. Giuffrè, Milan

Battini S (2008) Le due anime del diritto amministrativo globale. In: Il diritto amministrativo oltre i confini. Omaggio degli allievi a Sabino Cassese. Giuffré, Milan, pp. 1–22

Bobbio N (1994) Contributo ad un dizionario giuridico. Giappichelli, Turin.

Bronfman M (2006) Fair and Equitable Treatment: An Evolving Standard. Max Planck Yearbook of United Nations Law 10:609–680

Cannizzaro E (2016) Diritto internazionale, 3rd edn. Giappichelli, Turin

Cassese A (1995) Self-Determination of Peoples. A Legal Reappraisal. Cambridge University Press, Cambridge

Cassese A (2005) International Law, 2nd edn. Oxford University Press, Oxford

Charpentier J (1963) De la non-dicrimination dans les investissements. Annuaire français de droit international 9:35–63

Ciurtin H (2015) Beyond the Norm: The Hermeneutic Function of Treaty Preambles in Investment Arbitration and International Law. Romanian Arbitration Review 36:64–80

Collins D (2016) An Introduction to International Investment Law. Cambridge University Press, Cambridge

Conforti B, Labella A (2012) An Introduction to International Law. Nijhoff, Leiden

Cordero Moss GC (2008) Full Protection and Security. In: Reinisch A (ed) Standards of Investment Protection. Oxford University Press, Oxford, pp. 131–150

Crawford J (2012) Brownlie's Principles of Public International Law, 8th edn. Oxford University Press, Oxford

Crawford J (2013) Chance, Order, Change: The Course of International Law. Recueil des Cours 365:9–389

Crivellaro A (2001) La rilevanza dei preamboli nell'interpretazione dei contratti internazionali. Diritto del commercio internazionale 15:777–791

D'Amato A (1988) Custom and Treaty: A Response to Professor Weisburd. Vanderbildt Journal of International Law 21:459–472

Dedov D (2014) The Rule of Law and Legal State Doctrines as a Methodology of the Philosophy of Law. In: Silkenat JR, Hickey Jr JE, Barenboim PD (eds) The Legal Doctrines of the Rule of Law and the Legal State (Rechtsstaat). Springer, Heidelberg, pp. 61–70

Di Benedetto S (2013) International Investment Law and the Environment. Edward Elgar, Cheltenham

Diebold NF (2011) Standards of Non-Discrimination in International Economic Law. International and Comparative Law Quarterly 60:831–865

Diehl A (2012) The Core Standard of International Investment Protection. Fair and Equitable Treatment. Wolters Kluwer, Alphen aan den Rijn
Doehring K (2004) Völkerrecht, 2nd edn. CF Müller, Heidelberg
Dörr O, Schmalebach K (2012) Vienna Convention on the Law of Treaties. Springer, Heidelberg
Dumberry P (2013) The Fair and Equitable Treatment Standard: A Guide to NAFTA Case Law on Article 1105. Kluwer Law International, Alphen aan den Rijn
Dumberry P (2016) Has the Fair and Equitable Treatment Standard Become a Rule of Customary International Law? Journal of International Dispute Settlement 7:1–24
Dworkin R (1977) Taking Rights Seriously. Harvard University Press, Harvard
Fatouros AA (1962) Government Guarantees to Foreign Investors. Columbia University Press, New York
Fietta S (2005) Most Favoured Nation Treatment and Dispute Resolution under Bilateral Investment Treaties: A Turning Point? International Arbitration Law Review 4:131–138
Focarelli C (2015) Trattato di diritto internazionale. Utet, Turin
Franck TM (1995) Fairness in International Law and Institutions. Oxford University Press, Oxford
Gaja G (2008) General Principles of Law. Max Planck Encyclopedia of Public International Law, Online Edition. Available at http://opil.ouplaw.com
Gazzini T (2009) General Principles of Law in the Field of Foreign Investments. Journal of World Investment & Trade 10:103–119
Gosalbo-Bono R (2010) The Significance of the Rule of Law and Its Implications for the European Union and the United States. University of Pittsburgh Law Review 72:229–360
Guastini R (2011) Principi di diritto. Digesto delle discipline privatistiche, Sezione civile, Aggiornamento. Utet, Turin, pp. 645–653
Hachez N (2013) What Elements of the Rule of Law Can Be Put to Use at International Level. Revue Belge du droit international 47:307–324
Happ R (2016) Why Investment Arbitration Contributes to the Rule of Law: Without Knowing Where We Came from We Cannot Know Where We are Heading. European Investment Law and Arbitration Review 1: 278–287
Heiskanen V (2008) Arbitrary and Unreasonable Measures. In: Reinisch A (ed) Standards of Investment Protection. Oxford University Press, Oxford, pp. 87–110
Iovane M (2008) La participation de la société civile à l'élaboration et à l'application du droit international de l'environnement. Revue générale de droit international public 112:465–519
Jacob M, Schill S (2015) Fair and Equitable Treatment: Content, Practice, Method. In: Bungenberg M, Griebel J, Hobe S, Reinisch A (eds) International Investment Law. Beck/Hart/Nomos, Munich/Oxford/Baden-Baden, pp. 700–763
Juillard P (1994) L'évolution des sources du droit des investissements. Recueil des Cours 250:9–216
Kahn P (1968) The Law Applicable to Foreign Investments: The Contribution of the World Bank Convention on the Settlement of Investment Disputes. Indiana Law Journal 44:1–32
Kishoiyian B (1993) The Utility of Bilateral Investment Treaties in the Formulation of Customary International law. Northwestern Journal of International Law & Business 14:327–375
Kläger R (2011) 'Fair and Equitable' Treatment in International Investment Law. Cambridge University Press, Cambridge
Kohona PTB (1987) Investment Protection Agreements: An Australian Perspective. Journal of World Trade Law 21:79–103
Krieger H, Nolte G (2016) The International Rule of Law – Rise or Decline? Points of Departure. KFG Working Papers Series, No 1. Available at SSRN: https://ssrn.com/abstract=2866940
Lanfranchi F (1968) Il trattamento dello straniero nelle clausole relative allo stabilimento degli accordi bilaterali in vigore tra l'Italia e gli altri Stati. Rivista di diritto internazionale privato e processuale 4:331–350
Leben C (1999) L'évolution du droit international des investissements. In: Dupuy PM, Leben C (eds) Un accord multilateral sur l'investissement: d'un forum de négociation à l'autre? Pedone, Paris, pp. 7–32

Mann FA (1981) British Treaties for the Promotion and Protection of Investments. British Yearbook of International Law 52:241–254

Mann FA (1982) The Legal Aspects of Money, 4th edn. Oxford University Press, Oxford

Mauro MR (2003) Gli accordi bilaterali sulla promozione e la protezione degli investimenti. Giappichelli, Turin

McLachlan QC C (2008) Investment Treaties and General International Law. International and Comparative Law Quarterly 57:361–40.

Mo JS (1991) Some Aspects of the Australia-China Investment Protection Treaty. Journal of World Trade Law 25:43–80

Montt S (2009) State Liability in Investment Treaty Arbitration. Global Constitutional and Administrative Law in the BIT Generation. Hart, Oxford

Morelli G (1967) Nozioni di diritto internazionale, 7th edn. Cedam, Padua

OECD (2004) Fair and Equitable Treatment Standard in International Investment Law, OECD Working Papers on International Investment, 2004/03. OECD Publishing. http://dx.doi.org/10.1787/675702255435

Orakhelashvili A (2008) The Normative Basis of 'Fair and Equitable Treatment': General International Law on Foreign Investment? Archiv des Völkerrechts 46:74–105

Paparinskis M (2013) The International Minimum Standard and Fair and Equitable Treatment. Oxford University Press, Oxford

Pech L (2009) The Rule of Law as a Constitutional Principle of the European Union. Jean Monnet Working Paper 04. Available at SSRN: https://ssrn.com/abstract=1463242

Quadri R (1968) Diritto internazionale pubblico, 5th edn. Liguori, Naples

Rawls J (2001) Justice as Fairness: A Restatement. Harvard University Press, Cambridge

Reisman M (2015) Canute Confronts the Tide: States versus Tribunals and the Evolution of the Minimum Standard in Customary International Law. ICSID Review 30:616–634

Sacerdoti G (1997) Bilateral Treaties and Multilateral Instrument on Investment Protection. Recueil des Cours 269:251–460.

Salmond JW (1924) Jurisprudence. Sweet & Maxwell, London

Santulli C (2015) Le traitement juste et equitable: stipulation particuliere ou principe generale de bonne conduit? Revue Générale de Droit International Public 119:69–85

Savarese E (2011) Treaty-Based Investment Arbitration and the MFN Clause: The Possible Common Denominator between Jurisdiction and Admissibility. Italian Yearbook of International Law 21:241–257

Schachter O (1984) Compensation for Expropriation. American Journal of International Law 78:121–130

Schill S (2010) Fair and Equitable Treatment, the Rule of Law, and Comparative Public Law. In: Schill S (ed) International Investment Law and Comparative Public Law. Oxford University Press, Oxford, pp. 151–182

Schill S (2012) General Principles of Law and International Investment Law. In: Gazzini T, De Brabandere E (eds) International Investment Law. The Sources of Rights and Obligations. Nijhoff, Lcidcn, pp. 133–181

Schreuer C (2007) Fair and Equitable Treatment (FET): Interactions with other Standards. Transnational Dispute Management 5. www.transnational-dispute-management.com

Schreuer C (2008) Introduction: Interrelationship of Standards. In: Reinisch A (ed) Standard of Investment Protection. Oxford University Press, Oxford, pp. 1–7

Schreuer C (2010) Full Protection and Security. Journal of International Dispute Settlement 1:353–369

Schreuer C, Malintoppi L, Reinisch A, Sinclair A (2009) The ICSID Convention: A Commentary, 2nd edn. Oxford University Press, Oxford

Shihata IFI (1993) Legal Treatment of Foreign Investments: 'The World Bank Guidelines'. Nijhoff, Dordrecht

Sornarajah M (2010) The International Law on Foreign Investment, 3rd edn. Cambridge University Press, Cambridge

Strozzi G (1992) I 'Principi' dell'ordinamento internazionale. La Comunità internazionale 47:162–187

Thomas JC (2002) Reflections on Article 1105 of NAFTA: History, State Practice and the Influence of Commentators. ICSID Review 17:21–101

Treves T (2005) Diritto internazionale. Problemi fondamentali. Giuffré, Milan

Treves T (2012) Customary International Law. Max Planck Encyclopedia of Public International Law, Online Edition. Available at http://opil.ouplaw.com

Tudor I (2008) The Fair and Equitable Treatment Standard in the International Law of Foreign Investment. Oxford University Press, Oxford

Valenti M (2014) The Protection of General Interests of Host States in the Application of the Fair and Equitable Treatment Standard. In: Sacerdoti G, Acconci P, Valenti M, De Luca A (eds) General Interests of Host States in International Investment Law. Cambridge University Press, Cambridge, pp. 26–57

Vitanyi B (1982) Le positions doctrinales concernant le sens de la notion de 'principles généraux de droit reconnus par le nations civilisées'. Revue générale de droit international public 86:46–116

Vos JA (2013) The Function of Public International Law. TMC Asser Press, The Hague

Watts A (1994) The International Rule of Law. German Yearbook of International Law 36:15–45

Weeramantry JR (2012) Treaty Interpretation in Investment Arbitration. Oxford University Press, Oxford

Weiler T (2013) The Interpretation of International Investment Law. Equality, Discrimination and Minimum Standards of Treatment in Historical Context. Nijhoff, Leiden

Zolo D (2007) The Rule of Law: A Critical Reappraisal. In: Costa P, Zolo D (eds) The Rule of Law. History, Theory and Criticism. Springer, Heidelberg, pp. 3–7

Chapter 3
FET and Due Process of Law

Contents

Abstract This chapter aims to determine the exact content of due process of law within the context of the law on foreign investment. In that respect, following an in-depth analysis of the existing literature, the opinion is put forward whereby due process is a general principle of international law with its own foundations in the international legal order itself and which may be understood, as an FET element, in terms of denial of justice and procedural fairness in administrative proceedings.

F.M. Palombino, *Fair and Equitable Treatment and the Fabric of General Principles*, https://doi.org/10.1007/978-94-6265-210-1_3

Keywords Due process of law · Definition · Denial of justice · Administrative proceedings · Right to be heard · Country risk

3.1 Introduction

If regarded as an FET element, due process of law is susceptible to be seen in terms of denial of justice and fairness in administrative proceedings. *In terms of denial of justice*, what counts for the State responsibility to be ascertained is not the absence of a decent system of justice, but rather a judicial misinterpretation or misapplication of national law which proves 'manifestly unjust'; whoever decides to invest part of his capital in a foreign country does so in the wake of the *whole regulatory framework* existing in that country, therefore having regard not only to the rules that make the investment convenient, but also to those governing the judicial system and which may be relevant when a dispute between the investor and the host State arises. *In terms of fairness in administrative proceedings*, due process requires the host State to ensure the investor's participation in these proceedings, should the challenged measure cause a serious economic loss. Arguably, due process as an FET element has gone so far as to embody a general principle specific to international investment law.

3.2 Due Process as a General Principle of International Law

One of the main (and only in appearance less problematic) constituent elements of FET includes due process of law, especially in terms of denial of justice, viz. the traditional international wrong concerning the treatment of aliens which a State can incur for the breach of the principle. Support for this proposition may be found in a number of arbitral decisions whereby the concepts of due process and denial of justice are closely linked; accordingly, a failure to guarantee the former will often result in the occurrence of the latter.[1]

[1] *Waguih Elie George Siag and Clorinda Vecchi v. Egypt*, ICSID Case No. ARB/05/15, Award of 1 June 2009, para 452. In the same vein, Article 5, para 2(a), of the 2012 US Model BIT should be considered: 'fair and equitable treatment' includes the obligation not to deny justice in criminal, civil, or administrative adjudicatory proceedings in accordance with the principle of due process embodied in the principal legal systems of the world.'

Insofar as denial of justice is regarded as a rule of general international law—in the form of a principle common to domestic systems[2] or of a custom[3]—and with a clear-cut content, it may be argued that the FET content, at least in part, would be clearly defined as well. This argument seems to be reflected in the preparatory works to the 2013 Resolution rendered by the IIL in the matter of investments[4] and more recently in the 2015 Indian Model Bilateral Investment Treaty (Article 3).[5] But the argument is unconvincing in terms of both the content and the legal nature of due process of law as an FET element. *In terms of its content*, not only has due process taken on a meaning so broad as to include also the right to procedural fairness in administrative proceedings—as the 2009 ASEAN Comprehensive Investment Agreement[6] clearly confirms, but the very notion of denial of justice remains fairly uncertain; the only aspect to appear clear-cut in arbitral practice is that the occurrence of this delict may be established only where the investor has exhausted all internal remedies to challenge the allegedly unlawful decision (or has proved that such remedies would be futile).[7] *In terms of the legal nature of due*

[2] Borchard 1940, pp. 445 et seq.: 'Long before article 38 of the Permanent Court of International Justice made the 'general principles of law recognized by civilized stated' a source of international law, foreign offices and arbitral tribunals had relied on such general principles to work out a loose minimum which they applied constantly in interstate practice [...] It is well known that aliens may be denied numerous privileges [...] and may be restricted [...] in municipal law. Yet the alien must enjoy police and judicial protection for such rights as the local law grants and its arbitrary refusal is a denial of justice. Bad faith, fraud, outrage resulting in injury, cannot be defended on the ground that it is custom of the country to which nationals must almost submit'. Della Cananea 2009, pp. 133 et seq., takes the same position. As to the practice, the US Model BIT cited *supra* note 1, and its reference to the principle of due process as 'embodied in the principal legal systems of the world' is equally of assistance.

[3] More in detail, the existence of a custom in the matter at issue would be suggested by the difficulty of referring to the concepts of denial of justice adopted at the national level. Indeed, on the one hand '[t]he malleability of the words *denial of justice* have led States to adopt narrower or broader definitions, as their interests dictate'; on the other hand, 'some national laws contain their own long-established doctrines of denial of justice, defined in a manner different from that of international law, and sometimes inconsistent with it' (Paulsson 2005, pp. 13 et seq.). In the same vein, *see* Diehl 2012, p. 455: 'Denial of justice in international law cannot be equated with the notion developed in most national legal systems, where it has the limited meaning of a refusal to hear a grievance. Under national law, a litigant who has been given full access to the procedures provided within the system including appeal mechanisms—cannot ask for more justice or different justice. In other words: The matter is *res judicata*, the system has given all it has to offer.'

[4] *Supra* Sect. 1.5, para 130 states as follows: 'The violation of [due process] determines an international wrongful act of denial of justice. The denial of justice can be interpreted on the basis of customary international law [...] This requirement is considered to be so fundamental that in the practice of US BIT and FTA is specifically indicated.'

[5] This Article, as already observed, clearly speaks of denial of justice under customary international law.

[6] Article 11, para 2(a), states that 'fair and equitable treatment requires each Member State not to deny justice in any legal or administrative proceedings in accordance with the principle of due process.'

[7] In this regard, Paulsson 2005, p. 108, observes as follows: 'Perhaps the strongest argument for this special treatment of claim of denial of justice is that it avoids interference with the fundamental

process, reliance by legal writers on both general principles common to domestic systems and custom is questionable. On the one hand, the concept here referred to may expand and contract from State to State and is tied to the idiosyncrasies of each legal system, hence the inadequacy of the above principles. On the other hand, a number of awards increasingly advance the opinion whereby a distinction must be drawn between a denial of justice claim based on customary law and one based on the FET clause: should a claim for denial of justice fail under custom, the competent arbitral tribunal would not be exonerated 'from carefully appraising the alleged facts and deciding whether they amount to a breach of the fair and equitable treatment standard.'[8]

In this author's view, for the whole matter to be rightly assessed, the assumption from which one must move is the following: due process broadly understood embodies a general principle of international law that, as such, can be inferred by way of induction and generalization from a number of customary and conventional rules.[9] In effect, these rules not only involve due process, but may also be classified under three major groups. A first set of provisions, which are provided for in most

(Footnote 7 continued)

principle that States should to the greatest extent possible be free to organize their national legal systems as they fit [...] If aliens are allowed to bypass those mechanisms and bring international claims for denial of justice on the basis of alleged wrongdoing by the justice of the peace of any neighbourhood, international law would find itself intruding intolerably into internal affairs.' For an in-depth analysis of this point, also for the references therein, *see* recently Savarese 2012, pp. 169 et seq. More in general, it is worth remembering that, at least in principle, the local remedies rule does not represent a procedural requirement for the admissibility of claims in investment treaty arbitration (Douglas 2009, para 59). This may be inferred, for example, from the wording of Article 26 of the 1965 Washington Convention. This provision on the one hand states that 'Consent of the Parties to arbitration under this Convention shall, unless otherwise stated, be deemed consent to such arbitration to the exclusion of any other remedy'; on the other hand, but *by way of exception*, it recognizes that 'a Contracting State may require the exhaustion of local administrative or judicial remedies as a condition of its consent to arbitration under this Convention.' Further, some investment treaties expressly provide for a local remedies rule. This is the case of the 1991 Argentina-Spain BIT. Its Article X, para 2, states that where a dispute cannot be settled amicably 'it shall, at the request of either party, be submitted to the competent tribunals of the Party in whose territory the investment was made'. For the arbitral practice, for example, *see infra* Sect. 3.4.1

[8] *See*, for instance, *Franck Charles Arif v. Moldova*, ICSID Case No. ARB/11/23, Award of 8 April 2013, paras 423 et seq. In the same vein, one may mention *Flughafen Zürich A.G. and Gestión e Ingeniería IDC S.A. v. Venezuela*, ICSID Case No. ARB/10/19, Award of 18 November 2014, para 378: 'Y aunque la denegación de justicia no estuviera contenida en el estándar de TJE [fair and equitable treatment], adicionalmente, la denegación de justicia representa en todo caso un ilícito sancionado por el Derecho internacional consuetudinario.'

[9] The existence of a notion of international due process has been advanced, for example, by Kotuby 2013.

human rights treaties (both universal[10] and regional),[11] seeks to ensure the individual's right to a fair trial and embody, in the view of some authors, a veritable custom in criminal matters.[12] Further relevant norms of general international law refer to some fundamental canons of international adjudication, like that protecting the juridical equality between parties in their capacity as litigants[13] as well as that of *audi alteram partem.*[14] Last but not least, international norms reflecting concerns of due process are those providing for the right to fairness in administrative/ law-making proceedings, the scope of which extends to both individuals (at national and international levels), and States insofar as they are part of international organizations (of which both the EU[15] and the WTO[16] are good examples) acting as law-makers.

In light of the foregoing, the present chapter will investigate the two main manifestations of due process, namely denial of justice and fairness in administrative proceedings, and establish whether, as FET elements, they have taken on a specific content.

---

[10] *See*, for example, Article 14 of the UN Covenant on Civil and Political Rights. Its para 1 states as follows: 'All persons shall be equal before the courts and tribunals. In the determination of any criminal charge against him, or of his rights and obligations in a suit at law, everyone shall be entitled to a fair and public hearing by a competent, independent and impartial tribunal established by law. The press and the public may be excluded from all or part of a trial for reasons of morals, public order (ordre public) or national security in a democratic society, or when the interest of the private lives of the parties so requires, or to the extent strictly necessary in the opinion of the court in special circumstances where publicity would prejudice the interests of justice; but any judgement rendered in a criminal case or in a suit at law shall be made public except where the interest of juvenile persons otherwise requires or the proceedings concern matrimonial disputes or the guardianship of children'.

[11] *See*, e.g., Article 6 of the European Convention on Human Rights: 'In the determination of his civil rights and obligations or of any criminal charge against him, everyone is entitled to a fair and public hearing within a reasonable time by an independent and impartial tribunal established by law. Judgment shall be pronounced publicly but the press and public may be excluded from all or part of the trial in the interests of morals, public order or national security in a democratic society, where the interests of juveniles or the protection of the private life of the parties so require, or to the extent strictly necessary in the opinion of the court in special circumstances where publicity would prejudice the interests of justice.'

[12] *See* Dorigo and Pustorino 2009. For a confirmation of this opinion in case law, *see Al-Warraq v. Indonesia*, UNCITRAL, Final Award of 15 December 2014, paras 556 et seq.

[13] Equality of parties, in turn, may be translated in three further principles: 'recognizing the litigants' sovereign sensibilities, securing active involvement by the litigants in the communicative process, and assuring that neither party derives any special procedural advantage over the other' (Gaffney 1999, p. 1184).

[14] On fundamental canons of international adjudication more generally, *see* Mani 1980; Pedrazzi 2004 and Palombino 2010.

[15] Rose-Ackerman et al. 2014, pp. 216 et seq.

[16] Gaffney 1999.

3.3 FET and Denial of Justice. The Meaning of the Term 'Denial of Justice' in Academic Writing

As a matter of theory, the way by which the term 'denial of justice' has been defined varies greatly.[17] In the broadest sense, the term would be employed in connection with any wrongful conduct related to the administration of civil and criminal justice as regards an alien and carried out by any of the three branches of the State, viz. executive, legislative or judicial.[18] Accordingly, the kind of conducts flowing into this notion (which has been codified in a number of soft law instruments[19] and finds support in judicial practice)[20] end up being very wide and include, *inter alia*, 'denial of access to court, inadequate procedures, and unjust decisions.'[21]

---

[17] On the whole matter, *see* Focarelli 2009.

[18] *See* Fitzmaurice 1932, pp. 108–9: '[E]very injury involving the responsibility of the State committed by a court or judge acting officially, or alternatively every such injury committed by any organ of the government in its official capacity in connection with the administration of justice, constitutes and can properly be styled a denial of justice, whether it consists in a failure to redress a prior wrong, or in an original wrong committed by the court or other organ itself.'

[19] Historically speaking, there have been several attempts at codifying denial of justice so conceived. First of all, one may mention the resolution adopted by the *Institut de droit international* on the *Responsabilité international des États à raison des dommages causes sur leur territoire à la personne et aux biens des étrangers* (1927). Articles 5 and 6 of that resolution state as follows: 'L'Etat est responsable du chef de déni de justice: 1° Lorsque les tribunaux nécessaires pour assurer la protection des étrangers n'existent ou ne fonctionnent pas; 2° Lorsque les tribunaux ne sont pas accessibles aux étrangers; 3° Lorsque les tribunaux n'offrent pas les garanties indispensables pour assurer une bonne justice [...] L'Etat est également responsable si la procédure ou le jugement constituent un manquement manifeste à la justice, notamment s'ils ont été inspirés par la malveillance à l'égard des étrangers, comme tels, ou comme ressortissants d'un Etat déterminé.' Article 9 of the Draft Convention on the international responsibility of States for injuries to aliens, prepared by the Harvard Law School is equally revealing: 'Denial of justice exists where there is a denial, unwarranted delay or obstruction of access to courts, gross deficiency in the administration of judicial or remedial process, failure to provide those guarantees which are generally considered indispensable to the proper administration of justice, or a manifestly unjust judgment. An error of a national court which does not produce manifest injustice is not a denial of justice' (in American Journal of International Law, Supplement: Codification of International Law, 1929, pp. 131 et seq., spec. p. 134). Finally, Article 3.i of the 1967 OECD Draft Convention on the protection of foreign property should be mentioned: '[Denial of justice] implies that whenever a State seizes property, the measures taken must be free from arbitrariness. Safeguards existing in its Constitution or other laws or established by judicial precedent must be fully observed; administrative or judicial machinery used or available must correspond at least to the minimum standard required by international law.'

[20] *See Cotesworth and Powell, Great Britain v. Colombia* (1875), in Moore 1898, pp. 2050 et seq., as well as the practice cited in paras 3.5–3.7; *Robert E. Brown (U.S.) v. Great Britain*, Award of 23 November 1923, in *Reports of International Arbitral Awards*, vol. VI, p. 120.

[21] Cf. García-Amador et al. 1974, p. 180. Kohona 1987, p. 96; Crawford 2012, pp. 619–620; Francioni 2009.

On the other hand, some commentators tend to limit the scope of denial of justice in terms of either (i) the relevant wrongful acts or (ii) the State organs committing it.[22] As to the first tendency, special reference is made to the opinion whereby the State's refusal to grant an alien access to court would be the only case of denial of justice. This argument, which reflects the predominant Latin American view,[23] has also been followed by some Italian scholars. One may mention Dionisio Anzilotti who, on the one hand, regards the State's refusal to exercise jurisdiction as the main scope of denial of justice; on the other hand, in order to make the wrongful act attributable to the forum State, he considers pointless whether the act has its origins in law provisions precluding access to justice or in the misapplication of these provisions by judicial authorities.[24]

With regard to the tendency to circumscribe the set of organs whose conduct may embody the delict in question, the traditional distinction of German origin between denial of justice (*Justizverweigerung*) and denial of law (*Rechtsverweiverung*), i.e. the different type of activities (judicial or legislative) that may result in a violation of the State obligation to protect an alien, seems useful.[25] A strict interpretation of this distinction, indeed, allows two hypotheses to be

[22] Such a circumstance may be clearly inferred from the *Third Restatement of the Foreign Relations Law of the United States* (The American Law Institute, *Restatement of the Law, the Foreign Relations Law of the United States*, 3rd edn, 1987, vol. 2, para 711, comm a), insofar as it pinpoints that the term 'denial of justice' is commonly used in a narrow sense 'to refer only to injury consisting of, or resulting from, denial of access to courts, or denial of procedural fairness and due process in relation to judicial proceedings, whether criminal or civil.'

[23] Such an opinion has been expressed, for example, by Guerrero in his 1926 Report to the League of Nations Committee for the Progressive Codification of International Law. Articles 6 and 7 of the Report state as follows: '6. The duty of the State as regards legal protection must be held to have been fulfilled if it has allowed foreigners access to the national courts and freedom to institute the necessary proceedings whenever they need to defend their rights. It therefore follows: (a) That a State has fulfilled its international duty as soon as the judicial authorities have given their decisions, even if those authorities merely state that the petition, suit or appeal lodged by the foreigner is not admissible; (b) That a judicial decision, whatever it may be, and even if vitiated by error or injustice, does not involve the international responsibility of the State. 7. On the other hand, however, a State is responsible for damage caused to foreigners when it is guilty of a *denial of justice*. *Denial of justice* consists in refusing to allow easy access to the courts to defend those rights, which the national law accords them. A refusal of the competent judge to exercise jurisdiction also constitutes a *denial of justice*.' The same opinion can be found in the 1961 Report of the Inter-American Juridical Committee: 'The obligation of the State regarding judicial protection shall be considered as having been fulfilled when it places at the disposal of foreigners the national courts and the legal remedies essential to implement their rights. A State cannot initiate diplomatic claims for the protection of its nationals nor bring an action before an international tribunal for this purpose when the means of resorting to the competent courts of the respective State have been made available to the aforementioned nationals' (Whiteman 1963–1973, p. 727).

[24] Anzilotti 1964, p. 396.

[25] *See* Hatshek 1923, p. 397; Strupp 1925. In the past, this distinction had been drawn, with the view to claiming that denial of justice always entails State responsibility, whereas denial of law does so under exceptional circumstances only. For a critique of this distinction, *see* Quadri 1936, pp. 220 et seq., in the footnotes.

identified: (i) the situation where State responsibility stems from a judicial misapplication of national law which proves manifestly unjust (*denial of justice*); and (ii) the situation where State responsibility stems from the (substantive and procedural) rules in force domestically, namely rules that the judge concerned cannot but apply (*denial of law*). Perhaps some authors, like Jan Paulsson, tacitly rely on this distinction when they consider that the failure of a State, *in its law-making function*, to provide a decent judicial system does not entail any denial of justice:

> There may be extreme cases where the proof of the failed process is that the substance of a decision is so egregiously wrong that no honest or competent court could possibly have given it. Such cases would sanction the State's failure to provide a decent system of justice. They do not constitute an international appellate review of national law. A national court's breach of other rules of international law, or of treaties, is not a denial of justice, but a direct violation of the relevant obligation imputable to the State like any acts or omissions by its agents.[26]

Of course, the distinction between denial of justice and denial of law is also valid in the field of foreign investments, thus meaning that only a grave judicial misapplication or misinterpretation of national law (*denial of justice*) would be relevant. However, an argument of this kind is anything but unquestionable and requires rigorous assessment from the angle of arbitral case law.

3.4 The Meaning of the Term 'Denial of Justice' in International Investment Law: The *Azinian* Case

The first award to be considered is that passed by an ICSID tribunal in *Azinian*.[27] The award was the result of a decision by the Mexican City of Naucalpan to terminate without cause a contract with DESONA, a company in charge of operating a landfill and waste management system for the city. The company's shareholders (Robert Azinian, Kenneth Davinian and Ellen Baca), as American citizens, invoked their rights before the competent Mexican courts, but without success. Accordingly, they initiated an arbitration proceeding under the ICSID's 1978 Additional Facility Rules,[28] claiming that the concession cancellation amounted to a violation of NAFTA Chapter Eleven in terms of expropriation (Article 1110) and minimum standard of treatment (Article 1105).

---

[26] Paulsson 2005, p. 98. On this matter, *see* also Douglas 2014.

[27] *Robert Azinian v. Mexico*, ICSID Case No. ARB(AF)/97/2, Award of 1 November 1999.

[28] The *Azinian* award has been the first one to be rendered under the Additional Facilities Rules. As already said *supra* Chap. 1, Sect. 1.4, they apply to disputes where either the State party to the dispute or the State whose national is party to the dispute, but not both, is not a contracting State to the ICSID Convention. In this case, the Claimants are nationals of an ICSID Contracting State (the United States of America), whereas the Respondent (the United Mexican States) is not an ICSID Contracting State.

It is worth noting that the applicant did not claim any denial of justice in his pleadings. But in order to remove any doubt in the matter, the tribunal acted *ultra petitum* and still pronounced on the existence of this offence.[29] In detail, moving from the premise that denial of justice would fulfil a typical violation of the due process principle, in the tribunal's view this delict could be successfully invoked on the one hand 'if the relevant courts refuse to entertain a suit, if they subject it to undue delay, or if they administer justice in a seriously inadequate way'; on the other hand in the presence of a 'clear and malicious misapplication of the law.'

This statement is contained in a mere *obiter dictum*. Nevertheless, the idea whereby courts would be the only organs capable of committing a denial of justice is straightforward in the words of the decision and, to borrow the German terminology, seems to exclude the relevance of the different figure of denial of law.

3.4.1 The Mondev *Case*

The same idea advanced in *Azinian* emerges in the *Mondev* decision as well. In the late 1970s, in order to rehabilitate and develop the peripheral area known as the 'Combat Zone', the city of Boston, the Boston Redevelopment Authority (BRA) and Lafayette Place Associates (LPA)—which was formed by a Canadian commercial real estate development and management company, Mondev International Ltd.—entered into a tripartite Agreement, governed by the laws of the Commonwealth of Massachusetts and providing for a two-phase development. Phase I was completed in November 1985. Phase II, on the contrary, was never finalized. The Agreement granted LPA a conditional option to purchase the Phase II property upon notice of the City's intention to demolish a parking structure. LPA exercised its option in time, but a number of reasons prevented this phase from being completed. Further, on January 1, 1989, LPA leased its rights in the project to a Canadian developer, the Campeau Corporation; this corporation, however, also encountered resistance on the part of local authorities and eventually went bankrupt.

In order to claim both a breach of the contract under the Agreement and a tortious interference of BRA with its contractual relations with Campeau, LPA lodged an appeal before the competent Massachusetts domestic courts. The appeal, however, was ultimately dismissed by the Supreme Judicial Court (SJC). Two arguments underpin its decision. First, LPA failed to establish an actual breach of the contract, especially because it had not manifested the willingness and ability to perform it. Second, the allegation of tortious interference with contractual relations could not be upheld because BRA, as a public employer, was immune from suit under Section 10(c) of the Massachusetts Torts Claims Act; in line with this provision, indeed, a public agency which is not an 'independent body politic and corporate' is immune from 'any claim arising out of an intentional tort, including

[29] Paragraph 101.

assault, battery, false imprisonment, false arrest, intentional mental distress, malicious prosecution, malicious abuse of process, libel, slander, misrepresentation, deceit, invasion of privacy, interference with advantageous relations or *interference with contractual relations*';[30] thus, the interference of a public agency with contractual relations never amounts to a wrongful act and does not generate any right of action in favour of the party which suffers it.

In 1999, Mondev filed a claim under NAFTA Chapter Eleven, contending *inter alia* a violation of Article 1105 ('Minimum Standard of Treatment') in terms of denial of justice. Once again, however, its appeal was dismissed.[31] Going more into detail, the *Mondev* tribunal firstly assessed whether the judicial decisions passed by the Massachusetts courts could be regarded as manifestly unjust. To this aim, following the *Azinian*[32] as well as the *ELSI*[33] precedents, it argued as follows:

> The test is not whether a particular result is surprising, but whether the shock or surprise occasioned to an impartial tribunal leads, on reflection, to justified concerns as to the judicial property of the outcome, bearing in mind on the hand that international tribunals are not courts of appeal, and on the other hand that Chapter 11 of NAFTA (like other treaties for the protection of investments) is intended to provide a real measure of protection. In the end, the question is whether, at an international level and having regard to generally accepted standards of the administration of justice, a tribunal can conclude in the light of all the available facts that the impugned decision was clearly improper and discreditable, with the result that the investment has been subjected to *unfair and inequitable treatment*. This is admittedly a somewhat open-ended standard, but it may be that in practice no more precise formula can be offered to cover the range of possibilities.[34]

In this light, Mondev's argument, whereby the SJC would have departed significantly from its precedents, was considered unconvincing. In the tribunal's view, not only was it doubtful whether the SJC had done so, but in any case its decision fell within the limits of common law adjudication. Hence, there was nothing 'to shock or surprise even a delicate judicial sensibility.'[35]

Let us turn now to the question of whether the BRA's statutory immunity for intentional torts under the Massachusetts Tort Claims Act amounted to a denial of justice. In this regard—as the decision highlights, where the doctrine of foreign State

---

[30] Emphasis added.

[31] *Mondev International Ltd. v. United States*, ICSID Case No. ARB (AF)/99/2, Award of 11 October 2002. On the whole affair, *see* Krueger 2003.

[32] *See supra* note 27.

[33] International Court of Justice, *Elettronica Sicula S.p.a. (ELSI) (United States v. Italy)*, Judgment of 20 July 1989, para 128: 'Arbitrariness [...] is a wilful disregard of due process of law, an act which shocks, or at least surprises, a sense of judicial property'.

[34] Para 127 of the judgment.

[35] Para 133 of the judgment.

immunity is not relevant for the present case,[36] there would exist a closer analogy with a number of ECtHR decisions concerning statutory immunities of State agencies before their own courts. In line with these decisions, the right of access to justice under Article 6, para 1, ECHR would represent above all a procedural guarantee, which can be invoked as far as other civil rights protected by the Convention itself or by the forum State are concerned.[37] The same provision, however, may never be used in order to create by way of interpretation 'a substantive civil right which has no legal basis in the State concerned.'[38]

By the same token, the *Mondev* tribunal was of the view that Article 1105(1), as well as the right of access to justice which it implicitly envisages, cannot be read so as to create a new substantive right to sue BRA for tortious interference with contractual relations; as already seen, indeed, a right of this kind has no basis in the Massachusetts law.[39]

More in general,

> the tribunal is not persuaded that the extension to a statutory authority of a limited immunity from suit for interference with contractual relations amounts in this case to a breach of Article 1105 (1). Of course such an immunity could not protect a State Party from a claim for conduct which was substantively in breach of NAFTA standards – but for this NAFTA provides its own remedy, since it gives an investor the right to go directly to international arbitration in respect of conduct occurring after NAFTA's entry into force. In a Chapter 11 arbitration, no local statutory immunity would apply. On the other hand, within broad limits, the extent to which a State decides to immunize regulatory authorities from suit for interference with contractual relations is a matter for the competent organs of the State to decide.[40]

For the above reasons, Mondev's claims were dismissed in their entirety.

[36] 'The tribunal is not persuaded that the doctrine of foreign State immunity presents any useful analogy to the present situation. That immunity is concerned not with the position of State agencies before their own courts, but before the courts of third States, where considerations of interstate relations and the proper allocation of jurisdictional competence are raised' (para 142 of the judgment).

[37] Para 143 of the judgment.

[38] Idem.

[39] In this regard, the remarks made by de Visscher 1935, pp. 395–396, are of assistance: '[O]n ne saurait assimiler à un déni de justice l'absence de recours judiciaire ou administratif contre les mesures prises par les autorités supérieures de l'Etat, la législature ou le gouvernement, en tant que cette absence résulte de la législation générale de l'Etat et non d'une mesure de discrimination contre les étrangers. L'absence de recours contre ces mesures n'exclut pas évidemment pas la responsabilité internationale du chef de dommages qui résultent de ces mesures elles-mêmes; mais dans l'état actuel de l'organisation constitutionnelle des pays, même les mieux organisés, elle ne peut, en règle générale, être envisagée comme un manquement au devoir de protection judiciaire équivalant à un déni de justice.'

[40] Para 154 of the judgment.

3.4.2 *The* Loewen *Case*

The concept of denial of justice as it emerged in *Mondev* seems to be confirmed by the later and quite controversial decision in *Loewen*.[41] In the early Nineties, a Canadian firm, Loewen, began to aggressively acquire a number of funeral homes across Canada and the United States, causing various harms to the local companies operating in the same sector. In this light, a local Mississippi funeral home operator, O'Keefe, sued Loewen before the competent State Court, claiming the unlawful and anticompetitive nature of its conduct. Eventually, the jury upheld the claimant's request and issued a damage award of $500 million, of which $400 million was punitive damages.[42] On the other hand, according to the Mississippi rules of civil procedure, for the decision to be appealed, Loewen was required by the State Court to post a bond (*cautio iudicatum solvi*) equal to 125% of the total award (namely $650 million); accordingly, faced with the risk of bankruptcy in any event, it settled the case with O'Keefe for $175 million. Bearing this in mind, Loewen filed a claim under NAFTA Chapter Eleven, contending an FET violation before an ICSID tribunal. As a result of non-exhaustion of domestic remedies, its claim was nevertheless dismissed.

In detail, the tribunal was persuaded that the conduct of the trial by the domestic judge 'was so flawed that it constituted a miscarriage of justice amounting to a manifest injustice as that expression is understood in international law.'[43] But, for a FET violation to be upheld, it was necessary to prove that all the available domestic remedies had been exhausted.

In this regard, it is worth recalling that in the terms of NAFTA Article 1121, para 1(b), a disputing investor may submit a claim under Article 1116 ('Claim by an Investor of a Party on Its Own Behalf') to arbitration only if:

> the investor and, where the claim is for loss or damage to an interest in an enterprise of another Party that is a juridical person that the investor owns or controls directly or indirectly, the enterprise, waive their right to initiate or continue before any administrative tribunal or court under the law of any Party, or other dispute settlement procedures, any proceedings with respect to the measure of the disputing Party that is alleged to be a breach referred to in Article 1116, except for proceedings for injunctive, declaratory or other extraordinary relief, not involving the payment of damages, before an administrative tribunal or court under the law of the disputing Party.

[41] *Loewen v. United States*, ICSID Case No. ARB/98/3, Award of 26 June 2003. For a comment on the decision, *see* Wallace 2005; Acconci 2004.

[42] As is well known, punitive damages are intended to deter the defendant from engaging in conducts similar to those underpinning the lawsuit.

[43] *See* para 54 of the judgment.

In the tribunal's view, although the purpose of this article appears somewhat ambiguous, it does not imply any dispensation of the local remedies rule.[44] Therefore, the real question was whether the rule had been effectively respected, and more squarely to what extent the settlement accepted by Loewen could be regarded as premature in respect of the possibility of acceding to additional remedies. In order to solve the question, the very concept of *availability of the remedy* was dealt with:

> 168. Availability is not a standard to be determined or applied in the abstract. It means reasonably available to the complainant in the light of its situation, including its financial and economic circumstances as a foreign investor, as they are affected by any conditions relating to the exercise of any local remedy.
>
> 169. If a State attaches conditions to a right of appeal which renders exercise of the right impractical, the exercise of the right is neither available nor effective nor adequate. Likewise, if a State burdens the exercise of the right directly or indirectly so as to expose the complainant to severe financial consequences, it may well be that the State has by its own actions disabled the complainant from affording the State the opportunity of redressing the matter of complaint. The scope of the need to exhaust local remedies must be considered in the light of these considerations.

To sum up, in the terms of the decision, the availability of remedies needs to be assessed on a case-by-case basis and ruled out where there is sufficient proof that the right of appeal was neither effective nor adequate. Nonetheless—as the tribunal recognizes—this proof had not been given; of course, in order to challenge the decision of first instance, Loewen should have been required to pay a very onerous bond, but it had at least a further means of legal protection at its disposal: the possibility of a petition for a *writ of certiorari* before the US Supreme Court.[45]

The decision in *Loewen* has been strongly criticized by some scholars, who contend that the imposition of a *cautio iudicatum solvi* would end up frustrating the

[44] 'It would be strange indeed if *sub silentio* the international rule were to be swept away. And it would be very strange if a State were to be confronted with liability for a breach of international law committed by its magistrate or low-ranking judicial officer when domestic avenues of appeal are not pursued, let alone exhausted. If Article 1121 were to have that effect, it would encourage resort to NAFTA tribunals rather than resort to the appellate courts and review processes of the host State, an outcome which would seem surprising, having regard to the sophisticated legal systems of the NAFTA Parties. Such an outcome would have the effect of making a State potentially liable for NAFTA violations when domestic appeal or review, if pursued, might have avoided any liability on the part of the State. Further, it is unlikely that the Parties to NAFTA would have wished to encourage recourse to NAFTA arbitration at the expense of domestic appeal or review when, in the general run of cases, domestic appeal or review would offer more wide-ranging review as they are not confined to breaches of international law.'

[45] By *writ of certiorari* any party to a civil or criminal case can file a petition for review of the case by the Supreme Court.

right of access to justice.[46] As may be inferred from the above, security for costs entails that a claimant is obligated to deposit a certain amount in order to have his claim heard. Such a circumstance, however, should not be overestimated. Until the first half of the twentieth century, the fact that in several States access to justice by an alien was subordinated to a *cautio iudicatum solvi* did not amount by its very nature to a denial of justice. Indeed, it mainly served the purpose of avoiding the situation where an alien, or more in general an individual who was not habitually resident in the forum, did not have sufficient assets therein, with the consequence that an eventual final judgment issued against him could not be enforced.[47] Nonetheless, the rule on security deposit 'has largely lost its prominence.'[48] With respect to nationals of an EU Member State, it is no longer permitted.[49]

More in general, due to the growing protection of human rights at the international level, two remarks must be made. First, the payment of a bond is lawful so long as it does not regard the judicial position of the alien only; the principle of equal access to justice for both citizens and aliens is increasingly emerging in

[46] Francioni 2009, p. 735, observes as follows: '*Loewen* is not only a bad precedent for access to justice: it is also a bad precedent for the investment community, which can hardly benefit from the extreme and unrealistic application of the rule of prior exhaustion of local remedies when the risk of grave loss is imminent and a miscarriage of justice has been acknowledged. All the more so in a case such as this where the alien is facing the threat of the execution of an exorbitant verdict of punitive damages—which remain highly contested in international law—and when further judicial protection is barred by an excessive bond.'

[47] The provision of a *cautio iudicatum solvi*, on the other hand, was regarded as lawful by the majority of writers. Anzilotti 1906, pp. 5 et seq., in particular p. 26, note 2, was of this view: 'Nous laissons ici de côté la question de savoir si l'état peut, sans violer le droit international, imposer à l'étranger, qui veut avoir recours à la justice, des obligations qui ne regardent pas les nationaux. Au point de vue du droit positif actuel, nous ne croyons pas qu'il sont possible de nier cette possibilité d'une manière absolue (qu'on se rappelle la caution *judicatum solvi*). Mais ce qu'il faut affirmer, c'est que les restrictions à la faculté des étrangers de s'adresser aux tribunaux ne doivent jamais être de nature à rendre le recours impossible: cela constituerait sans aucun doute le déni de justice.' Support for this proposition may also be found in Verdross 1931, pp. 383–384: 'il est généralement admis que l'Etat de séjour puisse exiger des étranger, à défaut de conventions spéciales, la caution des frais du procès (*cautio iudicatum solvi*).'

[48] Kiestra 2014, p. 122.

[49] This can be inferred both from Article II-47 of the 2007 Charter of Fundamental Rights of the European Union ('*Right to an effective remedy and to a fair trial*—Everyone is entitled to a fair and public hearing within a reasonable time by an independent and impartial tribunal previously established by law. Everyone shall have the possibility of being advised, defended and represented') and the case law of the CJUE relying on the non-discrimination principle. One may mention ECJ, *David Charles Hayes and Jeannette Karen Hayes v. Kronenberger GmbH.*, Judgment of 20 March 1997, para 25 ('Article 6 of the [EC] Treaty must be interpreted as precluding a Member State from requiring security for costs to be furnished by a national of another Member State who has brought an action in one of its civil courts against one of its nationals where that requirement may not be imposed on its own nationals who have neither assets nor a residence in that country, in a situation where the action is connected with the exercise of fundamental freedoms guaranteed by Community law.')

general international law.[50] Second, even where the forum State legislation provides for a security deposit regardless of nationality, some categories of individuals, in particular refugees[51] and stateless persons,[52] are exempted in any event; in this case, indeed, the security deposit requirement would make the right of access to justice meaningless.

Well, the *Loewen* case falls neither in the first hypothesis (since in this case the payment of a deposit could be ordered regardless of the nationality) nor in the second (insofar as Loewen was a multinational corporation, with assets at its disposal in the forum State). That said, the decision under scrutiny may be criticized in any event, but for reasons fairly different from those advanced by the majority of writers. The Mississippi Law vests the judge with the power to order the payment of a deposit equal to 125% of the total award, but also to reduce it (or not to ask for it), should a fair cause occur. To put it another way, security for costs may have a legitimate aim, but the proportionality of the restriction has to be assessed on a case-by-case basis. In the case at issue, the manifest discriminatory nature of the national judicial proceeding ended up having an impact on the deposit calculation as well; hence, the ICSID tribunal could have highlighted this circumstance and, as a result, ascertained an FET violation.

3.4.3 Arbitral Case Law in the Aftermath of Mondev *and* Loewen

At first sight, the case law in the aftermath of *Mondev* and *Loewen* does not entirely exclude the possibility of attributing a denial of justice to the legislator. Reference is especially made to the judgment in *Iberdrola*[53] and the notion of denial of justice as accepted therein. In line with this notion, 'there is not only denial of justice in relation to the actions of the judiciary, but also, among other hypotheses, when a State prevents an investor's access to the courts of that State; in that case there will

[50] Reference is made, *inter alia*, to Article 14 of the UN Covenant on Civil and Political Rights, according to which 'All persons shall be equal before the courts and tribunals'.

[51] Article 16, para 2, of the 1951 Convention relating to the status of refugees states as follows: 'A refugee shall enjoy in the Contracting State in which he has his habitual residence the same treatment as a national in matters pertaining to access to the Courts, including legal assistance and exemption from *cautio judicatum solvi*.'

[52] Article 16, para 2, of the 1951 Convention relating to the status of the stateless persons states as follows: 'A stateless person shall enjoy in the Contracting State in which he has his habitual residence the same treatment as a national in matters pertaining to access to the Courts, including legal assistance and exemption from *cautio judicatum solvi*.'

[53] *Iberdrola v. Guatemala*, ICSID Case No. ARB/09/15, Award of 17 August 2012.

be denial of justice even if the act comes from the [...] legislative body.'[54] In spite of this, a denial of justice by the legislator has been ascertained neither in *Iberdrola* nor in investor-State case law more generally, and all the relevant decisions in the matter end up sanctioning the grave judicial misapplication of national law, rather than the local justice system in its entirety.

One example is the decision in *Pey Casado*.[55] The facts underlying this case go back to a claim for compensation made by the Spanish citizen, Mr. Pey Casado. This was brought as a result of the confiscation of a newspaper sympathetic to President Allende (*El Clarin*) which the claimant had acquired during the Pinochet regime. However, for seven years, the Chilean courts dealing with the case did not pronounce any decision and the government itself, rather than recognize the claimant's ownership rights, indemnified only the heirs of the company's former shareholders. In this light, according to the 1994 Chile-Spain BIT, Mr. Pey Casado instituted an arbitration proceeding before the ICSID, seeking damages for the illegal expropriation. According to the arbitral tribunal, the behaviour assumed by the Chilean authorities, and in particular the excessive length of the proceedings brought by the applicant, amounted to a denial of justice and therefore to an FET violation.[56]

Of course this is not to say that any judicial deficiencies amount *per se* to a denial of justice. In *Jan de Nul*,[57] for example, it was established that the period of 10 years to obtain a first instance judgment was 'certainly unsatisfactory', but it did not rise to the level of a denial of justice, considering that 'the issues were complex and highly technical, that two cases were involved, that the parties were especially productive in terms of submissions and filed extensive reports'.[58] Again, in *Philip Morris*, the claimant's argument whereby it had been denied a fair trial since two different domestic courts had ruled contrary to each other was dismissed by the tribunal; in the view of the latter '[o]utright conflicts within national legal systems

[54] Idem, para 444.

[55] *Victor Pey Casado et al. v. Chile*, ICSID Case No. ARB/98/2, Award of 8 May 2008. On the subsequent development of the case, *see* Schreurer 2014.

[56] Para 659 of the judgment states as follows: '[L]a ausencia de resolución por parte de los tribunales civiles chilenos en cuanto a las pretensiones del Sr. Pey Casado se considera una denegación de justicia. En efecto, la ausencia de una decisión de primera instancia en cuanto al fondo de las demandas de las partes demandantes durante siete años [...] debe calificarse come una denegación de justicia por parte de los tribunales chilenos. De hecho, los plazos procesales extraordinariamente largos constituyen una de las formas clásicas de denegación de justicia.' For an additional case of judicial misapplication of national law, see *Dan Cake (Portugal) S.A. v. Hungary*, ICSID Case No. ARB/12/9, Decision on Jurisdiction and Liability of 24 August 2015, paras 142 et seq.

[57] *Jan de Nul v. Egypt*, ICSID Case No. ARB/04/13, Award of 6 November 2008.

[58] Para 204.

may be regrettable but they are not unheard of' and not serious enough in themselves 'to constitute a denial of justice.'[59]

3.4.4 Denial of Justice as a Manifestation of the German Model of **Justizverweigerung**

A careful appraisal of the case law so far considered sheds light on the fact that denial of justice, as an FET element, is anchored in the German model of *Justizverweigerung* only and does not include the different concept of denial of law. As already said, this concept refers to the situation where State responsibility does not stem from a misapplication of law by its own courts, but rather from a conduct attributable to the legislator, that is to say a conduct consisting of the (substantive and procedural) rules in force and which any judge is required to respect. Now, whoever decides to invest part of his capital in a foreign country (especially in the case of multinational enterprises), does so in the wake of the *whole regulatory framework* existing in that country, therefore having regard not only to the rules making the investment convenient, but also to those governing the judicial system, which may be relevant when a dispute between this investor and the host State arises.

> All business transactions involve some degree of risk. When business transactions occur across international borders, they carry additional risks not present in domestic transactions. These additional risks, called country risks, typically include risks arising from a variety of national differences in economic structures, policies, socio-political institutions, geography, and currencies.[60]

Significantly enough, Andrea Giardina, serving as rapporteur of the already quoted 2013 IIL Resolution in matter of investments, made the point clear that the breach of due process of law 'might be attributed to the host State judiciary [...]', but not to the legislator.

---

[59] *Philip Morris et al. v. Uruguay*, ICSID Case No. ARB/10/7, Award of 8 July 2016, para 529. For a critical assessment of this conclusion, *see* the concurring and dissenting opinion appended by the co-arbitrator Gary Born, paras 6 et seq.

[60] Meldrum 2000, p. 33. According to the same author, six types of country risk may be identified: (1) *Economic Risk.* A significant change in the economic structure or growth rate that produces a major change in the expected return of an investment; (2) *Transfer Risk.* The risk arising from a decision by a foreign government to restrict capital movements; (3) *Exchange Risk.* An unexpected adverse movement in the exchange rate; (4) *Location or Neighbourhood Risk.* Spillover effects caused by problems in a region, in a country's trading partner, or in countries with similar perceived characteristics; (5) *Sovereign Risk.* A government becomes unwilling or unable to meet its loan obligations, or reneges on loans it guarantees; (6) *Political Risk.* Risk of a change in political institutions stemming from a change in government control, social fabric, or other non-economic factor. On this point, *see* also Hirsch 2011.

In a nutshell, the business risk that an investor takes on covers also the possible deficiencies of the local justice system, i.e. a system which he 'should reasonably have known at the time of the investment,'[61] and the effects that this circumstance may produce in the lawsuits involving him. This idea is not new to international case law, and a significant precedent can be found in the PCIJ judicial practice.[62] On the other hand, the two leading decisions on the topic, *Mondev* and *Loewen*, as well as the case law in their aftermath, support such a conclusion: in *Mondev* the existence of a national rule conferring immunity from jurisdiction to public agencies was not regarded as contrary to FET; in *Loewen* the provision of a *cautio iudicatum solvi* did not frustrate—in the terms of the decision—the right of access to justice and so on.

The above remarks help clarify the legal nature of denial of justice as an FET element. On closer inspection, the judge concerned has always assumed the existence of a general principle providing for due process of law. On the basis of this principle, and in the wake of the features peculiar to the matter of foreign investments, that same judge has formulated the rule of denial of justice. Finally, by way of a constant and uniform case law, this rule has become 'stable' going so far as to be subsumed under FET.

---

[61] *Electrabel S.A. v. Hungary*, ICSID No. ARB/07/19, Decision on Jurisdiction, Applicable Law and Liability of 30 November 2012, para 7.78.

[62] Reference has first to be made to the case *Oscar Chinn* (*United Kingdom v. Belgium*), Judgment of 12 December 1934, p. 84: 'Mr. Chinn, a British subject, when, in 1929, he entered the river transport business, could not have been ignorant of the existence of the competition which he would encounter on the part of Unatra, which had been established since 1925, of the magnitude of the capital invested in that Company, of the connection it had with the Colonial and Belgian Governments, and of the predominant role reserved to the latter with regard to the fixing and application for transport rates.' The same rationale underpins most of the decisions rendered in matter of FET. One may mention *Generation Ukraine, Inc v. Ukraine*, ICSID Case No. ARB/00/9, Award of 16 September 2003, para 20.37: '[I]t is relevant to consider the vicissitudes of the economy of the state that is host to the investment in determining the investor's legitimate expectations, the protection of which is a major concern of the minimum standards of treatment contained in bilateral investment treaties. The Claimant was attracted to the Ukraine because of the possibility of earning a rate of return on its capital in significant excess to the other investment opportunities in more developed economies. The Claimant thus invested in the Ukraine on notice of both the prospects and the potential pitfalls. Its investment was speculative. Perhaps for this very reason, the Claimant was cautious about contributing substantial sums of its own money to the enterprise, preferring to seek capital from third parties to finance the construction of the building. By 31 October 1997, the Claimant had undoubtedly experienced frustration and delay caused by bureaucratic incompetence and recalcitrance in various forms. But equally, the Claimant had managed to secure a 49-year leasehold over prime commercial property in the centre of Kyiv without having participated in a competitive tender and without having made any substantial payment to the Ukrainian authorities.' Finally, similar remarks may be found in the recent volume published by the UNCTAD on FET, 2012. Its pp. 71–72, in particular, state as follows: 'Investors should also be aware and take into account the level of the country's development and administrative practices [...] It is normal that the prospects of greater profits are accompanied by greater risks, including in the regulatory sphere.'

3.5 FET and Procedural Fairness in Administrative Proceedings. The Foreign Investor's Participation in Public Decisions

The right to procedural fairness in administrative proceedings has to be considered in the same line of thought. Once again, it is worth stating that under international law on foreign investment due process has taken on a meaning so broad as to include not only denial of justice, but also fairness in administrative proceedings, especially conceived as the right to be heard (*audi alteram partem*). Such a result, which may be inferred from both the wording of some BITs[63] and several arbitral awards,[64] is unsurprising and echoes the circumstance whereby due process (and the guarantees related thereto) has gone much further than the limits of the judicial function and has become the typical way by which to exercise the administrative function as well.[65]

Historically speaking, support for this proposition may be first traced back to the US legal system. The Fifth and Fourteenth Amendments of the American Constitution require that neither the federal government nor the States deprive any person of life, liberty or property without *due process of law*. In principle, this is a clause dealing with the administration of justice. Since the beginning of its case law, however, as a result of the proliferation of administrative decisions susceptible to cause some harm to individuals, the US Supreme Court has always regarded due process as a rule equally applicable to administrative proceedings. Evidence of such a broad application of the rule is reflected in a number of decisions whereby actions requiring some right to be heard include, *inter alia*, deprivation of welfare benefits and dismissal of a government employee.[66]

English case law should be assessed in the same terms when applying the principle of natural justice, i.e. a concept that is very similar to due process and represents the basis of procedural protection in the English legal system. Notably, despite the fact that the right to be heard (as a constituent element of the principle)

---

[63] One example is Article 11 of the 2009 ASEAN Comprehensive Investment Agreement, *supra* footnote 6.

[64] A similar conclusion may be inferred, *inter alia*, from *Rumeli Telekom A.S. et al. v. Kazakhstan*, ICSID Case No. ARB/05/16, Award of 29 July 2008, para 623: 'Courts are not the only State organs the conduct of which can amount to a denial of justice. Administrative organs can also engage the State's international responsibility by denying justice.' And indeed: the award speaks of denial of justice, but it implicitly refers to the different principle of fair administrative proceeding; not by chance, with a view to exemplifying the case at issue, the tribunal mention the two well-known decisions in *Amco*, that is to say, two decisions where the violation of such a principle has been ascertained. On this point, *see infra*.

[65] Buffoni 2008, p. 38.

[66] 397 U.S. 254 (1970). In this case, in particular, the Supreme Court held that the Fourteenth Amendment due process clause required a State agency to provide an evidentiary hearing before terminating a person welfare's benefits after the agency determined that the individual was no longer eligible for such benefits.

was only guaranteed within judicial proceedings from the second half of the nineteenth century, the same guarantee has been progressively extended to administrative proceedings. As well as in the US case, this is a consequence of a large number of administrative decisions able to have major consequences for individuals. Accordingly, in *Ridge v. Boldwin*, natural justice has been considered to be a principle of *universal application* equally valid with reference to any proceedings leading to a discretionary decision.[67]

On the other hand, it is worth noticing that the extension of due process to administrative proceedings is no longer a feature typical of common law countries only. Although belatedly the same result has also been reached in civil law countries, like the Italian legal system. Reference has to be made to the Italian Administrative Procedure Act which does nothing but extend to administrative procedures one of the main rules governing adjudication, namely the *audi alteram partem* principle.[68]

Finally, this rule belongs to the general principles of EU law, and may be applied in any proceedings, regardless of their judicial or administrative nature. In *Transocean Marin Paint Association*, the Court of Justice of the European Union (CJEU) stated that, generally speaking, 'a person whose interests are perceptibly affected by a decision taken by a public authority must be given the opportunity to make his point of view known.'[69] Likewise, one may mention the decision passed by the Court of First Instance (which was replaced by the General Court on 1 December 2009) in *Lisrestal*: 'it is settled law that respect for the rights of the defence in all proceedings which are initiated against a person and are liable to culminate in a measure adversely affecting that person is a fundamental principle of Community law which must be guaranteed, even in the absence of any specific rules concerning the proceedings in question.'[70] Last but not least, the same principle has been recognized in Article 41 of the Charter of Fundamental Rights of the European Union ('Right to good administration'); in the terms of its para 2, indeed, every person has the right to be heard, before any individual measure which would affect him or her adversely is taken.[71]

Apparently, the above remarks seem to sustain the existence of a general principle common to domestic systems, which guarantees the *audi alteram partem* principle in the relationship between individuals and the administrative power. Such

---

[67] *Ridge v. Boldwin* [1964] AC 40.

[68] *See* Law No. 241, 7 August 1990 and subsequent amendments. A number of national decisions further support such a conclusion. One may mention Italian Court of Cassation, first civil section, 20 May 2002, No. 7341.

[69] Judgment of 23 October 1974, para 15.

[70] Judgment of 6 December 1994, para 42.

[71] Bifulco 2001.

a view, however, proves unconvincing. Indeed, depending on the legal order where it is invoked, the principle scrutinised here tends to undertake a different content. One divergence, for example, concerns the fact that while in some countries (such as the United States, Sweden and Japan) administrative procedural acts 'provide for a hearing, in some civil law countries only a possibility to make written submissions is required.'[72] On the other hand, the circumstances under which the principle may be applied vary significantly from case to case; thus, where in some cases what counts is the 'nature' of the activities performed by the administration, in other cases one has to establish whether a person has a reasonable expectation to be heard in a given proceeding. Unsurprisingly, also within the context of the EU legal order (i.e. a context where the *audi alteram partem* rule belongs to the category of general principles of law), the way this rule is applied by the Court of Justice is shrouded in ambiguity: despite the fact it is regarded as a general principle, it solely applies 'to certain categories of procedure (particularly those producing adverse effects) but not all of them (even if an unfavourable effect was indeed produced)'.[73] Similarly, the existence of a customary international law provision in the matter should be excluded; beyond some specific treaty regimes[74] and a narrow number of judgments,[75] the rule in question has been broadly and consistently applied precisely within the area of foreign investments. Needless to say, its features have to be determined with reference to this area only.

Once again, the reasoning followed by arbitral tribunals turns out to be the same. The *audi alteram partem* rule has been inferred, by way of induction, from the

[72] Della Cananea 2010, p. 71.

[73] Della Cananea 2011, p. 100.

[74] One example in this regard lies in Articles 6 et seq. of the Aarhus Convention on Access to Information, Public Participation in Decision-Making and Access to Justice in Environmental Matters. These Articles actually state that the public concerned shall be adequately informed in an environmental decision-making procedure and benefits from a number of guarantees, such as that guaranteeing the participation in the procedure and the submission of comments and questions. The Agreement on Implementation of Article VI of 1994 GATT is equally revealing. Article 6, para 1, of this agreement ('Evidence') states as follows: 'All interested parties in an anti-dumping investigation shall be given notice of the information which the authorities require and ample opportunity to present in writing all evidence which they consider relevant in respect of the investigation in question.'

[75] Reference can be made to the judgment passed by the International Tribunal for the Law of the Sea in *Juno Trader* (*San Vincent and the Grenadines v. Guinea-Bissau*), Judgment of 18 December 2004. Its para 77 states as follows: 'The obligation of prompt release of vessels and crews includes elementary considerations of humanity and *due process of law*. The requirement that the bond or other financial security must be reasonable indicates that a concern for fairness is one of the purposes of this provision.' (emphasis added) The separate opinion of judge Treves confirms the impression that due process, in this case, was understood in terms of fairness in administrative proceedings: 'In the present case, the essential fact seems to me to be that between the time of the arrest of the ship and the time of the application to the tribunal (and also up to the hearing before the tribunal) all domestic procedures held in the case (whatever other possibilities might have been open under the local law) have been *inaudita altera parte* (namely, without giving the accused party the possibility of being heard).' In this regard, *see* Cassese 2006, pp. 120 et seq.

general principle of due process, and adapted to the features peculiar to the international law on foreign investment. Subsequently, thanks to a constant and uniform case law, this rule has become a 'stable' FET element.

3.5.1 *The Conditions Under Which the Right to Be Heard Can Be Violated: The Right Should Be Provided for by the Host State Legal System*

In administrative proceedings involving foreign investors, a violation of the *audi alteram partem* principle, conceived as an FET element, may be claimed under the presence of two cumulative conditions. For the first condition to occur, the host State's legal order is required to expressly or tacitly provide for this principle. Otherwise, the same argument advanced with reference to denial of justice should be relied on: it is assumed that the investor is and must be aware of the State's normative framework and takes the risks that are connected to it. While a large number of judgments regard this requirement as crucial,[76] some decisions do the opposite. Reference is especially made to the *Genin* case.[77]

The dispute originated from the cancellation by the Central Bank of Estonia of an operating licence held by EIB (Estonian Innovation Bank), a financial institution incorporated under the laws of Estonia and in which the claimants (Mr. Genin, a national of the United States, and two companies owned by him) were shareholders. The claimants' argument was that 'no notice was ever transmitted to EIB to warn that its licence was in danger of revocation unless certain corrective measures were taken, and no opportunity was provided to EIB *to make representation* in that regard.'[78] Nonetheless, the arbitral tribunal regarded the national authorities' action as lawful. And this on the assumption that Article 16 of the Credit Institution Act does not require any form of public participation in administrative decisions for a revocation to take place.

This decision is far from persuasive. As the tribunal itself clarifies through an argument ending up being contradictory, the action taken by the Estonian authorities was consistent with the Estonian law on the one hand, whereas it could be regarded as contrary to generally accepted banking and regulatory practice on the other hand. And indeed, along this practice, whoever may suffer loss as a result of a licence revocation should have the opportunity to be heard before the organ that

[76] This practice has been commented in Sect. 3.4.1 et seq.

[77] *Genin et al. v. Estonia*, ICSID Case No. ARB/99/2, Award of 25 June 2001.

[78] Idem, para 358. The same para states as follows: 'When the Council of the Bank of Estonia was convened on 9 September 1997 to discuss the revocation of EIB's licence, no representative of EIB was invited to respond to the submission made by P. Negri, head of Banking Supervision, and A. Schmidt, head of the Legal Department, as to why revocation of EIB's license was necessary or appropriate in the circumstance.'

deals with revocation and, if need be, to challenge it in court before it is publicly announced.[79] Such a circumstance, in this author's view, indicates that the host State's legal order protects, albeit tacitly, the *audi alteram partem* rule; accordingly, the procedures followed by national authorities in this case amounted to an unfair administrative proceeding. Not by mere coincidence, in a situation very akin to that surrounding the *Genin* trial, in 2016 the *Urbaser* tribunal came to the opposite solution: it asserted a lack of transparency by the host State (which, in respect to the renegotiation of a supply contract, failed to provide its counterpart with a transparent treatment) and regarded such a lack as a violation of the FET standard.[80]

3.5.2 *The Administrative Decision Should Cause a Serious Economic Loss to the Investor*

The fact that the *audi alteram partem* rule is provided for in some way in the host State's legal order, but is not guaranteed in a given administrative proceeding involving a foreign investor, does not necessarily entail an FET violation. To this end, arbitral case law requires an additional requirement: the decision passed *in absentia* must be able, at least potentially, to cause a serious economic loss to the investor. Support for this proposition may firstly be found in the two long-standing, but quite instructive, decisions in *Amco*.[81] The facts underlying this case can be summarized as follows.

In 1968, Amco, an American company, and P.T. Wisma, an Indonesian company, signed a leasing and management contract whereby the former was tasked with developing a hotel complex on a site in Indonesia owned by the latter, and this for a period of thirty years. In 1980, however, as a result of a number of disagreements between the two parties, PT Wisma took full control and management of the hotel with the assistance of the Indonesian army; and the Republic of Indonesia unjustifiably cancelled the investment licence. On this assumption, Amco initiated an ICSID proceeding against Indonesia.

---

[79] 'The tribunal considers […] that certain procedures followed by the Estonian authorities in the present instance, while they do conform to Estonian law and do not amount to a denial of due process, can be characterized as being contrary to generally accepted banking and regulatory practice. They include the following: (1) No formal notice was given to EIB that its licence would be revoked unless it complied with the Bank of Estonia's demands within a reasonable time; (2) no representative of EIB was invited to the session of the Bank of Estonia's Council that dealt with the revocation to respond to the charges brought by the Governor; (3) the revocation of the license was made immediately effective, giving EIB no opportunity to challenge it in court before it was publicly announced': para 364 of the Award.

[80] *Urbaser S.A. et al. v. Argentina*, ICSID Case No. ARB/07/26, Award of 8 December 2016, paras 842 et seq.

[81] *Amco I v. Indonesia*, Award of 20 November 1984 (in International Legal Materials 24, 1985, pp. 1022 et seq.) and *Amco II v. Indonesia*, ICSID Case No. ARB/81/1, Award in the Resubmitted Case of 5 June 1990 (in ICSID Reports 1, 1993, pp. 569 et seq.)

In both decisions under scrutiny, the arbitral tribunal ascertained a violation of the right to procedural fairness in the administrative proceeding, as provided for in Indonesian law, leading to the revocation of the licence. In its view, despite the fact that a sanction as heavy as a revocation had been envisaged against the claimant and that accordingly the risk of seriously damaging his investment existed, no formal notice was given to him;[82] such a circumstance amounted to a violation of due process in any event, that is to say, regardless of whether and to what extent that remedy could affect the outcome of the proceeding.[83]

The award in *Metalclad* is to be considered in the same vein.[84] Metalclad was a U.S. company which had bought a piece of land in Mexico, with a view to operating a landfill for hazardous waste. Even though the federal government had authorized the construction of the landfill and promised that no additional permit was needed, shortly after the start of works Metalclad was notified by the local municipality that it was prevented from operating. This was also the result of an Ecological Decree, which regarded the landfill site as a protected natural area. In the

[82] Thus, in *Amco I*, it was argued that 'the warning (or warnings) are an element of due process, rightly in the opinion of the tribunal, established by Indonesia law to protect the investor, *in particular where a sanction as heavy—and indeed irremediable—as a revocation is envisaged against him*. In the instant case, this protection was not made available to the Claimants, who were thus deprived of due process, contrary to Indonesian law as well as contrary to general principles of law. Moreover, infringement of the due process principles is met again when examining the manner in which the revocation was prepared, quite apart from the issue of the absence of any warning', paras 198–199; emphasis added. In this passage, the tribunal seems to regard the fair administrative proceeding rule as a general principle of law. Nonetheless, insofar as there existed a national rule providing for this rule, any reference to the category of principles was *ad adiuvandum* only.

[83] According to the respondent State, in particular, 'warning or warnings would have been useless in the circumstances of this case and consequently, that even if admitted, the lack of warning would be irrelevant—since no remedy could have been brought by the Claimants to their alleged failures, which led to the revocation': para 202(i). Nonetheless, the tribunal was of the view that '[w]hether this is so in fact, and whether or to what extent such remedy was needed will be seen when examining hereunder the alleged failures on which the revocation was based. Suffice it to recall here that the purpose of the warning, or warnings, is not only to allow such remedies, but also to offer to the investor the opportunity to discuss the alleged failures, in order to demonstrate either that they do not exist, or that they do not justify revocation. It could not be argued, in this respect, that discussion and defence would not have changed the administration's mind; because such argument would mean that the administration had decided in advance not to take into account any argument of the investor whatsoever, which would itself amount to a refusal of due process': idem.

[84] *Metalclad Corporation v. Mexico*, ICSID Case No. ARB(AF)/97/11, Award of 30 August 2000.

view of the tribunal, the whole procedure lacked transparency,[85] insofar as the claimant was denied any possibilities to defend his position before the municipality.[86] An FET violation was ascertained accordingly, above all considering the grave damage suffered by the investor.

The decision in *Middle East Cement Shipping* corroborates the same line of thought.[87] In this case, the investor's ship (Poseidon) was seized and auctioned without due notification; indeed, both the attachment order and notice for an auction were applied by the competent authority on board of Poseidon (having found neither the debtor nor his representative), notified to the chief of the Suez port's Police, and published in a local newspaper. Bearing in mind that such a serious sanction should have been notified to the claimant by a direct communication, the tribunal found the auction procedure contrary to due process of law and therefore to the FET principle.[88]

Finally, the award in *Tecmed* needs to be considered.[89] This case involved a Spanish company (Tecmed), with two Mexican subsidiaries, which had obtained a licence to operate a hazardous waste landfill. On November 1998, however, because of a number of breaches in the handling of the landfill, Tecmed's request to renew the license was rejected by the competent federal authority. Once again, considering that the foreign investor had a reduced or nil participation in the taking of the decisions affecting it and that as a result of such decisions the investment was completely lost, the tribunal found an FET violation in terms of procedural fairness.[90]

---

[85] Para 76 of the decision states as follows: 'Prominent in the statement of principles and rules that introduces the Agreement is the reference to "transparency" (NAFTA *Article 102(1)*). The tribunal understands this to include the idea that all relevant legal requirements for the purpose of initiating, completing and successfully operating investments made, or intended to be made, under the Agreement should be capable of being readily known to all affected investors of another Party. There should be no room for doubt or uncertainty on such matters. Once the authorities of the central government of any Party (whose international responsibility in such matters has been identified in the preceding section) become aware of any scope for misunderstanding or confusion in this connection, it is their duty to ensure that the correct position is promptly determined and clearly stated so that investors can proceed with all appropriate expedition in the confident belief that they are acting in accordance with all relevant laws'.

[86] '[T]he permit was denied at a meeting of the Municipal Town Council of which Metalclad received no notice, to which it received no invitation, and at which it was given no opportunity to appear': idem, para 91

[87] *Middle East Cement Shipping and Handling Co.S.A. v. Egypt*, ICSID Case No. ARB/99/6, Award of 12 April 2002, para 143.

[88] 'The tribunal has found […] the auction procedure applied here to have not been 'under due process of law' (Article 4a) of the BIT) and specifically the notification procedure to have not been sufficient': idem, para 147.

[89] *Técnicas Medioambiente Tecmed S.A. v. Mexico*, ICSID Case No. ARB (AF)/00/2, Award of 29 May 2003.

[90] Idem, para 122.

3.6 Conclusion

What has been remarked in this chapter begins to shed light on the core idea underlying the whole volume. Due process of law is a general principle of international law that, as such, primarily plays a 'directive' role. Accordingly, its application in the field of foreign investments is not automatic, but demands a complex interpretive activity by the judge concerned. By this activity, due process has been conceived in terms of denial of justice (in line with the German model of *Justizverweigerung*) and of procedural fairness in administrative proceedings. Put simply, due process is contextual: 'different legal contexts legitimately require different procedural standards and operate according to different principles and values.'[91] In the next two chapters an attempt will be made to establish whether and to what extent a reasoning of this kind is the same followed by arbitral case law in connection with the other two fundamental elements falling under FET, namely legitimate expectations and proportionality.

References

Acconci P (2004) The Requirement of Continuous Nationality and Customary International Rules on Foreign Investments. Italian Yearbook of International Law 14:225–236

Anzilotti D (1906) La responsabilité international des États: la raison des dommages soufferts par des étrangers. Revue générale de droit international public 13:5–29

Anzilotti D (1964) Corso di diritto internazionale, vol. I, 4th edn. Cedam, Padua

Bifulco R (2001) Articolo 41. In: Bifulco R, Cartabia M, Celotto A (eds) L'Europa dei diritti. Commento alla Carta dei diritti fondamentali dell'Unione europea. Il Mulino, Bologna, pp. 284–293

Borchard E (1940) The 'Minimum Standard' of the Treatment of Aliens. Michigan Law Review 38:445–461

Buffoni L (2008) Il rango costituzionale del 'giusto procedimento' e l'archetipo del 'processo'. Forum dei Quaderni costituzionali 2:1–43

Cassese S (2006) Oltre lo Stato. Laterza, Rome-Bari

Crawford J (2012) Brownlie's Principles of Public International Law, 8th edn. Oxford University Press, Oxford

De Visscher C (1935) Le déni de justice en droit international. Recueil des Cours 52:365–442

Della Cananea G (2009) Al di là dei confini statuali. Principi generali del diritto pubblico globale. Il Mulino, Bologna

Della Cananea G (2010) Minimum Standards of Procedural Justice in Administrative Adjudication. In: Schill S (ed) International Investment Law and Comparative Public Law. Oxford University Press, Oxford, pp. 39–74

Della Cananea G (2011) The Genesis and Structure of General Principles of Global Public Law. In: Chiti E, Mattarella BG (eds) Global Administrative Law and EU Administrative Law. Relationships, Legal Issues and Comparison. Springer, Heidelberg

Diehl A (2012) The Core Standard of International Investment Protection. Fair and Equitable Treatment. Kluwer Law International, Alphen aan den Rijn

[91] Howell 2016, p. 2.

Dorigo S, Pustorino P (2009) Diritto a una tutela giurisdizionale effettiva e revision dei processi penali. Diritti umani e diritto internazionale 3:85–110
Douglas Z (2009) The International Law of Investment Claims. Cambridge University Press, Cambridge
Douglas Z (2014) International Responsibility for Domestic Adjudication: Denial of Justice Deconstructed. International and Comparative Law Quarterly 63:867–900
Fitzmaurice G (1932) The Meaning of the Term 'Denial of Justice'. British Yearbook of International Law 13:93–114
Focarelli C (2009) Denial of Justice. Max Planck Encyclopedia of Public International Law, Online Edition. Available at http://opil.ouplaw.com
Francioni F (2009) Access to Justice, Denial of Justice and International Investment Law. European Journal of International Law 20:729–747
Gaffney JP (1999) Due Process in the World Trade Organization: The Need for Procedural Justice in the Dispute Settlement System. American University International Law Review 14:1173–1221
Garcìa-Amador FV, Sohn LB, Baxter RR (1974) Recent Codification of the Law of State Responsibility for Injuries to Aliens. Oceana, Dobbs Ferry
Hatshek J (1923) Völkerrecht als System rechtlich bedeutsamer Staatsakte. Deichert, Leipzig
Hirsch M (2011) Between Fair and Equitable Treatment and Stabilization Clause: Stable Legal Environment and Regulatory Change in International Investment Law. The Journal of World Investment & Trade 12:783–806
Hovell D (2016) Due Process in the United Nations. American Journal of International Law 110:1–48
Kiestra LR (2014) The Impact of the European Convention on Human Rights on Private International Law. TMC Asser Press, The Hague
Kohona PTB (1987) Investment Protection Agreements: An Australian Perspective. Journal of World Trade Law 21:79–103
Kotuby Jr CT (2013) General Principles of Law, International Due Process, and the Modern Role of Private International Law. Duke Journal of Comparative & International Law 23:411–443
Krueger D (2003) The Combat Zone: Mondev International Ltd v. United States and the Backlash against NAFTA Chapter 11. Boston University International Law Journal 21:399–426
Mani VS (1980) International Adjudication: Procedural Aspects. Nijhoff, The Hague
Meldrum DH (2000) Country Risk and Foreign Direct Investment. Business Economic 34:33–40
Moore JB (1898) History and Digest of the International Arbitrations to Which the United States Has Been a Party, vol. II. Government Printing Office, Washington
Palombino FM (2010) Judicial Economy and Limitation of the Scope of the Decision in International Adjudication. Leiden Journal of International Law 23:909–932
Paulsson J (2005) Denial of Justice. Oxford University Press, Oxford
Pedrazzi M (2004) Uguaglianza delle parti e contraddittorio nel processo internazionale. In: Studi di diritto internazionale in onore di Gaetano Arangio Ruiz, Vol. II. Editoriale Scientifica, Naples, pp. 1129–1156
Quadri R (1936) La sudditanza nel diritto internazionale. Cedam, Padua
Rose-Ackerman S, Egidy S, Fowkes J (2014) Due Process Lawmaking. Cambridge University Press, Cambridge
Savarese E (2012) La nozione di giurisdizione nel sistema ICSID. Editoriale Scientifica, Naples
Schreuer C (2014) Victor Pey Casado and President Allende Foundation v Republic of Chile. ICSID Review 2014 29:321–327
Strupp K (1925) Rechts- und Justizverweigerung, Rechtsverzögerung. In: Hatschek J, Strupp K (eds) Wörterbuch des Völkerrechts und der Diplomatie, Vol. II. De Gruyter, Berlin, pp. 340–341
UNCTAD (2012) Fair and Equitable Treatment. UNCTAD Series on Issues in International Investment Agreements II. A Sequel. United Nations, New York/Geneva
Verdross A (1931) Les règles internationales concernant le traitement des étrangers. Recueil des Cours 37:323–412

Wallace D (2005) Fair and Equitable Treatment and Denial of Justice: Loewen v US and Chattin v Mexico. In: Weiler T (ed) International Investment Law and Arbitration. Cameron May, London, pp. 669–700

Whiteman MM (1963–1973) Digest of International Law. Department of State Publication, Washington

Chapter 4
FET and Legitimate Expectations

Contents

Abstract This chapter is intended to investigate the nature and the scope of legitimate expectations in international investment law. It is argued that legitimate expectations embody a general principle of international law with its own foundations in the international legal order itself and that such principle, as an FET element, may demand protection under three types of State conduct: contractual commitment, unilateral promise, and legislation.

Keywords Legitimate expectations · Definition · Public law · Contract · Promise · Legislation

F.M. Palombino, *Fair and Equitable Treatment and the Fabric of General Principles*, https://doi.org/10.1007/978-94-6265-210-1_4

4.1 Introduction

The manifold expressions and concretizations of the principle of legitimate expectations as one of the FET major components have been accurately identified by arbitral tribunals. Three main types of State conduct would be susceptible to generate a legitimate expectation: (i) contractual commitment; (ii) unilateral promise, and (iii) legislation. The first form of legitimate expectations occurs when the breach of a contract by the host State is combined with a reference to other elements, as in the case where the State changes the course of conduct in the fulfilment of its contractual commitments. Expectations by promise demand safeguarding, under the requirement that promise be given intentionally by an administrative authority, and one which is entitled to do so. Finally, expectations by legislation postulates the occurrence of a qualified conduct of the legislator, that is to say a normative act specifically aimed to induce foreign investments and on which the foreign investor relied in making his investment (the so-called expectation by 'induction'). Arguably, legitimate expectations as an FET element have gone so far as to embody a general principle specific to international investment law.

4.2 Legitimate Expectations as a General Principle of International Law

At first glance, the rationale behind the principle of legitimate expectations rests on the need to protect the individual's reliance on the conduct of another party.[1] Accordingly, the principle is firstly applied in the area of private law, an area where its protection refers to legal relations—such as those between private citizens—that take place on an equal footing. Yet the relevance of the principle proves much broader. Unless one were to adopt an absolutist view of the State's power and its activity—according to which the public interest should always prevail over the private one—in any modern and democratic legal systems private parties' legitimate expectations demand safeguarding, even where they are the result of State conduct. And indeed, in such cases, what the principle calls for is a fair balance

[1] We may wonder whether a distinction can be drawn between the reliance theory and that of legitimate expectations. In the European legal systems, the answer seems to be in the negative, especially because expectations often prompt reliance. By contrast, in common law countries, the said distinction is still regarded as useful. Some argue that, even though a casual-circumstantial link between expectations and reliance generally exists, this 'is not proof of its necessity, nor it should blind us to the fact that expectations do not always lead to reliance […] Ensuring independent protection of the expectation interest means that the remedy granted is not contingent on the existence of a reliance interest. The scope of the expectation is not determined by the extent of reliance but the value of the expectations' (Barak-Erez 2005, pp. 587 et seq.). As far as international investment law is concerned, reliance and expectations are discussed and dealt with together by arbitral tribunals. Arguably, this is a consequence of the undeniable vagueness of this distinction.

between the individual interest in maintaining a given legal situation which has been relied on for the purpose of his assessments and decisions and the State's power to modify this situation, i.e. to exercise the typical power to regulate in the public interest.[2]

Notably, this very principle plays a crucial role also in the field of international law, but its legal nature continues to be shrouded in ambiguity. Several authors regard legitimate expectations as part of the body of general principles common to domestic systems. Yet their lines of argument are not altogether convincing. In detail, while the principle is provided for by the overwhelming majority of both civil and common law countries, its scope as well as the conditions under which it may be guaranteed, especially from the standpoint of public law, differ greatly according to each country and, of course, each country's peculiar legal tradition. In Germany, for example, the principle (which is known as '*Vertrauensschutz*'—literally protection of trust) is enshrined at the constitutional level, and applies not only to decisions and representations made by public authorities, but to legislative measures as well.[3] On the contrary, in other countries, the scope of the principle tends to be narrower. One may mention the case of England, where 'expectations' mainly give rise to procedural rights: individuals are entitled to participate in the decision-making process of public bodies, but they are not safeguarded from changes of legislation.[4] The Italian legal order represents an additional revealing example in the same line of thought.[5] Lastly, some countries, such as France, do not provide for any express protection of legitimate expectations, which is probably due to the presence of other principles (such as that of legal certainty) having a similar function.[6]

Curiously enough, the lack of consistency as to the way the principle is applied domestically does not prevent some authors from regarding it as a general principle of law in the traditional meaning under Article 38, para 1(c), of the ICJ Statute.[7]

---

[2] *See* Merusi 2001.

[3] This very notion of expectations ended up entering the European Administrative Law as well. In *Algera*, the EU Court of Justice ruled that 'an administrative measure conferring individual rights on the person concerned cannot in principle be withdrawn, if it is a lawful measure; in that case, since the individual right is vested, the need to safeguard confidence in the stability of the situation thus created prevails over the interest of an administration desirous of reversing its decision' (Case 7/56 and 3-7/57, *Algera c. Common Assembly*, 1957 E.C.R. 56 (E.C.J. 1957)). In this regard, *see* more generally Gigante 2008.

[4] Forsyth 1985.

[5] *See* Merusi 2006, p. 33 ss.

[6] The French *Conseil d'État* has always refused to hold the principle of legitimate expectations. On this point, *see* Snodgrass 2006, p. 27.

[7] *See* Snodgrass 2006, especially p. 2 ('[p]rotection for investors' legitimate expectations can be justified as reflecting a 'general principle of law recognized by civilized nations' as that phrase is used to describe a source of international law, and that the methodology for recognizing a general principle can be applied to develop a more highly articulated expression of that principle to guide the protection given investors' legitimate expectations in future cases'); Brown 2009, p. 6. ('[E]ven though there are differences from one legal system to another, the fact that a principle is applied differently should not necessarily prevent its acceptance as a general principle of law within the meaning of Article 38(1)(c) of the *ICJ Statute*'; Diehl 2012, p. 173. On legitimate expectations in the international law on foreign investment, *see*, in addition to the previous references, Fietta 2006; Walter 2008.

Support for this contention has been found, for example, in the circumstance whereby 'there is very little dispute about the status of *res judicata* as a general principle of law, even though that principle is applied somewhat differently in common law systems and civil law systems (and, indeed, even among different common law systems).'[8]

An argument of this kind, however, is unpersuasive[9] and all the more so the example used to sustain it. The status of *res judicata* in contemporary international

[8] Brown 2009, p. 6. A similar opinion has also been advanced by Potestà 2013, p. 98: '[O]ne could [...] conclude that to establish at least an emerging general principle of protection of legitimate expectations would not seem to be an unrealistic endeavour. Thus, it is this general principle that will inform the content of fair and equitable treatment in investment treaty law.' Finally, it is helpful to consider the separate opinion rendered by Thomas Wälde in *Thunderbird* (*International Thunderbird Gaming Corporation v. Mexico*, UNCITRAL (NAFTA) Arbitration Proceedings, Award of 26 January 2006). He does not specifically claim the existence of a principle common to domestic systems, but the importance of a comparative public law inquiry is notwithstanding outlined: 'The principle of protection of 'legitimate expectation' or, in common law, estoppel, has also been applied in comparative contract law, mainly to deny formal rights invoked by a party if such invocation contradicts previous statements and conduct that made the other party trust in the particular expectation so created. But contract law—presuming the existence of two equal parties in a commercial contract—is less relevant than comparative public law with respect to the judicial review of governmental conduct. For example, in its well-established jurisprudence, the European Court of Justice held 'legitimate expectations' to be a key principle of the relation between State and individuals. The principle requires public authorities (including the European Commission) to respect legitimate expectations it has created with individuals, in particular if such expectations have become the basis for investment [...] The principle of legitimate expectation is also recognised in several developed systems of administrative law. The common principles of the principal administrative law systems are in my view an important point of reference for the interpretation of investment treaties to the extent investment treaty jurisprudence is not as yet firmly established. But its exact scope and implication are not well established' (paras 27 et seq.).

[9] One may mention Sornarajah 2010, pp. 354–355: '[A]s a general principle, legitimate expectations provide only procedural protection, requiring that an expectation created by administrative conduct should not be violated unless a hearing is given to the person who had that expectation. The principle has rarely been used as a substantive principle because of practical difficulties. Governments make assurances as to policies on taxation, agriculture and other areas. Administration would become difficult if, at each change of policy to suit new circumstances, the State has to pay damages to affected parties. It is an error to state that there is a general principle of law that violations of legitimate expectations give rise to substantive remedies [...] It is unlikely that such a rule can be maintained in any system.' The same opinion may be ascribed to Zeyl 2011, p. 209, who observes that 'recognizing substantive expectations as part of the general principles of law is at this point premature and amounts to a misstatement of a general principle of law.' Last, but not least, a reference should be made to the separate opinion passed by Judge Nikken with regard to the decision in *Suez* and *AWG Group v. Argentine Republic* (ICSID Case No. ARB/03/19, Decision on Liability of 30 July 2010). In his view, in particular, '[t]he concept of legitimate expectations is no stranger to the different legal systems, which, to varying degrees and on the basis of good faith, consider the party to a legal relationship that engages in self-contradiction to the detriment of the other party reprehensible. In human relationships, in general, your word is your bond and whoever betrays the trust of another must be penalized. However, the specific formulation of this concept varies in the different legal systems. Not even the English law concept of estoppel has a uniform wording or matches the same principle in other Anglo-Saxon countries. Neither is the doctrine of *actos propios* (close to estoppel) in the contract law of some civil law countries identical nor the doctrine of *confianza legítima* (*confiance legitime*) in the administrative law of those same countries' (para 22).

law is anything but undisputed;[10] and this precisely as a result of the various forms the principle may take in national legal systems. Hence, a number of prominent scholars prefer to regard it as part of the different body of principles peculiar to international law only.[11] On the other hand, the practice of the ICJ, especially the 2007 judgment in *Genocide Convention*,[12] could be cited to the same effect; para 115 of the judgment clearly recognizes the belonging of *res judicata* to general principles of international law.[13] For reasons similar to those referred to above, this specific source of law has been invoked also with a view to defining the legal nature of legitimate expectations. According to Michael Byers,

> all rules of international law involve legitimate expectations. Apart from the role played by acquiescence, *rules of customary international law* involve legitimate expectations because any change from a voluntary pattern of behaviour to a customary rule involves the transformation and legitimisation of patterns of behaviour, around which expectations of a legal character necessarily develop. *Treaty rules* involve legitimate expectations because they are based on the general customary rule of *pacta sunt servanda*, which requires that treaty obligations be upheld in good faith. In short, States expect other States to abide by their treaty obligations. This expectation may be considered as legitimate – i.e., legally justifiable – because States usually behave accordingly *and* regard their behaviour as having legal relevance.[14]

The last-mentioned contention proves the most convincing. In the same way as due process of law, legitimate expectations may be regarded as a general principle of international law that prescribes a direction to be followed and, alongside, vests the judge with the power of inferring (from the principle) the rules applicable to a given case. Notably, with the apparent exception of the decision in *Total*[15] and the

---

[10] Zarra 2016, pp. 124 et seq., pp. 135–136.

[11] Quadri 1968, p. 127.

[12] *Application of the Convention on the Prevention and the Punishment of the Crime of Genocide (Bosnia and Herzegovina v. Serbia and Montenegro)*, Judgment of 26 February 2007.

[13] 'There is no dispute between the Parties as to the existence of the principle of *res judicata* even if they interpret it differently as regards judgments deciding questions of jurisdiction. The fundamental character of that principle appears from the terms of the Statute of the Court and the Charter of the United Nations. The underlying character and purposes of the principle are reflected in the judicial practice of the Court. That principle signifies that the decisions of the Court are not only binding on the parties, but are final, in the sense that they cannot be reopened by the parties as regards the issues that have been determined, save by procedures, of an exceptional nature, specially laid down for that purpose. Article 59 of the Statute, notwithstanding its negative wording, has at its core the positive statement that the parties are bound by the decision of the Court in respect of the particular case. Article 60 of the Statute provides that the judgment is final and without appeal; Article 61 places close limits of time and substance on the ability of the parties to seek the revision of the judgment.' Put differently, the Court does not engage in an examination of the status of the principle in national legal systems, but rather assumes the existence of a general principle of international law, with its own foundations in the international legal order, viz., in the Statute of the ICJ itself and the Charter of the United Nations.

[14] Byers 1999, p. 107.

[15] On this case, and the way it should be read, *see infra* Sect. 4.5.2.

case law following it, this very approach has been adopted in investor-State arbitration, within which the safeguard of expectations is firmly rooted and one of the major components of the FET standard.[16] The judge has claimed the existence of a general principle in this matter and, *by way of deduction*, a number of different rules have been found, depending on whether the investor's expectations arose from (i) contractual commitment, (ii) unilateral promise, or (iii) legislation. Subsequently, by a consistent case law, these rules have become stable going so far as to be subsumed under FET.[17] A *caveat* is required in any event: FET clauses are not equivalent to stabilization clauses, which means that State legislative or regulatory changes apparently frustrating investors' legitimate expectations are not sufficient *per se* to generate an obligation of compensation.[18]

---

[16] *Electrabel S.A. v. Hungary*, ICSID No. ARB/07/19, Decision on Jurisdiction, Applicable Law and Liability of 30 November 2012, para 7.75: 'It is widely accepted that the most important function of the fair and equitable treatment standard is the protection of the investor's reasonable and legitimate expectations.'

[17] From the very beginning of our inquiry, the autonomous value of the principle of legitimate expectations has been claimed. Nonetheless, both in national and international legal systems, the question has proven to be challenging, and is intimately connected to the more general debate concerning the good faith principle. Generally speaking, good faith would have a twofold dimension, subjective and objective. *Subjectively*, it implies 'honesty in fact', that is to say, the situation where the person who infringes a certain right is not aware of doing so. *Objectively*, it is regarded as a legally imposed standard of behaviour which is not construed by reference to the subjective perceptions of the party in question. Now, if one assumes that the second variant of good faith covers the protection of legitimate expectations as well, this latter principle would lack an autonomous nature accordingly (Merusi 2006, p. 145). The same opinion has been advanced by several scholars of international law. Kolb 2006, p. 16, for instance, observes as follows: '[G]ood faith has an objective sense: it is here a powerful general norm, a general principle of law. [...] The substance of good faith as a general principle decomposes itself in several more concrete aspects. [...] First, the principle of good faith requires the protection of *legitimate expectations* which a certain course of conduct has provoked in another person.' In the sense that legitimate expectations would be a concretization of the principle of good faith, *see* also Ziegler and Baumgartner 2015, pp. 17–18. However, it is arguable that, at least within the international legal order, reliance embodies an autonomous principle, and more precisely a general principle of international law aimed at protecting the certainty of legal relations. Support for this proposition may be found not only in the legal doctrine mentioned beforehand (*see supra* para 4.1), but also in the arbitral practice in matter of foreign investments. In line with this practice, it may be the case that a State acts in good faith, but nevertheless violates the reliance principle. On this assumption, the autonomous value of these two principles must be necessarily admitted. To put it differently: either reliance is regarded as a more concrete aspect of good faith (with the consequence that a State conduct in good faith is automatically consistent with the reliance principle) or one has to submit the existence of two principles working independently from each other (Diehl 2012, pp. 356 ss., spec. p. 358: 'In sum, the principle of good faith is not to be seen as a foundation of the protection of legitimate expectations, but as a guiding interpretive principle which helps to apply and clarify the FET standard').

[18] Hirsch 2011, p. 292.

4.3 The Circumstances Under which an Investor's Expectation May Be Regarded as 'Legitimate'

Before inquiring into the State conducts that may give rise to an investor's expectation, one should ask when the latter is to be regarded as *legitimate* in this particular field of law. Of course the reasonableness of the expectation may be evaluated in both objective and subjective terms.

In objective terms, tribunals are required to consider whether the alleged expectation is that of a diligent or prudent investor, that is to say, the investor should take into account 'all circumstances, including not only the facts surrounding the investment, but also the political, socioeconomic, cultural and historical conditions prevailing in the host State.'[19] Put differently, what is relevant is once again the so-called country risk in the traditional meaning of this concept;[20] this explains why the *Parkerings-Compaignie*t tribunal rejected an FET claim for the changing of the legal regime existing at the time of the investment: at that time (1998), 'the political environment in Lithuania was characteristic of a country in transition from its past being part of the Soviet Union to candidate for the European Union membership. Thus, legislative changes, far from being unpredictable, were in fact to be regarded as likely.'[21] Additionally, the investor's expectations

> must have been affected in essential parts. Such important level of interest may result from the trust the investor had in promises and undertakings made by or on behalf of the host State in support of the investment and its promotion. When the host State's representatives were aware or must have been aware that certain specific commitments or guarantees were decisive for the investor's decision to proceed with the investment, the disregard or violation of such undertakings are generally to be considered as triggering the State's responsibility under the fair and equitable treatment standard.[22]

In subjective terms

> an expectation will be […] unreasonable if such expectation conflicted with other knowledge the individual has about the law and/or representations made by the host State. Therefore, an investor may not argue that his investment fails merely because of laws, policies or practices which were in place at the time of the investment, and which were, or ought to have been, well known to him before making the investment.[23]

---

[19] *Duke v. Ecuador*, ICSID Case No. ARB/04/19, Award of 18 August 2008. More recently, the same remark may be found in *Charanne B.V. and Construction Investments S.A.R.L. v. Spain*, Arbitration Institute of the Stockholm Chamber of Commerce, Award of 21 January 2016, para 505: '[I]n order to exercise the right of legitimate expectations, the Claimants should have made a diligent analysis of the legal framework for the investment.'

[20] *See* Chap. 2, Sect. 2.7.

[21] *Parkerings-Compagniet AS v. Lithuania*, ICSID Case No. ARB/05/8, Award, 11 September 2007, para 335.

[22] *Urbaser S.A. et al. v. Argentina*, ICSID Case No. ARB/07/26, Award of 8 December 2016, para 627.

[23] Téllez 2012, p. 3.

Among the decisions supporting such a proposition, the one rendered in *Urbaser* is of particular assistance inasmuch as it regards FET as a clause including 'the actual social and economic environment of the host State, which is also part of the expectations the investor has to acknowledge when making its business decision.'[24]

4.4 FET and Expectation by Contractual Commitment

Should some specific circumstances occur, an investor's expectation might be firstly generated by a contractual commitment: if one assumes that in any legal system contracts represent the most important means by which to create legal stability and predictability, this is equally true as far as a contract between the host State and an investor is concerned.[25]

More squarely, administrative authorities are used to entering into contracts with private individuals. By doing so, the administration creates a legitimate expectation as to the fact that the arrangements contained therein will be performed. Such a contention seems to be self-evident, but it raises a crucial question at both the national and international levels. *In terms of national law*, the question is whether administrative authorities are required to perform (or may derogate from) contracts in the same way as private individuals, should a public interest of fundamental importance demand protection. For this question to be answered, a distinction needs to be drawn between *patrimonial contracts* and *public power contracts*: while the former are concerned with purely private actions of the administration, the latter imply the exercise of public law powers. Needless to say, such a distinction fulfils an important function as to the duty to perform. Even though a departure from the contract by the administration is admissible in any event, in relation to a public power contract, the margin for non-performance is wider.

> At the moment when a public law power must be exercised (for example where a decision must be taken to issue a permit), the administrative authority concerned must make a careful examination of all relevant facts and interests and must balance the different interests. The authority is not relieved of this obligation merely because a contract has previously been concluded. If the interests of a third party could be affected disproportionality by the granting of the permit, the administrative authority is bound to take this into account. It is conceivable that as a result of balancing the interests the administrative authority may be compelled to default on the contract. A person cannot be bound by a contract to which he is not party. Naturally, if the administrative authority decided not to perform a public power contract it would then be obliged [...] to pay compensation.[26]

---

[24] *Supra* note 23, para 623.

[25] Dolzer and Schreuer 2012, p. 140.

[26] Berge and Widdershoven 1998.

In terms of international law, the question is whether the *mere* breach by a State of an administrative contract with a foreign investor entails *per se* an internationally wrongful act. Bearing in mind the ILC works on State responsibility,[27] the question should be answered in the negative, but for reasons different from those linked to the public nature of the contract. Indeed, as was clearly observed by René-Jean Dupuy serving as the sole arbitrator in the celebrated *Texaco* award,[28] the very concept of administrative contract is hardly applicable to the agreement between the host State and a foreign investor. Two reasons underlie such a conclusion. First, as a result of the rights and powers they may confer on the host State' s administration (such as the power to modify the contract should the protection of a public interest require doing so), contracts of this kind generally prove unbalanced. Second, while the doctrine of administrative contracts is adopted in several countries (such as France), 'it is unknown in many other legal systems which are as important as the French system and it has not been accepted by international law notwithstanding wishes which *de lege ferenda* may have been expressed in this field. The distinction made by certain legal systems between "civil contracts" and "administrative contracts" cannot therefore be regarded as corresponding to a "general principle of law".[29] More plausibly, the reason justifying the ILC's solution in the matter is that the breach of a contract by the host State is part of the economic risk underlying any investments. That said, one must ask (i) whether non-performance of a contract between the host State and a foreign investor is contrary to the legitimate expectations of the latter, and entails, as such, an FET violation; if the answer is in the

[27] One remark in this sense may already be found in the Fourth Report on State Responsibility presented by García-Amador, as special rapporteur of the UN ILC, UN doc. A/CN.4/119 (1959), in *Yearbook of International Law Commission*, 1959, Vol. II, Chap. III, 1959, p. 30, para 123: 'Diplomatic protection and international case law have traditionally accepted almost as dogma the idea that mere non-performance by a State of its obligations under a contract with an alien individual does not in itself necessarily give rise to international responsibility.' The same view is reflected in the Commentary to Article 4 of the 2001 Draft Articles on State Responsibility, UN doc. A/56/10 (2001), in *Yearbook of International Law Commission*, Vol. II, Second Part, 2001, pp. 19 et seq, especially p. 41, para 6: '[O]f course the breach by a State of a contract does not entail a breach of international law.' As to the legal doctrine, *see* Schreuer 2005, p. 380: 'A simple breach of contract is part of normal business risk, and an investor may have to anticipate such an occurrence without recourse to a treaty remedy. Also, a breach of contract resulting from serious difficulties on the part of the government to comply with its financial obligations cannot be equated with unfair and inequitable treatment.' In similar terms, *see* Potestà 2013, p. 101: 'even if the investor has an expectation that the contract will be fulfilled, a disappointment of such expectation cannot per se be equated to a violation of the fair and equitable treatment standard in the treaty. To reason otherwise would mean that invocation of legitimate expectations would turn the fair and equitable treatment standard into a general umbrella clause, which can hardly be a tenable interpretation.'

[28] *Texaco v. Libya* (1978), *Ad Hoc* Award of 19 January 1977, in 17 International Law Materials 1, paras 54–56. On this judgment, *see* Cantegreil 2011.

[29] Idem, para 57.

affirmative, (ii) to what extent FET may be used as a kind of 'umbrella clause'[30] which, as such, brings contractual commitments under the protective umbrella of the treaty where it is provided for and accordingly 'elevates contractual breaches to treaty breaches.'[31]

According to Santiago Montt, the existence of contractual obligations would make the very idea of legitimate expectations pointless; indeed, the rights and interests arising from the contract should be protected 'in the framework of the contract, and not pursuant to the international investment law principle of legitimate expectations [...] Specific assurances should be assessed in the context of the contract, and their violation should be seen, at best, as a potential breach of contract (or domestic law).'[32] Other authors take a different position, claiming that 'contractual commitment by a government formalises a legitimate expectation with the foreign investor. The investor, in reliance on such commitment, takes the commercial risk by investing his capital, technology and managerial skills into a project';[33] therefore, from this perspective, a breach of the commitment undermines that legitimate expectation and amounts to an FET violation.[34]

Against this backdrop, arbitral practice seems to corroborate a view placed halfway between those mentioned thus far. This is the view according to which the applicability of the FET standard to contract claims would depend on the particular circumstances of the case.[35] Thus, this applicability must be excluded sometimes. In *Waste Management*, for example, the failure of the City of Acapulco to make payments under a concession agreement was not regarded as a violation of FET (as provided for in NAFTA Article 1105), since the City had acted in a situation of undeniable difficulty:

> [E]ven the persistent non-payment of debts by a municipality is not to be equated with a violation of Article 1105, provided that it does not amount to an outright and unjustified repudiation of the transaction and provided that some remedy is open to the creditor to

[30] On the meaning of umbrella clauses, *see* the recent judgment in *Garanti Koza LLP v. Turkmenistan*, ICSID Case No. ARB/11/20, Award of 19 December 2016, paras 328 et seq.

[31] This sentence is to be credited to Schreuer 2005, p. 379. On the coordination between contract claims and treaty claims, *see* Mauro 2016; Zarra 2016, pp. 3 et seq. In case law, a revealing judgment is that recently passed in *Ampal-American Israel Corp et al. v. Egypt*, ICSID Case No. ARB/12/11, Decision on Jurisdiction of 1 February 20016, paras 249 et seq.

[32] Montt 2012, p. 363.

[33] Wälde and Kolo 2001, p. 844.

[34] The same authors, idem, observe as follows: '[A breach of the commitment] needs to be taken into account in determining whether the breach is confiscatory. The existence of a commitment by the government may not extinguish the government's authority to change or enact new [...] laws. But where such regulation severely impacts on the investment (e.g. by rendering it no longer profitable to operate, or adding exorbitant costs on the investor—which were not contemplated at the time of the investment), then that breach of commitment weighs in on the side of the factors indicating expropriation.'

[35] The tribunal in *Hamester v. Ghana*, ICSID Case No. ARB/07/24, Award, 18 June 2010, para 337, concluded that 'it is not sufficient for a claimant to invoke contractual rights that have allegedly been infringed to sustain a claim for a violation of the FET standard.'

> address the problem. In the present case the failure to pay can be explained, albeit not excused, by the financial crisis which meant that at key points the City could hardly pay its own payroll. There is no evidence that it was motivated by sectorial or local prejudice.[36]

At other times, the circumstances of the case reveal an FET violation.[37] One may mention the cases where the government unjustifiably refuses to comply with its financial obligations, as in *SGS*,[38] or changes the course of conduct in the fulfilment of its contractual commitments. This last hypothesis is exemplified by the decision in *MTD*.[39] In this case, a Malaysian company had entered into an investment contract with Chile's foreign investment agency regarding an urban development project. However, the existing normative framework prevented the project from being successfully carried out: in accordance with the host State laws in force, all the necessary permits were denied by the competent local authorities. The tribunal found that Chile's incoherence in dealing with the whole affair (entering into an investment contract on the one hand and denying the necessary permits on the other hand) frustrated the investor's legitimate expectations and amounted, as such, to an FET violation.[40]

The same conclusion may be inferred from the more recent case in *Perenco*.[41] According to the tribunal:

> where a State has duly considered a legislative/regulatory policy [...] governmental decisions taken thereafter must, during the lifetime of such contractual arrangements maintain fidelity to that policy framework. This is not to say that the policy framework is frozen and cannot be changed because this is not so unless the State has expressly stabilised its law *vis-à-vis* its contractual counterparty. But even [...] where there is no full stability clause in its contracts, any changes to the policy framework must still be made mindful of the State's

[36] *Waste Management, Inc. v. Mexico*, ICSID Case No. ARB(AF)/00/3, Award of 30 April 2004, para 115.

[37] A general statement in this sense may be found in *Mondev International Ltd. v. United States*, ICSID Case No. ARB (AF)/99/2, Award of 11 October 2002. Paragraph 134 of the decision states as follows: 'Indeed a governmental prerogative to violate investment contracts would appear to be inconsistent with the principles embodied in Article 1105 and with contemporary standards of national and international law concerning liability for contractual performance.' In *Flemingo DutyFree v. Poland*, UNCITRAL, Award of 12 August 2016, para 529 et seq., the tribunal found that a termination in bad faith of a contract resulted in an FET violation.

[38] *SGS v. Philippines*, ICSID Case No. ARB/02/6, Decision on Jurisdiction, 29 January 2004, para 162: 'Whatever the scope of Article IV standard [fair and equitable treatment] may turn out to be—and that is a matter for the merits—an unjustified refusal to pay sums admittedly payable under an award or a contract at least raises arguable issues under Article IV.'

[39] *MTD v. Chile*, ICSID Case No. ARB/01/7, Award of 25 May 2004.

[40] Idem, para 166: 'The tribunal is satisfied, based on the evidence presented to it, that approval of an investment by the FIC for a project that is against the urban policy of the Government is a breach of the obligation to treat an investor fairly and equitably.' On the other hand, the fact that the permit had been denied by the competent local authorities is not significant. As it is well-known, indeed, the State has to be identified with the machinery of government as a whole, i.e. all the organs which directly or indirectly take part in the government activity. *See* Conforti 2015, pp. 15–16.

[41] *Perenco Ecuador Limited v. Ecuador*, ICSID Case No. ARB/08/6, Decision on Remanding Issues of Jurisdiction and Liability of 12 September 2014.

> contractual commitments [...] Particularly after changes in government occur, States must seek to act consistently with, and governments cannot wilfully repudiate, long-term commercial relationships with foreign investors concluded by their predecessors. New governments must bear in mind why the State engaged in such relationships in the first place, because resource extraction and other capital-intensive investments with substantial 'upfront' costs generally require a medium to long-term period of operations in order to be able to generate a reasonable return on investment. Such investments must be able to withstand deviations in governmental policy that could undermine their contractual framework.[42]

Moving from these assumptions, the measures demanding assessment in this case included windfall profit taxes at 50 and 99%. In the tribunal's view, while the former had not breached the FET clause,[43] the latter had done so.[44]

To sum up,

> [a] simple breach of the contract is part of normal business risk, and an investor may have to anticipate such an occurrence without recourse to a treaty remedy. Also, a breach of contract resulting from serious difficulties on the part of the government to comply with its financial obligations cannot be equated with unfair and inequitable treatment. On the other hand, a wilful refusal by a government authority to abide by its contractual obligations, abuse of government authority to evade agreements with foreign investors and action in bad faith in the course of contractual performance may well lead to a finding that the standard of fair and equitable treatment has been breached.[45]

4.5 FET and Expectation by Promise. Promise and National Legal Systems

The foreign investor's legitimate expectations may also be generated by a promise of the administration. As a rule, in private law, promise requires that a party (the promisor) undertakes to another party (the promisee) the fulfilment of a certain action. Its features, however, vary greatly from civil law to common law countries.

In civil law countries promise is binding only where (i) it is made within the context of a contract (namely, a veritable agreement between two parties creating

[42] Idem, paras 562 et seq.

[43] Idem, para 591: 'The market conditions in which the State acted were, in the tribunal's view, quite extraordinary and the widespread array of measures taken by other States during this time satisfies the tribunal that seeking an adjustment of the economic rent derived from exhaustible natural resources was not per se arbitrary, unreasonable or idiosyncratic'.

[44] Idem, paras 606–607: '[T]he application of the law at 99% rendered a participation contract essentially the same as a service contract [...] In the tribunal's view, moving beyond 50–99% with the application of Decree 662 amounted to a breach of Article 4 of the Treaty.' *See* also *Garanti Koza LLP, supra* footnote 31, where the tribunal concluded that the inconsistency of behaviour between different organs of the respondent State with regard to its contractual obligations amounted to an FET violation.

[45] Schreuer 2005, p. 380. For a similar view, *see* Alvik 2011, pp. 261 et seq.

obligations enforceable by law); or (ii) its bindingness is expressly provided for by law.[46] From a very different perspective one has to appraise the US doctrine of *promissory estoppel*, the aim of which is notably to protect private investments. This doctrine always prevents one party from withdrawing a promise made to a second party, where the latter has reasonably relied on that promise; should the promise be withdrawn, the promisee would have a cause of action in tort.[47]

Now, while in private law promise may be conceived in terms of two specific and contrasting models, in public law its features are more difficult to grasp. It is commonly argued that an administrative promise occurs where a public official undertakes that certain decisions will (or will not) be taken.[48] In detail, as to the legal nature of a promise of this kind (i.e. whether it embodies a real administrative act) and to the circumstances under which it may create legal obligations, the existing practice is too scant to reach any definitive solutions, especially in terms of comparative law. Nonetheless, some general guiding principles can be identified.

For an administrative promise to be binding, there are at least two criteria that must be fulfilled. First, with regard to acts that have the potential to create legitimate expectations, a distinction is needed between a promise intentionally given by an administrative authority, *the sole kind of promise to possess such an aptitude*, and the mere provision of certain information. As it has been rightly observed

> [i]n the case of a promise, there is in principle a kind of decision which precedes a final decision. Here, the interests concerned will often have been balanced in preliminary deliberations by the administrative authority concerned. This is not the case of the mere provision of information. An administrative authority provides information in response to a particular question and, in doing so, takes account of what it considers relevant in the particular case.[49]

---

[46] One example may be found in Arts 1987–1988 of the Italian Code of Civil Law.

[47] *See* Pardolesi 2009. An exemplification of the doctrine may be found in the 1965 Wisconsin Supreme Court decision in *Hoffman v. Red Owl Store* (26 Wis. 2d 683, 133 N.W. 2d 267). The facts underlying this case go back to a claim for compensation concerning the potential extension of a franchise. In the early 1960s, Mr. Joseph Hoffman, who owned and operated a bakery, sought to obtain a Red Owl supermarket franchise in Wisconsin. The franchisor assured him that the amount of money at his disposal ($18.000) was sufficient, but in the end the negotiations fell apart; indeed, Red Owl raised the amount of investment beyond what Mr. Hoffman was able to afford. Accordingly, the latter sued the former for reliance damage, lost profits and expenses. Now, despite the fact that the parties had never reached agreement on essential factors necessary to create a valid contract and with a view to upholding the claimant's request, the Wisconsin Supreme Court relied on the promissory estoppel doctrine. More squarely, under Section 90 of the *Restatement (First) of Contracts*, '[a] promise which the promisor should reasonably expect to induce action or forbearance of a definite and substantial character on the part of the promisee and which does induce such action or forbearance is binding if injustice can be avoided only by enforcement of the promise.' This article, which exemplifies promissory estoppel, was regarded as applicable in the case at issue. And indeed, in its terms, the promise is not required to be so comprehensive in scope as to meet the requirements of an offer that would create a binding contract if accepted by the promisee.

[48] Merusi 2001, pp. 167 et seq.

[49] Berge and Widdershoven 1998, pp. 445–446.

Second, as to the promisor, he is required to be the competent administrative authority. Hence, a promise given by an official who later proves to be unauthorized to do so will not create any legitimate expectations. In spite of what has been observed, some writers advance a different view in matter of promise, and limit its bindingness to the sole case where it is given in the context of a public law power contract.[50] Yet, little support for this proposition may be found in judicial practice.

In summary, the existence of a general principle common to domestic systems with regard to promise must be rejected; the question here is a different one, i.e. whether, in the same matter, there exists a custom applicable in the relationship between sovereign States as well as between the latter and a foreign investor.

4.5.1 *Promise and International Law*

In international law, the question relating to the legal nature of promise (which somewhat replaces the terms of the debate arising in private law) is still of keen interest to scholars, and the range of opinions on the issue is evidence of this.

According to a 'conservative' view, which is in favour of a strict interpretation of the principle *pacta sunt servanda*, the binding nature of promise should be ruled out as a matter of principle. Indeed, such a nature would be inconsistent with the structure and features typical of the international legal order: an order within which not only restrictions on State sovereignty, but also the way States assume obligations, are conceived restrictively. Therefore, a promise would be binding only to the extent that the promisee is willing to agree with its content. In these terms, however, promise ends up amounting to one element of a veritable contractual legal transaction; and what binds the parties concerned is such a transaction, rather than the promise itself.[51] Two additional circumstances seem to sustain such a view. First, Article 38, para 1, of the ICJ Statute, among the sources of international law, does not expressly or tacitly mention promise (nor refer to unilateral acts in general), while giving great relevance to agreements.[52] Second, it is argued that:

> the fact that, while in national legal orders contract is, universally and indisputably (in spite of certain obvious limits), held as being the typical means of establishing, regulating and cancelling any kind of legal relationship whatsoever, the same is not true for unilateral acts. These are generally thought to have legal effects only in certain cases expressly provided for by the legislator.[53]

Contrariwise, a number of writers regard promise as a binding act, by giving substance, at the most, to the will of the promisee. More in detail, the rationale behind this approach rests on the existence of the principle whereby any State

[50] Grellert 1964.

[51] Sereni 1962, p. 1352; Morelli 1967, p. 289; Barile 1983, pp. 151–153.

[52] Quadri 1968, p. 573.

[53] Carbone 1975, p. 166.

promise that is intended to be legally binding without acceptance is binding (*promissio est obligatio*). This opinion was originally advanced by an Italian scholar (Giorgio Bosco), precisely with a view to contesting the absolute nature of the principle *pacta sunt servanda* in the international legal order,[54] and finds support in the current legal doctrine as well.[55] On closer inspection, however, an opinion of this kind proves unpersuasive inasmuch as it leads to an illogical result: if one assumes that the mere will of a State would be able to make a promise binding, by the same will that promise might always be revoked. In this light, the overwhelming majority of writers end up claiming the existence of a general principle in matter of legitimate expectations, and regard promise as a concrete aspect of it. As to the 'object' of the principle, however, no agreement exists.

According to a first opinion, the principle would protect the will expressed by the promisor. [56] Yet this is nothing but a refined version of the view claiming that *promissio est servanda*, and in respect of which the same criticism applies. On the other hand, in a more realistic fashion, a group of authors call for an 'intermediate' model, whereby promise should be regarded as binding in principle, but only under some specific circumstances. This view is primarily to be ascribed to Sergio Maria Carbone,[57] who points out as follows:

> [A]n international promise has binding effects only when it concurs with other factors in creating a situation which is, in the interest of the promisee, legally protected by international law; and only on such perspective account must be taken of the promisee's expectations among all the circumstances in which the promisor's intention to be legally bound has been expressed thus giving way to the promisee's reliance that promise will be fulfilled. This implies that international law requires the promisee to show [...] his expectation which, together with the promisor's intention of being legally binding, are the only relevant evidence of a situation protected, in the interests of the promisee, by international law.[58]

In a nutshell, for a binding promise to exist, a dual element is required: a *subjective element*, viz. the clear will of the promisor to accomplish the promise; an *objective element*, viz. the occurrence of additional circumstances (such as the public taking of the commitment), insofar as they help give rise to a legally protected situation.[59] Support for this view, which ends up being very akin to the

---

[54] Bosco 1938.

[55] *See* Cassese 2005, p. 185: 'Promise is a unilateral declaration by which a State undertakes to behave in a certain manner. This obligation is assumed independently of any reciprocal undertaking by other States (otherwise the declaration would amount to one element of a contractual legal transaction).'

[56] De Nova 1956, p. 11.

[57] Carbone 1967 and 1975.

[58] Carbone 1975, p. 168.

[59] Several authors share the same view. *See*, for instance, Eckart 2012, p. 295: 'Even without the Court's Statute being revised to reflect legal realities, the lacuna presented by promises not being listed amongst the sources of law might fade away over time, should the principles which have primarily been established by the World Court's case law continue to be accepted and thereby entrenched as customary international law through the practice of States.'

doctrine of promissory estoppel, can be found both in case law and in the ILC works on the matter of unilateral acts of States.

As to case law, one may firstly mention the two well-known 1974 ICJ decisions regarding nuclear experiments in the waters of the South Pacific.[60] In both decisions, what underpins the Court's reasoning is the existence of a general principle protecting reliance in the relations between foreign States: 'Trust and confidence are inherent in international cooperation, in particular in an age when this cooperation in many fields is becoming increasingly essential'.[61] On this assumption, the promise is able to bind the promisor, but only where some specific circumstances occur, as it would be the fact that the unilateral declaration's *content* goes so far as to create a legitimate expectation on the part of the promisee.[62] According to the Court, all these circumstances were present in the case under review: the declaration of the French Government announcing its intention to terminate the nuclear tests was *unequivocal* and, being *publicly* addressed to the international community *as a whole*, it generated the legitimate expectations of the latter.[63]

In its subsequent case law, the ICJ has no longer recognized the existence of a binding promise. Nonetheless, the same jurisprudence has better clarified what elements make a promise binding, especially from the standpoint of the promisee. Reference is especially made to the case concerning the frontier dispute between Burkina Faso and Mali.[64] In this case, the Court was required to establish whether the statement of the Mali's Head of State (11 April 1975) concerning the possible acceptance of the solution to the dispute, as suggested by the Mediation

[60] *Nuclear Tests (Australia v. France)*, Judgment of 20 December 1974 and *Nuclear Tests (New Zealand v. France)*, Judgment of 20 December 1974.

[61] *See* para 46 of the decision *Australia v. France* and para 49 of the decision *New Zealand v. France*, where it is further stated: 'Thus, interested States may take cognizance of unilateral declarations and place confidence in them, and are entitled to require that the obligation thus created be respected.' For a comment on these decisions, *see* Carbone 1975 and Rubin 1977.

[62] As to the form (oral/written) of the statement, contrariwise, no special requirements are imposed: 'With regard to the question of form, it should be observed that this is not a domain in which international law imposes any special or strict requirements. Whether a statement is made orally or in writing makes no essential difference, for such statements made in particular circumstances may create commitments in international law, which does not require that they should be couched in written form. Thus the question of form is not decisive.': para 45 of the decision *Australia v. France* and para 48 of the decision *New Zealand v. France*.

[63] Paragraphs 50–51 of the decision *Australia v. France* and paras 52–53 of the decision *New Zealand v. France* clarify as follows: 'The unilateral statements of the French authorities were made outside the Court, publicly and *erga omnes* [...] As was observed above, to have legal effects, there was no need for these statements to be addressed to a particular State, nor was acceptance by any other State required [...] In announcing that the 1974 series of atmospheric tests would be the last, the French Government conveyed to *the world at large*, including the Applicant, its intention effectively to terminate these tests [...] The objects of these statements are clear and they were addressed to *the international community as a whole*, and the Court holds that they constitute an undertaking possessing legal effect' (emphasis added). The fact that this unilateral declaration had an *erga omnes* effect is of relevance. On this point, *see infra*.

[64] *Frontier Dispute*, Judgment, ICJ Reports 1986, 22 December 1986, 554, paras 39–40.

Commission of the Organization of African Unity, embodied an international promise. The question was answered in the negative, in view of the radical differences existing between this case and the case concerning nuclear experiments. In the latter case, as said above, France undertook a commitment towards the international community as a whole; accordingly, an intention to be bound could not be expressed otherwise than by a unilateral declaration.[65] Contrariwise, in *Burkina Faso v. Mali*,

> there was nothing to hinder the Parties from manifesting an intention to accept the biding character of the conclusions of the Organization of African Unity Mediation Commission by the normal method: *a formal agreement on the basis of reciprocity*. Since no agreement of this kind was concluded between the Parties, the Chamber finds that there are no grounds to interpret the declaration made by Mali's head of State on 11 April 1975 as a unilateral act with legal implications in regard to the present case.[66]

To put it differently, according to the Court, promise would have a residual character in respect of agreement, and should be relied on especially where, being addressed to the international community *as a whole*, it represents the sole means by which to undertake a certain commitment.

Bearing this in mind, the impression one gets is that, at least in the relationship between sovereign States, promise ends up being a lens through which the process of formation of customary international law may be evaluated: insofar as a State unilateral declaration entails an *erga omnes* effect, this has the potential to prove the progressive development or the existence of a custom by which the promisor feels bound anyway.[67] Remarkably, similar conclusions may be drawn from the 2006 ILC Guiding Principles applicable to unilateral declarations of States capable of creating legal obligations.[68]

Principle 1, in particular, clarifies that

> [d]eclarations publicly made and manifesting the will to be bound may have the effect of creating legal obligations. When the conditions for this are met, the binding character of such declarations is based on good faith; States concerned may then take them into consideration and rely on them; such States are entitled to require that such obligations be respected.

On the other hand, such a principle must be coupled with principles 7 (highlighting under which conditions a promise may be regarded as binding)[69] and 10 (which

[65] 'It is difficult to see how it could have accepted the terms of a negotiated solution with each of the applicants without thereby jeopardizing its contention that its conduct was lawful.'

[66] Paragraph 40. Emphasis added.

[67] Barile 1983, pp. 17 et seq. and 26 et seq.

[68] UN doc. A/61/10 (2006), in General Assembly Official Records, Sixty-first Session, Supplement n. 10, pp. 367 et seq.

[69] 'A unilateral declaration entails obligations for the formulating State only if it is stated in clear and specific terms. In case of doubt as to the scope of the obligations resulting from such a declaration, such obligations must be interpreted in a restrictive manner. In interpreting the content of such obligation, weight shall be given first and foremost to the text of the declaration, together with the context and the circumstances in which it was formulated.'

hinders a promise from being revoked, should that promise create the promisee's legitimate expectations).[70] In brief, the ILC principles seem to thoroughly reflect the concept of promise intended as a source of *international obligations*,[71] should some specific circumstances occur.

It is nonetheless worth noting that these principles, as well as not being binding, have been largely inspired by the *dicta* in the ICJ judgments in *Nuclear Tests*;[72] needless to say, what has been observed beforehand is equally true: the main function of promise in international relations is not to create obligations, but rather to contribute to the progressive development or evidence of customary international law, and any attempts to apply a concept like this with reference to the relationships between host States and foreign investors must be rejected. The ICSID decision in *El Paso Energy International Company* proves particularly instructive in that respect:

> The Claimant asserts that strong legal value should be attached to such unilateral declarations of Argentina, comparing them to those made by France in the *Nuclear Tests* cases between Australia and New Zealand, on the one hand, and France, on the other, where France in her pleadings, had presented unilateral declarations before the World Court and the ICJ had concluded that these declarations created binding obligations for France. It is

---

[70] 'A unilateral declaration that has created legal obligations for the State making the declaration cannot be revoked arbitrarily. In assessing whether a revocation would be arbitrary, consideration should be given to: (a) Any specific terms of the declaration relating to revocation; (b) The extent to which those to whom the obligations are owed have relied on such obligations; (c) The extent to which there has been a fundamental change of circumstances.'

[71] The idea whereby promise would be a source of *international obligations*, rather than of *international law*, is clearly confirmed by the ILC works. One may mention V.R. Cedeño, *First Report on Unilateral Acts of States*, UN doc. A/CN.4/486 (1998), in Yearbook of the International Law Commission, vol. II, Part one, 1998, p. 328, paras 69–71 ('69. Legal acts, that is, acts performed with the intent to produce effects in international law, are the main source of obligations in international law. A State can incur obligations through formal acts which are not necessarily sources of international law, within the meaning referred to in Article 38 of the Statute of the International Court of Justice, already discussed briefly here. 70. Article 38 of the Court's Statute does not mention unilateral acts of States among the sources of law that it lists. That, however, does not mean that such acts cannot give rise to international legal norms. 71. Differentiating formal sources from sources of obligations could help to distinguish acts which are unilateral in their form from those which are unilateral in their effects. Not all formal unilateral acts fall within the realm of treaties. Some of them, albeit not very many, can, as the doctrine by and large indicates, be classified as strictly unilateral acts'); International Law Commission, *Report on its Work of the Fifty-fourth Session*, UN doc. A/57/10 (2002), in General Assembly Official Records, *Fifty-seventh Session*, Supplement n. 10, 2002, p. 215, para 411 ('The Special Rapporteur indicated that he shared the view of the vast majority of members which believe that unilateral acts did indeed exist, that they were well-established institution in international law and that they could be binding on the author State, subject to certain conditions of validity. In his view, unilateral acts are not sources of law, within the meaning of Article 38 of the Statute of the International Court of Justice, but they could however constitute a source of obligations').

[72] This can be clearly inferred from the commentary on Draft Guiding Principle 1: 'The wording of Guiding Principle 1, which seeks both to define unilateral acts in the strict sense and to indicate what they are based on, is very directly inspired by the *dicta* in the Judgments handed down by the International Court of Justice on 20 December 1974 in the *Nuclear Tests* case.'

the tribunal's view, however, that what is involved here are two totally different types of unilateral declarations – one made before the highest judicial body in the world, the other in commercial meetings – and that no lesson can be drawn from the *Nuclear Tests* cases to give legal weight to investment-promoting road shows. In the tribunal's view, such political and commercial incitements cannot be equated with commitments capable of creating reasonable expectations protected by the international mechanism of the BIT.[73]

4.5.2 *Promise and International Investment Law*

Once again, the foregoing remarks suggest the whole issue be brought under the law on foreign investment, and to ascertain which solutions arbitral tribunals have adopted therein. The already mentioned decision in *Metalclad* offers a clear exemplification of the reasoning generally followed in case law.[74]

In this case the claimant was refused (by the municipality competent to do so) permission to build a hazardous waste landfill. This decision was, however, entirely inconsistent with the behaviour assumed by Mexico in the previous period; the host State, indeed, had given *repeated and specific* assurances concerning the fact that no authorization was necessary, and that in any case the concerned municipality would have had no reason in law to reject the request (hinting of being able to influence the decision). On this assumption, the elements of a legally binding promise were supposed to exist:

> Metalclad was entitled to rely on the representations of federal officials and to believe that it was entitled to continue its construction of the landfill. In following the advise of these officials, and filing the municipal permit application [...], Metalclad was merely acting prudently and in full expectation that the permit would be granted.[75]

A comparable conclusion was expressly reached by the *Cristallex International Corporation* tribunal.[76] The tribunal starts its analysis by elucidating that

> [a] legitimate expectation may arise in cases where the Administration has made a promise or representation to an investor as to a substantive benefit, on which the investor has relied in making its investment, and which later was frustrated by the conduct of the Administration. To be able to give rise to such legitimate expectations, such promise or representation – addressed to the individual investor – must be sufficiently specific, i.e. it must be precise as to its content and clear as to its form.[77]

---

[73] *El Paso Energy International Company v. Argentina*, ICSID Case No. ARB/03/15, Award of 31 October 2011, para 392.

[74] *Metalclad Corporation v. Mexico*, ICSID Case No. ARB(AF)/97/1, Award of 30 August 2000; see Chap. 3, Sect. 3.5.2.

[75] Idem, para 89.

[76] *Crystallex International Corporation v. Venezuela*, ICSID Case No. ARB(AF)/11/2, Award of 4 April 2016.

[77] Idem, para 547.

Bearing this in mind, according to the tribunal, the specific representation contained in a letter of the Venezuelan Ministry of Environment of 16 May 2007 created a legitimate expectation in Crystallex (an international corporation) that the permitting process for the exploitation of gold relating to the so-called *Las Cristinas* Project would go ahead.[78]

On the other hand, even where the existence of a binding promise is excluded by the tribunal concerned, the kind of reasoning usually adopted is always the same. From this angle, the decision in *Thunderbird* is fairly symptomatic.[79] The publicly held Canadian corporation Thunderbird engaged in the business of operating gaming facilities, and on August 2000, with a view to investigating potential opportunities in Mexico, presented a written request ('*Solicitud*') to the competent local authority. In particular, under Mexican law, a distinction must be drawn between machines involving gambling and those in which the principal factor of operation is the user's skilfulness: where the former are prohibited, the latter are not. Accordingly, since the gaming facilities proposed by Thunderbird fell in the last-mentioned category, the formal response given to the *Solicitud* did not pinpoint any reasons to prevent their use. Later on, however, following a changing of leadership of the same local authority, the Thunderbird's machines were prohibited, with the consequent closure of the facilities hosting them. Moving from this assumption, the Canadian corporation initiated UNCITRAL proceedings against Mexico, claiming (under NAFTA Chapter 11) an FET violation in terms of legitimate expectations; in the claimant's view, indeed, the formal response to the *Solicitud*—insofar as it implicitly authorized Thunderbird to use its machines—embodied a veritable binding promise capable, as such, of inducing the promisee to act in reliance on it. Hence, the arbitral tribunal assumed the existence of a general principle concerning legitimate expectations[80] and established which *regula juris* deducible from the latter could be applied within the NAFTA system. In particular, in the tribunal's view, the concept of reliance refers

> to a situation where a Contracting Party's conduct creates reasonable and justifiable expectations on the part of an investor (or investment) to act in reliance on said conduct, such that a failure by the NAFTA Party to honour those expectations could cause the investor (or investment) to suffer damages. The threshold for legitimate expectations may vary depending on the nature of the violation alleged under the NAFTA and the circumstances of the case.[81]

This is to say that where the circumstances of a particular case make State promises capable of generating the legitimate expectations of the promisee, these promises must be regarded as binding. Yet, according to the same tribunal, the

---

[78] Idem, para 575.

[79] *International Thunderbird Gaming Corporation v. Mexico*, UNCITRAL (NAFTA), Award of 26 January 2006.

[80] Para 147 of the decision refers to the concept of good faith), but in the terms specified by Diehl 2012, p. 358.

[81] Paras 147–148 of the decision.

Thunderbird affair did not meet such criteria: the *Solicitud* failed to give a complete picture concerning the nature of the contested machines, which, involving gambling anyway, proved to be inconsistent with the Mexican Law.[82]

Similar conclusions in matter of promise may be inferred from the decision in *Saluka*. In this case, the tribunal held that the claimant could not reasonably rely on any assurances issued by the Minister of Finance, provided that the latter was not entitled to bind future governments.[83]

Again, one may mention the decision passed by an UNCITRAL Tribunal in *Frontier Petroleum*.[84] The dispute was concerned with two letters by which the Czech Deputy Minister of Industry and Trade had represented to the investor the opportunity to start some negotiations. Since the latter failed, the tribunal was asked to establish whether the content of these letters had generated the claimant's legitimate expectations and triggered an FET violation. The question was answered in the negative. Those letters, indeed, represented a mere 'signal' to the Claimant as to the possibility that the State could negotiate, whilst they 'did not provide an adequate basis [...] to rely on some form of representation or expectation [and did] not exhibit the level of specificity necessary to generate legitimate expectations.'[85]

An additional decision to be considered in matter of promise is that delivered in *Total*.[86] Total, a French company engaged in the fields of gas and hydrocarbons, made a number of investments in Argentina and, like many other foreign investors, was seriously damaged by the economic crisis of 2001–2002. According to Total,

---

[82] 'In the tribunal's view, the information presented by EDM in the *Solicitud* is incomplete [...]. The tribunal is therefore of the opinion that the *Solicitud* is not a proper disclosure and that it puts the reader on the wrong track [...] Thunderbird has also argued that in the event of doubt, SEGOB should have made a request for additional information regarding the operation of the machines, or for an inspection of the machines. Yet Thunderbird was the moving party presenting a *Solicitud* to the Mexican administration; one would therefore expect that the moving party supply adequate information and make a proper disclosure. In the tribunal's view, the *Solicitud* did not give the full picture, even for an informed reader': paras 151 et seq. of the decision.

[83] *Saluka Investments BV v. Czech Republic*, UNCITRAL, Partial Award, 17 March 2006, para 351: 'Firstly, Nomura's expectation that the Government would not address the bad loan problem by support to the banks was initially said to have been based on an express assurance to that effect given by the then Minister of Finance. The Claimant has also argued that this was consistent with the obligations undertaken by the Czech Government in their pre-accession agreement with the European Commission (the Europe Agreement) to adhere to European Union norms on State aid. The Claimant has admitted, however, that whatever assurance the Minister of Finance may have given, he could not bind future Governments. Especially, he could not give any assurance that the privatisation of the other banks would proceed in the same way as the privatisation of IPB, i.e. without any State financial assistance. Nomura therefore had no basis for expecting that there would be no future change in the Government's policy towards the banking sector's bad loan problem or in the Government's willingness to adhere during the pre-accession period to the rules on State aid in the Europe Agreement.' For more details on this case, *see infra*.

[84] *Frontier Petroleum Services Ltd v. Czech Republic*, UNCITRAL, Final Award of 12 November 2010.

[85] Idem, para 468.

[86] *Total S.A. v. Argentina*, ICSID Case No ARB/04/1, Decision on Liability of 27 December 2010.

the 2002 Emergency Law and the interrelated regulations failed to protect the claimant's legitimate expectations stemming from some specific assurances given by Argentina, as well as from the general regulatory framework existing at the time of the investment; accordingly, it contended an FET violation. The appeal was upheld by the tribunal, but not due to the existence of a binding promise. Nonetheless, the reasoning underpinning the decision turns out to be extremely revealing. Reference is made to the passage of the decision which postulates the existence of a principle in matter of expectations and regards this principle as being common to domestic systems in the terms of Article 38, para 1(c), of the ICJ Statute.[87]

Against this background, however, the tribunal assesses national practice in a very superficial way[88] and ends up following a line of argument quite similar to that underlying the decision in *Thunderbird*, i.e. a pathway assuming the existence of a general principle of international law (that of reliance) and the related need for this principle to be further specified; thus, promise, as an aspect of reliance and provided that some circumstances are met, is seen as binding. In detail, such circumstances would be the same as those specified in the ILC Guiding Principles in matter of State unilateral acts; even though (i) the Guidelines deal with the legal effects of unilateral acts of States addressed to other subjects of international law, (ii) they are more akin to the principle of estoppel, rather than that of legitimate expectations,[89]

[87] In this regard, a clarification seems to be necessary. Para 128 of the decision states as follows: 'Since the concept of legitimate expectations is based on the requirement of good faith, one of the general principles referred to in Article 38 (1)(c) of the Statute of the International Court of Justice as a source of international law, the tribunal believes that a comparative analysis of the protection of legitimate expectations in domestic jurisdictions is justified at this point. While the scope and legal basis of the principle varies, it has been recognized lately both in civil and in common law jurisdictions within well defined limits.' At first glance, the tribunal regards legitimate expectations as a particular aspect of the principle of good faith in its objective facet. Yet, inasmuch as the decision highlights that the principle would be recognized in countries of both civil and common law, it clearly refers to legitimate expectations as a principle independent from that of good faith. This conclusion may be inferred from the legal literature cited therein (which exclusively deal with legitimate expectations) as well as from para 129, whereby the protection of expectations would reflect the importance of legal certainty. As has been seen above, this is a line of argument adopted with a view to claiming the autonomous nature of the principle of reliance (Merusi 2006, p. 145). On the other hand, what the tribunal stresses in para 130 is worthless: 'From a comparative law perspective, the tenets of the legal system of the European Community (now European Union), reflecting the legal traditions of twenty-seven European countries, both civil and common law [...] are of relevance, especially since the recognition of the principle of legitimate expectations there has been explicitly based on the international law principle of good faith.' On closer inspection, the decision cited by the same tribunal in order to corroborate a similar conclusion (Court of First Instance, *Opel Austria v. Council of the European Union*, Case T-115/94, Judgment, 22 January 1997) is evidence of the contrary; remarkably, its para 93 states that 'the principle of good faith is the corollary in public international law of the principle of protection of legitimate expectations'.

[88] *See* again paras 129–130 of the decision.

[89] On the relationship between legitimate expectations and estoppel in public international law, *see* again Eckart 2012, pp. 277 et seq.

and (iii) they do not cover the legal relations between States and individuals,[90] in the tribunal's view they do nothing but draw from concepts 'found in investment arbitral practice and in comparative law [...], such as the importance of factual circumstances, the relevance of content and intent, non-arbitrariness in case of revocation and the restrictive interpretation of unilateral acts invoked as a source of commitments for the issuing party.'[91]

Arguably, the reference to the ILC Guiding Principles was not intended to reveal the existence of a general rule in matter of promise, applicable by analogy to the matter of investments. Rather, it allowed the tribunal to increase the legitimacy of its decision and avoid dealing with this issue by referring to a specific domestic system; and indeed, even though the same tribunal engages in a (generic) comparative analysis, the notion of promise set forth herein does nothing but repeat the typical features prevailing in some national legal orders,[92] which means that for an

[90] *See* paras 131–132 of the decision: '131. Under international law, unilateral acts, statements and conduct by States may be the source of legal obligations which the intended beneficiaries or addressees, or possibly any member of the international community, can invoke. The legal basis of that binding character appears to be only in part related to the concept of legitimate expectations—being rather akin to the principle of 'estoppel'. Both concepts may lead to the same result, namely, that of rendering the content of a unilateral declaration binding on the State that is issuing it. According to the International Court of Justice, only unilateral acts that are unconditional, definitive and 'very specific' have binding force, which derives from the principle of good faith. This fundamental principle requires a State to abide by its unilateral acts of such a character and to follow a line of conduct coherent with the legal obligations so created. 132. The recent 'Guiding Principles applicable to unilateral declarations of States capable of creating legal obligations' ('the Guidelines'), which were formulated by the International Law Commission in 2006 as a restatement of international (inter-State) case law in the subject matter, are of interest here. We are aware that the Guidelines deal with the legal effects of unilateral acts of States addressed to other subjects of international law, and not with domestic normative acts relied upon by a foreign private investor. Still, we believe that the conditions required for unilateral declarations of a State to give rise to international obligations are of relevance here since the issue before the tribunal has to be resolved by application of international law.'

[91] *See* para 134 of the decision.

[92] Such a circumstance is not surprising. Where in a certain field of international law a provision to be applied does not exist, and a principle common to domestic legal systems lacks, the concerned tribunal is required to refer to one specific national legal order. Needless to say, such order should be the one whose legislation (in matter of promise, for instance) proves particularly appropriate with regard to the field of reference. A similar opinion was advanced by A. Cassese, as judge of the ICTY in *Erdemović*, IT-96-21, Appeals Chamber, Judgment of 7 October 1997. To his mind, 'it would be inappropriate mechanically to incorporate into international criminal proceedings ideas, legal constructs, concepts or terms of art which only belong, and are unique to a specific group of national legal systems, common-law or civil-law systems. Reliance upon one particular system may be admissible only where indisputably imposed by the very terms on an international norm, or where no autonomous notion can be inferred from the whole context and spirit of international norms' (para 4). An approach of this kind has been followed by the ICTY in matter of cumulation of offences. In this regard, *see* Palombino 2005, pp. 782 et seq.

administrative promise to be binding, it must be (i) sufficiently specific and (ii) given by the administrative authority which is entiitled to do so.[93]

The same conclusion may be found in the *Bilcon* case.[94] Bilcon of Delaware Inc., a U.S. company, had planned to invest in Nova Scotia by developing there a quarry and marine terminal at Whites Point quarry. The decision to invest was largely influenced by the repeated promises from various Canadian officials, in particular some technical officials and the Minister for natural resources, who assured that any potential environmental law concerns could be addressed through a fair process whereby Bilcon would be given the opportunity to mitigate or prevent any potential environmental impact. But things turned out differently. In terms of environmental feasibility, for several years the investor and the competent authorities failed to reach any agreement on the project, which was accordingly referred to a Joint Review Panel and negatively evaluated because of the possible environmental risks. The tribunal did not rely on the concept of legitimate expectations, but in ascertaining the host State's liability made clear that

> after all the specific encouragement the Investors and their investment had received from government to pursue the project, and after all the resources placed in preparing and presenting their environmental assessment case, the Investors and their investment were not afforded a fair *opportunity* to have the specifics of that case considered, assessed and decided in accordance with applicable laws.[95]

In other words, it is clear that the notion of promise was implicitly resorted to by the tribunal and that both requirements which make a promise binding (i.e. its specificity and the fact that it is given by the competent authority) were identified.

---

[93] Notably, the reasoning underpinning the *Total* decision, and particularly the idea whereby legitimate expectations would embody a principle common to domestic systems, has been followed in *Toto* (*Toto Costruzioni SpA v. Lebanon*, ICSID Case No. ARB/07/12, Award of 7 June 2012, para 166: 'The fair and equitable treatment standard of international law does not depend on the perception of the frustrated investor, but should use public international law and comparative domestic public law as a benchmark. As was recently also confirmed in Total S.A. v. Argentina, 'a comparative analysis of what is considered generally fair and unfair conduct by domestic public authorities in respect to private investors and firms in domestic law may also be relevant to identify the legal standards under BITs') and *Gold Reserve* (*Gold Reserve Inc. v. Venezuela*, ICSID Case No. ARB(AF)/09/1, Award of 22 September 2014, para 576: 'With particular regard to the legal sources of one of the standards for respect of the fair and equitable treatment principle, i.e. the protection of 'legitimate expectations', these sources are to be found in the comparative analysis of many domestic legal systems. This has been succinctly stated recently by other ICSID tribunals, for example in *Total v. Argentina* and in *Toto Construzioni Generali SpA v Republic of Lebanon*. Based on converging considerations of good faith and legal security, the concept of legitimate expectations is found in different legal traditions according to which some expectations may be reasonably or legitimately created for a private person by the constant behaviour and/or promises of its legal partner, in particular when this partner is the public administration on which this private person is dependent'). Needless to say, the same remarks apply.

[94] *Bilcon of Delaware et al. v. Canada*, UNCITRAL (NAFTA), Award on Jurisdiction and Liability of 17 March 2015.

[95] Para 603.

4.6 FET and Expectation by Legislation. Expectation by Legislation in National Legal Systems

The last question to be dealt with is whether, in the law on foreign investment, legitimate expectations may be generated by provisions of *general* legislation, applicable to a plurality or a category of persons. As is well known, the 'reliance' theory firstly entails a limit to the retroactivity of legislation, therefore preserving the legal effects of situations that took place in the past (the so-called *proper retroactivity*). In these terms, legitimate expectations are protected in both common[96] and civil law[97] domestic systems, but in matter of investments the relevance of this aspect proves sporadic.[98] Nonetheless, as far as the legislator's activity is

[96] The US Supreme Court expressed this principle in the following terms: '[T]he presumption against retroactive legislation is deeply rooted in our jurisprudence, and embodies a legal doctrine centuries older than our Republic. Elementary considerations of fairness dictate that individuals should have an opportunity to know what the law is and to conform their conduct accordingly; settled expectations should not be lightly disrupted. For that reason, the 'principle that the legal effect of conduct should ordinarily be assessed under the law that existed when the conduct took place had timeless and universal appeal.' In a free, dynamic society, creativity in both commercial and artistic endeavours is fostered by a rule of law that gives people confidence about the legal consequences of their actions'; *Landgraf v. USI Film Products*, 511 U.S. 244, 265–66 (1994).

[97] One should mention the Italian legal system, within which non-retroactivity of the law embodies a fundamental value of legal culture. More in detail, in criminal matters, this principle benefits from privileged protection under Article 25, para 2, of the Constitution, whereby '[n]o punishment may be inflicted except by virtue of a law in force at the time the offence was committed.' In civil matters, the same principle may be inferred from Article 11 of Preliminary Provisions to the Italian Civil Code. But in this case the principle may suffer some exceptions, especially where the enactment of an *ex post facto* law is justified by the need to protect principles, rights and interests of constitutional standing. Judgment No. 264, passed by the Italian Constitutional Court on 19 November 2012, is symptomatic of this need. The Court (which was asked to consider a challenge to a legislation, in matter of pensions, with *retroactive effects*) held that the appellant had no *legitimate expectation* for his pension to be calculated in line with the previous arrangements, since the contested legislation was inspired by the principles of equality and solidarity, which prevailed within the balancing of constitutional interests (para 5.3, conclusions on points of law).

[98] *See ATA Construction, Industrial and Trading Company v. Jordan*, ICSID Case No. ARB/08/02, Award of 18 May 2010, para 128: 'By virtue of Article II of the New York Convention, Jordan's State courts are required to 'recognize an agreement in writing under which the parties undertake to submit to arbitration', and in such circumstances to 'refer the parties to arbitration, unless it finds that the said agreement is null and void, inoperative or incapable of being performed'. There has never been any allegation in this case by either party that the Arbitration Agreement at issue was *per se* 'null and void, inoperative or incapable of being performed'. It is arguable (but the tribunal takes no position on the point) that the extinguishment rule might be deemed to be prospectively compatible with Article II insofar as parties electing Jordan as the venue for an arbitration or electing Jordanian law as the law of the arbitration had notice of the rule and accepted it. But this argument cannot work retroactively. Retroactivity is the problem here. The new rule should cover only those arbitration agreements concluded after the coming into force of the Jordanian Arbitration Law in 2001 and not arbitration agreements existing before the 2001 Law came into force, such as the Arbitration Agreement at issue in this proceeding. In the tribunal's view, the Jordanian Court of Appeal and Court of Cassation could have complied with

concerned, the same theory may fulfil a further function, i.e. to protect the individual's expectations against laws *formally* providing for the future, but having negative effects on the position of those individuals to whom all the laws previously in force were directed (*improper retroactivity*).[99]

Where understood in these terms, expectation by legislation plays a crucial role in investment arbitration, and rests ultimately on the confidence individuals place in the constancy of the host State's legal framework that existed at the time of the investment.[100] It is a concept that finds its theoretical basis in the sociology of law, the best-known drafting of which is to be ascribed to the eminent scholar Max Weber and his book *Economy and Society*.[101] In his view, indeed, one of the main contributions of law to any social system is to make economic life more calculable; not by coincidence, along the same view, capitalism arose in Europe because European law showed a high degree of 'calculability.'[102]

Going more into detail, and assuming the lack in the matter of a general principle common to domestic systems, expectation by legislation (where it is provided for domestically) works in a twofold way, depending on whether one takes into account the features typical of (i) the supervening legislation or those of (ii) the previous legislation (i.e. that generating the legitimate expectation). In line with *variant (i)*, a supervening legislation radically changing the existing normative framework may create an expectation to be safeguarded, unless it serves the purpose of defending a fundamental public interest and does so without any discriminatory effects. *Variant (ii)* corresponds to the so-called expectation by 'induction'. In this case, the individual's expectations must be protected where the law that is going to be modified embodies a *previous qualified conduct* of the legislator, viz. a normative act put in

(Footnote 98 continued)

their duty in this case by refusing to apply retroactively the new rule introduced in the last sentence of Article 51 of the Jordanian Arbitration Law.' For a recent arbitral case discussing retroactivity, *see Charanne B.V. and Construction Investments S.A.R.L. v. Spain*, Arbitration Institute of the Stockholm Chamber of Commerce, Award of 21 January 2016, paras 543 et seq. For a comment on this judgment, *see* De Luca 2016.

[99] The distinction between proper and improper retroactivity must be traced back to the case law of the German *Bundesverfassungsgericht*. The same distinction, albeit tacitly, has been upheld by the Italian Constitutional Court. In this regard, *see* Merusi 2001, pp. 21 et seq.

[100] This kind of expectation is what Maynard 2016, pp. 99 et seq., calls 'legal stability obligation' and considers as distinct from the concept of expectations itself. This opinion, however, as well as being unable to shed new light on the FET content, is based on the false inference according to which legitimate expectations 'have their origins in the domestic administrative laws of States, whereas the Legal Stability Obligation has typically been inferred into the FET standard on the basis of a purposive interpretation of the perambulatory language of investment treaties' (p. 112); indeed, such obligation (which is nothing but a manifestation of expectation by legislation), albeit in a somewhat ambiguous manner, is fairly well-rooted in national legal systems (*see infra* Sect. 4.6.2). For a recent judicial confirmation of the interrelation between legitimate expectations and legal stability, *see Philip Morris et al. v. Uruguay*, ICSID Case No. ARB/10/7, Award, 8 July 2016, para 421.

[101] Weber 1922.

[102] Idem, pp. 847 and 855.

place with the specific aim of inducing a certain decision and on which the individual relied in assuming that decision.

The differences between these two variants of expectation seem to be straightforward. Nonetheless, establishing which of the two models effectively works in a certain domestic system is anything but easy: where in some countries such a concept has been fully dealt with from both a theoretical and practical point of view (like in Germany, where expectation by induction seems to apply),[103] in other countries (like Argentina)[104] it has not.

4.6.1 Expectation by Legislation and the Original Approach Developed in Investor-State Arbitration

The original approach followed in investor-State arbitration in the matter under discussion may be summarized as follows. Moving from the dual assumption that (i) expectation by legislation embodies an FET element and (ii) can as such limit the public authority conduct, arbitral tribunals supported the view whereby States have the right to modify the normative framework existing at the time of the investment, but only by means of non-discriminatory measures that clearly pursue public aims. The decision in *Tecmed* echoes this line of argument.[105]

In this case, the competent Mexican federal authority denied the applicant the renewal of a licence to operate a hazardous waste landfill. According to the tribunal, a decision of this kind amounted to an FET violation in terms not only of fairness in administrative proceedings,[106] but also of legitimate expectations of the investor. Indeed, the local authority, in order to refuse the renewal of the licence and despite the absence of any causal link between this decision and the aim to be pursued, incongruously relied on the environmental national legislation.[107] Such a circumstance, albeit tacitly, ended up giving rise to an arbitrary change of the normative framework existing at the time of the investment.

The decision in *Saluka* is symptomatic of the same approach.[108] The case arose from a crisis that in 1998 had affected the entire bank sector in the Czech Republic.

---

[103] *See* Merusi 2001, 23–24.

[104] Coviello 2004, pp. 21 et seq.

[105] *Técnicas Medioambiente Tecmed S.A. v. Mexico*, ICSID Case No. ARB (AF)/00/2, Award of 29 May 2003.

[106] *See* Chap. 3, Sect. 3.5.2.

[107] 'Upon making its investment, the fair expectations of the Claimant were that the Mexican laws applicable to such investment, as well as the supervision, control, prevention and punitive powers granted to the authorities in charge of managing such systems, would be used for the purpose of assuring compliance with environmental protection, human health and ecological balance goals underlying such laws': para 157 of the decision.

[108] *Saluka Investments BV v. Czech Republic*, UNCITRAL, Partial Award of 17 March 2006.

As a result, IPB, one of the banks involved in the crisis, was put under forced administration by the government. On this assumption, the Dutch company Saluka Investments BV, as a shareholder of the IPB, initiated an UNCITRAL arbitration under the 1991 Netherlands-Czech Republic BIT. It was argued that the supervening impossibility of disposing of the IPB shares amounted to an FET violation, especially in the light of two main circumstances: first, IPB was completely excluded from the program by means of which the Czech Republic assisted the other main banks operating in the country; second, the competent authorities had not taken any account of the proposals made in good faith by both the bank and its shareholders with a view to resolving the crisis. The tribunal regarded both arguments as persuasive and ascertained an FET violation, precisely with regard to the need to protect the investor's legitimate expectations. In detail,

> [a]n investor's decision to make an investment is based on the state of the law and the totality of the business environment at the time of the investment as well as on the investor's expectation that the conduct of the host State subsequent to the investment will be fair and equitable.[109]

In the view of the same tribunal, however, such a legitimate expectation must be balanced with the equally legitimate rights of the State to regulate domestic matters in the public interest,[110] but by means of non-discriminatory measures.[111] In these terms, the conduct by the Czech Republic, although justified by the current contingencies, was clearly discriminatory, insofar as it implied the exclusion of IPB from any State aid.[112]

[109] *See* para 301.

[110] 'The determination of a breach of Article 3.1 by the Czech Republic therefore requires a weighing of the Claimant's legitimate and reasonable expectations on the one hand and the Respondent's legitimate regulatory interests on the other' (para 306).

[111] A foreign investor protected by the Treaty may in any case properly expect that the Czech Republic implements its policies bona fide by conduct that is, as far as it affects the investor's investment, reasonably justifiable by public policies and that such conduct does not manifestly violate the requirements of consistency, transparency, even-handedness and non-discrimination. In particular, any differential treatment of a foreign investor must not be based on unreasonable distinctions and demands, and must be justified by showing that it bears a reasonable relationship to rational policies not motivated by a preference for other investments over the foreign-owned investment' (para 307).

[112] On this kind of expectation, *see* also *Bayindir Insaat Turizim Ticaret ve Sanayi A v. Pakistan*, ICSID Case No. ARB/03/29, Award of 27 August 2009: 'The tribunal agrees with Bayindir when it identifies the different factors which emerge from decisions of investment tribunals as forming part of the FET standard. These comprise the obligation to act transparently and grant due process, to refrain from taking arbitrary or discriminatory measures, from exercising coercion or from frustrating the investor's reasonable expectation with respect to the legal framework affecting the investment' (para 178).

4.6.2 *The Gradual Emergence of the Notion of 'Expectation by Induction': The Decision in* Suez et al. *and* AWG Group

Over the years, the original approach to expectation by legislation has been gradually abandoned in arbitral practice, and replaced with the 'by induction' model.[113] This model is not new to the international arena and is usually followed, for example, by the CJEU when establishing whether a private party can rely on legitimate expectations against the exercise of normative powers by the EU institutions.[114] But it is especially within investor-State arbitration that such a form of expectation has gained momentum. An *obiter dictum* in *Glamis*[115] is already symptomatic of this new trend, but the real turning point is undoubtedly the decision in *Suez* and *AWG*.[116] It is a decision whose importance goes beyond the reliance theory, and refers more in general to the FET normative content.

In 1993, together with a comprehensive program of privatization, Argentina released to a national company, the AASA, a concession of thirty years to operate the water distribution and waste water services system in the City of Buenos Aires and surrounding municipalities. AASA, in turn, was formed by a consortium of companies (including several foreign companies), which had been induced to invest their capital by the particularly advantageous regulatory framework underlying the Concession Contract. On April 17, 2003, some of the said companies initiated an ICSID arbitration against Argentina. And this thanks to the ICSID clauses provided for by the three BITs concluded between this State and the States of the companies.[117] To the view of the claimants, indeed, the radical change on the part of

[113] Our opinion is shared by Vicente 2013, p. 153 f., p. 189.

[114] In this regard, *see* Gigante 2008, pp. 80 et seq.

[115] *Glamis Gold Ltd. v. United States*, UNCITRAL, Award of 8 June 2009, para 22; where it is argued that an FET violation may depend on 'the creation by the State of objective expectations *in order to induce* investment and the subsequent repudiation of those expectations.'

[116] *Suez* and *AWG Group v. Argentina,* ICSID Case No. ARB/03/19, Decision on Liability of 30 July 2010. For a comment on this decision, *see* Palombino 2011.

[117] In detail, reference in made to Article 8, para 3, of the BIT Argentine-France (1991); Article 10, para 4, of the BIT Argentine-Spain (1991); and Article 8, para 3, of the BIT Argentine-United Kingdom (1990). It must be clarified that, according to the last-mentioned Article, '[w]here the dispute is referred to International arbitration, the investor and the Contracting Party concerned in the dispute may agree to refer the dispute either to: (a) the International Centre for the Settlement of Investments disputes […]; or (b) an International arbitrator or *ad hoc* arbitration tribunal to be appointed by a special agreement or established under the Arbitration Rules of the United Nations Commission on International Trade Law. If after a period of three months from written notification of the claim there is no agreement to one of the above alternative procedures, the Parties to the dispute shall be bound to submit it to arbitration under the Arbitration Rules of the United Nations Commission on International Trade Law as then in force'. The final part of this Article has been relied on in *AWG*, where Argentina allowed the dispute to be administered by ICSID, but on the base of the UNCITRAL Rules (paras 2 et seq. of the decision). Further, as already said, the same ICSID tribunal has dealt with the case under consideration in conjunction with the *Suez* case.

Argentina of the normative framework existing at the time of the investment (due to the aforementioned massive economic and financial crisis of 2001) would severely compromise the value of the investment, therefore sapping their confidence in the constancy of that framework and triggering an FET violation. In detail, the three BITs, on which the request for arbitration was founded, expressly require the host State to treat foreign investments fairly and equitably. Nonetheless, the norms referring to such an obligation do not have the same content: where Articles 4, para 1, of the Argentina-Spain BIT (1991)[118] and 2, para 2, of the Argentina-Great Britain BIT (1993)[119] rely on FET without any further specifications, Article 3 of the Argentina-France BIT (1993) states that such a treatment must be accorded in line with the principles of international law.[120]

According to the Respondent, a similar reference to international law led to the identification of FET with the minimum standard rule and, through a kind of osmosis, to reach the same conclusion with regard to the other BIT clauses. This argument, however, was not regarded as persuasive by the relevant tribunal. In its view, indeed, 'in accordance with the principles of international law' means just what it says:

> that the tribunal is to interpret fair and equitable treatment under Article 3 of the Argentina-France BIT in accordance with all relevant sources of international law and that it is not limited in its interpretation to the international minimum standard. The ordinary meaning of the words 'principles of international law' is 'the legal principles derived from all sources of international law.' Authoritative documents employing the term 'international law' contain no implication that the term is limited to the international minimum standard and amply support the tribunal's interpretation of the term 'international law.' Thus, Article 38 of the Statute of the International Court of Justice states that the function of the Court is to 'decide in accordance with international law [...]' and then proceeds in the broadest terms to list the basic sources of international law.[121]

On this assumption, the tribunal ascertained whether the FET normative content could be determined by interpreting the relevant BIT provisions pursuant to Article 31 of the VCLT. However, for the reasons discussed above,[122] that is to say the vagueness of the ordinary meaning of the words 'fair and equitable', and the difficulty to remedy this vagueness taking account of the objects and purposes of the three BITs, also this attempt proved useless.

---

[118] 'Each Party shall guarantee in its territory fair and equitable treatment of investments made by investors of the other Party.'

[119] 'Investments of investors of each Contracting Party shall at all times be accorded fair and equitable treatment and shall enjoy protection and constant security in the territory of the other Contracting Party.'

[120] 'Each Contracting Party shall undertake to accord in its territory and maritime zone just and equitable treatment, in accordance with principles of international law, to the investments of investors of the other Party and to ensure that the existence of the rights so granted is not impeded either de jure or de facto.'

[121] Para 185.

[122] *See* Chap. 2, Sect. 2.5.

At this juncture, the tribunal, benefiting from prior decisions as a subsidiary means for the determination of the rules of international law, decided to assess the correctness of the applicant's line of argument, namely the idea whereby the principle of legitimate expectations, as well as that of FET, had been violated in the present case. In particular, according to the tribunal, such prior decisions clearly regarded expectation by legislation as an FET constituent element. On closer inspection, however, a crucial element had not been sufficiently emphasized in those decisions and suggested disregarding them:

> that investors, deriving their expectations from the laws and regulations adopted by the host country, *acted in reliance upon those laws and regulations and changed their economic position as a result.* Thus it was not the investor's legitimate expectations alone that led tribunals to find a denial of fair and equitable treatment. It was the existence of such expectations created by host country laws, coupled with the act of investing their capital in reliance on them, and a subsequent, sudden change in those laws that led to a determination that the host country had not treated the investors fair and equitably.[123]

To put it differently, the kind of expectation relied on in the instant case is precisely that *by induction*: the judge, assuming once again the existence of a general principle in matter of legitimate expectations, identified the *regula juris* capable of solving the dispute in hand, and ascertained an FET violation accordingly.

> [T]he expectations of the Claimants with respect to their investment in the water and sewage system of Buenos Aires did not suddenly and surprisingly come into their minds the way Athena sprang from the head of Zeus. Argentina through its laws, the treaties it signed, its government statements, and especially the elaborate legal framework which it designed and enacted, deliberately and actively sought to create those expectations in the Claimants and other potential investors in order to obtain the capital and technology that it needed to revitalize and expand the Buenos Aires water and sewage system.[124]

4.6.3 The Decisions in Total, El Paso, Micula *and* Philip Morris

The already quoted decision in *Total*[125] is also symptomatic of the gradual emer gence in case law of the 'by induction' expectation model. In this regard, the following view was offered:

> The reasons and features for changes (sudden character, fundamental change, retroactive effects) and the public interest involved are thus to be taken into account in order to evaluate whether an individual who incurred financial obligations on the basis of the

[123] Para 226. Emphasis added.

[124] Para 227.

[125] *Total S.A. v. Argentina*, ICSID Case No. ARB/04/1, Decision on Liability of 27 December 2010; see *supra* Sect. 4.5.2.

> decisions and representations of public authorities that were later revoked should be entitled to a form of redress. However, it appears that only exceptionally has the concept of legitimate expectations been the basis of redress when legislative action by a State was at stake.[126]

Remarkably, in order to identify such exceptional circumstances, the tribunal refers to the previously discussed approach followed by the CJEU,[127] namely an approach which echoes the notion of expectation by induction.[128]

In the same vein, one should mention the decision in *El Paso*.[129] El Paso Energy, a U.S. company incorporated in the State of Delaware, had invested in four Argentinian companies involved in the electricity and hydrocarbons industries. Nonetheless, after it made its investment, Argentina adopted a series of measures (like the so-called 'pesification', i.e. the conversion of foreign currency contracts to peso denominations) aimed at countering the 2001 economic and financial crisis. These measures, according to El Paso, violated the 1991 Argentina-U.S. BIT in several respects, including the FET clause and the expectation by legislation provided for by the latter. Moving from this assumption, and bearing in mind the prior case law in the matter, the tribunal firstly highlighted that the reliance theory entails a fair balance between all the rights and interests at stake:

> [L]egitimate expectations cannot be solely the subjective expectations of the investor, but have to correspond to the objective expectation that can be deduced from the circumstances and with due regard to the rights of the State. In other words, a balance should be established between the legitimate expectation of the foreign investor and the right of the host State to regulate its economy in the public interest.[130]

On this premise, the appeal was upheld: in the tribunal's view, even though the measures adopted by Argentina, *if considered separately*, were legitimate, the same measures, *in their entirety*, amounted to an FET violation and embodied a composite wrongful act in the terms of Article 15 of the ILC Draft on State Responsibility.[131] In particular, along this Article, '[t]he breach of an international obligation by a State through a series of actions or omissions defined in aggregate as wrongful occurs when the action or omission occurs which, taken with the other actions or omissions, is sufficient to constitute the wrongful act'. In a similar fashion, in the instant case,

---

[126] *See* para 129.

[127] *See supra* Sect. 4.6.2.

[128] *See* para 130: 'According to Court of Justice of the European Union [...] private parties cannot normally invoke legitimate expectations against the exercise of normative powers by the Community's institutions, except under the most restrictive conditions.'

[129] *El Paso Energy International Company v. Argentina*, ICSID Case No. ARB/03/15, Award of 31 October 2011.

[130] *See* para 358.

[131] UN doc. A/56/10 (2001), in Yearbook of International Law Commission, Vol. II, Second Part, 2001, pp. 62 et seq.

> [a]lthough they may be seen in isolation as reasonable measures to cope with a difficult economic situation, the measures examined can be viewed as cumulative steps which individually do not qualify as violations of FET […] but which amount to a violation if their cumulative effect is considered.[132]

The line of argument followed in the decision proves particularly complex, but one may conclude that the variant of expectation underpinning it is that by induction anyway: such a form of expectation occurs where a specific normative act is intended to attract foreign capital; nonetheless, that very intention may also be inferred from a number of acts, *where considered cumulatively*.[133]

On the other hand, this is equally true with regard to the decision in *Suez* and *AWG*.[134] In this case, the will of the State to attract foreign capitals was ascertained having regard not to single and specific normative acts, but rather to the *whole legal framework* existing at the time of the investment.

The decisions in *Micula*[135] and *Philip Morris*[136] also deserve attention. Both decisions move from the assumption whereby expectations by legislation depend on the existence of specific normative acts by the host State *to induce* investors to make an investment. On this assumption, while in *Micula* the tribunal ascertained the existence of such acts,[137] in *Philip Morris* the opposite conclusion was reached.[138]

---

[132] *See* para 515.

[133] With a view to exemplifying this kind of reasoning, the tribunal also makes a comparison between the notion of *creeping expropriation* and that of *creeping violation* of FET: 'According to the case-law, a creeping expropriation is a process extending over time and composed of a succession or accumulation of measures which, taken separately, would not have the effect of dispossessing the investor but, when viewed as a whole, do lead to that result. A *creeping violation of the FET standard* could thus be described as a process extending over time and comprising a succession or an accumulation of measures which, taken separately, would not breach that standard but, when taken together, do lead to such a result' (para 518). Such a comparison, however, is not entirely convincing, especially where one considers how controversial the notion of *creeping expropriation* is. In this regard, the remarks made by Reisman and Sloane 2003, pp. 123–125, turn out to be quite revealing: 'Direct acts, analysed in isolation rather than in the context of the overall flow of events, may, whether legal or not in themselves, seem innocuous *vis-à-vis* a potential expropriation. Some may not be expropriatory in themselves. Only in retrospect will it become evident that those acts comprised part of an accretion of deleterious acts and omissions, which in the aggregate expropriated the foreign investor's property rights […] Because of their gradual and cumulative nature, creeping expropriations also render it problematic, perhaps even arbitrary, to identify a single interference (or failure to act where a duty requires it) at the "moment of expropriation".

[134] *Suez et al.* and *AWG Group v. Argentina*, ICSID Case No. ARB/03/19, Decision on Liability of 30 July 2010, para 227.

[135] *Ioana Micula at al. v. Romania*, ICSID Case No. ARB/05/20, Final Award, 11 December 2013.

[136] *Philip Morris et al. v. Uruguay*, ICSID Case No. ARB/10/7, Award, 8 July 2016.

[137] Para 677 (emphasis added). *See*, however, the separate opinion appended by judge G. Abi-Saab.

[138] Para 427. *See* also *Charanne B.V. and Construction Investments S.A.R.L. v. Spain*, Arbitration Institute of the Stockholm Chamber of Commerce, Award of 21 January 2016, para 495: 'A finding that there has been a violation of investor's expectations must be based on an objective

Last but not least, a normative confirmation of the approach here scrutinized is elaborated in the text of CETA: its Section D, Article 8.10, para 4, states that when applying the fair and equitable treatment obligation, 'a Tribunal may take into account whether a Party made a specific representation to an investor *to induce* a covered investment, that created a legitimate expectation, and upon which the investor relied in deciding to make or maintain the covered investment, but that the Party subsequently frustrated.'[139]

4.6.4 Expectation by Legislation and the State Power to Regulate

It has been argued that expectation by legislation may take on different forms and that arbitral tribunals increasingly resort to the 'by induction' model. But the question remains as to the impact of this model on the State power to regulate in the public interest, viz. 'the legal right exceptionally permitting the host State to regulate in derogation of international commitments it has undertaken by means of an investment agreement without incurring a duty to compensate.'[140]

In principle, as may also be inferred from the above, the investor

> is and must be aware of the State's commitment to deal with situations and problems that may emerge over the time and were impossible to anticipate. The fair and equitable treatment does not provide for a standard according to which the investor would remain completely isolated and immune from the host State's endeavours to deal with such situations in complying with public interests.[141]

Notwithstanding this, in the presence of a previous legislation put in place with the specific aim of inducing certain investments, FET can limit the State regulatory power from a threefold angle at least. First, this power may be exercised (precisely without any duty to compensate) only where the public interest demanding normative changes is of paramount importance. That would be the case, for example, of 'an epidemic threat to the health of a very large amount of people.'[142] Second, 'the basic expectations of the investor in respect of the fate of its investment are nevertheless taken care of by the host State when reacting to unforeseen

(Footnote 138 continued)

standard or analysis, as the mere subjective belief that could have had the investor at the moment of making the investment is not sufficient. Moreover, the application of the principle accordingly depends on whether the expectation has been reasonable in the particular case with relevance to representations possibly made by the host State *to induce the investment*' (emphasis added).

[139] Emphasis added.

[140] Titi 2014, p. 33.

[141] Idem.

[142] Idem.

circumstances.'[143] Third, when proceeding with deference to those interests, authorities are in any event required to 'restore their efficient preservation as soon as the circumstances so allow.'[144]

In this last regard, the *Suez/AWG* decision is of particular relevance. And indeed, in this case, an FET violation was ascertained not only as a result of the change to the legal framework existing at the time of the investment, but also because, despite the subsequent economic recovery, Argentina did not renegotiate any tariffs concerning water concession.[145] By the same token, in the decision in *Total*, Argentina was held responsible for an FET violation, because, from the entry into force of the 2002 Emergency law, it

> [r]epeatedly established new deadlines, causing protracted delays in the renegotiations of licenses and concessions (the tariff regime included) in the public utility sector for almost six years. At the same time, any automatic semi-annual adjustment (such as the one originally provided linked to the US PPI) had been discontinued.[146]

4.7 Conclusion

The analysis carried out in this chapter reveals that the (tacit or explicit) rationale behind arbitral decisions in matter of reliance ends up being always the same. For the principle of legitimate expectations to be applied, the judge has engaged in a complex interpretive activity, aimed at identifying a specific rule capable of securing a positive solution to the dispute in hand. All the forms of expectations included under FET have been identified by means of a reasoning of this kind, i.e. a reasoning whose *premise* lies in the existence of a general principle of international law protecting expectations, and whose *conclusion* lies in the circumstances under which a breach of a contract, a promise or legislation amounts to an FET violation.

---

[143] Idem.

[144] Idem.

[145] *Suez et al.* and *AWG Group v. Argentina*, ICSID Case No. ARB/03/19, Decision on Liability of 30 July 2010, para 242: 'Argentina sought to structure the 'renegotiation' process in such a way as to severely limit or indeed curtail the contractual freedom of AASA in order to arrive at a predetermined result desired by Argentina. In the opinion of the tribunal, such a process cannot in fairness be said to constitute a renegotiation as that term is generally understood. It was certainly not the kind of renegotiation or revision process that AASA and the Claimants were led to expect by the legal framework of the Concession and the events of the first eight years of the Concession.'

[146] *Total S.A. v. Argentina*, ICSID Case No. ARB/04/1, Decision on Liability of 27 December 2010, para 174.

References

Alvik I (2011) Contracting with Sovereignty. State Contracts and International Arbitration. Hart, Oxford
Barak-Erez D (2005) The Doctrine of Legitimate Expectations and the Distinctions between the Reliance and Expectation Interests. European Public Law 11 (4):583–602
Barile P (1983) Lezioni di diritto internazionale, 2nd edn. Cedam, Padua
Berge GT, Widdershoven R (1998) The Principle of Legitimate Expectations in Dutch Constitutional and Administrative Law. In: Hondius EH (ed) Netherlands Report to the Fifteenth International Congress of Comparative Law. Intersentia, Antwerp, pp. 421–452
Bosco G (1938) Il fondamento giuridico del valore obbligatorio del diritto internazionale. Rivista di diritto pubblico 30:626–636
Brown C (2009) The Protection of Legitimate Expectations As a 'General Principle of Law': Some Preliminary Thoughts. Transnational Dispute Management 6:1–10
Byers M (1999) Custom, Powers and the Power of Rules. International Relations and Customary International Law. Cambridge University Press, Cambridge
Cantegreil J (2011) The Audacity of the Texaco/Calasiatic Award: René-Jean Dupuy and the Internationalization of Foreign Investment Law. European Journal of International Law 22:441–458
Carbone SM (1967) Promessa e affidamento nel diritto internazionale. Giuffrè, Milan
Carbone SM (1975) Promise in International Law: A Confirmation of its Binding Force. The Italian Yearbook of International Law, vol. I:166–172
Cassese (2005) International Law, 2nd edn. Oxford University Press, Oxford
Conforti B (2015) Diritto internazionale, 10th edn. Editoriale Scientifica, Naples
Coviello PJJ (2004) La protección de la confianza del administrado. Abeledo Perrot, Buenos Aires
De Luca A (2016) Lodo favorevole alla Spagna a conclusione del primo degli investment arbitration sorti da impianti fotovoltaici: un precedente rilevante? (Lodo 21 gennaio 2016). Diritto del commercio internazionale 30:250–275
De Nova R (1956) Considerazioni sulla neutralità permanente dell'Austria. Comunicazioni e Studi 8:1–32
Diehl A (2012) The Core Standard of International Investment Protection. Fair and Equitable Treatment. Kluwer Law International, Alphen aan den Rijn
Dolzer R, Schreurer C (2012) Principles of International Investment Law, 2nd edn. Oxford University Press, Oxford
Eckart C (2012) Promises of States under International Law. Hart, Oxford
Fietta S (2006) The "Legitimate Expectations" Principle under Article 1105 NAFTA – International Thunderbird Gaming Corporation v. The United Mexican States. The Journal of World Investment and Trade 7:423–432
Forsyth CF (1985) The Provenance and Protection of Legitimate Expectations. Cambridge Law Journal 47:238–260
Gigante M (2008) Mutamenti nella regolazione dei rapporti giuridici e legittimo affidamento. Tra diritto comunitario e diritto interno. Giuffrè, Milan
Grellert (1964) Zusicherung in Beamtenrecht. Uhlig, Bonn
Hirsch M (2011) Between Fair and Equitable Treatment and Stabilization Clause: Stable Legal Environment and Regulatory Change in International Investment Law. The Journal of World Investment & Trade 12:783–806
Kolb R (2006) Principles as Sources of International Law (With Special Reference to Good Faith). Netherlands International Law Review 53:1–36
Mauro MR (2016) Conflitti di competenza e coordinamento tra fori nel diritto internazionale degli investimenti: *contract claims v. treaty claims*, Diritto del commercio internazionale 30:725–761
Maynard S (2016) Legitimate Expectations and the Interpretation of the 'Legal Stability Obligation'. European Investment Law and Arbitration Review 1:99–114

Merusi F (2001) Buona fede e affidamento nel diritto pubblico. Dagli anni 'trenta' alla 'alternanza'. Giuffrè, Milan

Merusi F (2006) Affidamento. In: Cassese S (ed) Dizionario di diritto pubblico, vol. I. Giuffrè, Milan, pp. 144–147

Montt S (2012) State Liability in Investment Treaty Arbitration. Global Constitutional and Administrative Law in the BIT Generation. Hart, Oxford

Morelli G (1967) Nozioni di diritto internazionale, 7th edn. Cedam, Padua

Palombino FM (2005) Should Genocide Subsume Crimes Against Humanity? Some Remarks in the Light of the *Krstić* Appeal Judgment. Journal of International Criminal Justice 3 :778–789

Palombino FM (2011) 'Fair and Equitable Treatment' degli investimenti stranieri e affidamento da atto normative in un recente lodo arbitrale. Diritto del Commercio internazionale 25:836–852

Pardolesi P (2009) Promissory estoppel: affidamento e vincolatività della promessa. Cacucci, Bari

Potestà M (2013) Legitimate Expectations in Investment Treaty Law: Understanding the Roots and the Limits of a Controversial Concept. ICSID Review 28: 88–122

Quadri R (1968) Diritto internazionale pubblico, 5th edn. Liguori, Naples

Reisman WM, Sloane RD (2003) Indirect Expropriation and Its Valuation in the BIT Generation. The British Yearbook of International Law 74:115–150

Rubin AP (1977) The International Legal Effects of Unilateral declarations. American Journal of International Law 71:1–30

Schreurer C (2005) Fair and Equitable Treatment in Arbitral Practice. Journal of World Investment & Trade 6:357–386

Sereni AP (1962) Diritto internazionale, vol. III. Giuffrè, Milan

Snodgrass E (2006) Protecting Investors' Legitimate Expectations: Recognizing and Delimiting a General Principle. ICSID Review 21: 1–58

Sornarajah M (2010) The International Law on Foreign Investment, 3rd edn. Cambridge University Press, Cambridge

Téllez FM (2012) Conditions and Criteria for The Protection of Legitimate Expectations Under International Investment Law. ICSID Review 27:432–442

Titi A (2014) The Right to Regulate in International Investment Law. Nomos/Dike/Hart, Baden-Baden/Zürich/St. Gallen/Oxford

UNCTAD (2012) Fair and Equitable Treatment. UNCTAD Series on Issues in International Investment Agreements II. A Sequel. United Nations, New York/Geneva

Vicente MO (2013) Princípio da proteção da confiança como garantia dinâmica. In: Tavares da Silva S, de Fátima Ribeiro M (eds) Trajéctorias de Sustentabilida de Tributação e Investimento. Istituto Jurídico da Faculdade de Direito da Universidad de Coimbra, Coimbra, pp. 153–207

Wälde T, Kolo A (2001) Environmental Regulation, Investment Protection and Regulatory Taking in International Law. International and Comparative Law Quarterly 50:811–848

Walter AV (2008) The Investor's Expectations in International Investment Arbitration. In: Reinisch A, Knahr C (eds) International Investment Law in Context. Eleven, The Hague, pp. 173–200

Weber M (1922) Wirtschaft und Geselschaft. Mohr, Tubingen

Zarra G (2016) Parallel Proceedings in Investment Arbitration. Giappichelli/Eleven, Turin/The Hague

Zeyl T (2011) Charting the Wrong Course: The Doctrine of Legitimate Expectations in Investment Treaty Law. Alberta Law Review 49:203–236

Ziegler AR, Baumgartner J (2015) Good Faith as a General Principle of (International Law). In: Mitchell AD, Sornarajah M, Voon T (eds) Good Faith and International Economic Law. Oxford University Press, Oxford, pp. 10–37

Chapter 5
FET and Proportionality

Contents

Abstract This chapter expounds on the contours of proportionality as an FET element. It is argued that (i) proportionality embodies a general principle of international law with its own foundations in the international legal order itself and (ii) the balancing process that this principle, as an FET element, involves, always takes into account certain circumstances which mainly rest on the business risk taken by the investor on the one hand and the kind of prejudice the investment may suffer on the other hand.

Keywords Proportionality · Definition · Suitability · Necessity · Balance · Business risk

F.M. Palombino, *Fair and Equitable Treatment and the Fabric of General Principles*, https://doi.org/10.1007/978-94-6265-210-1_5

5.1 Introduction

Proportionality is a general principle of international law, the normative content of which proves both 'fixed' and 'flexible'. Its fixed part crosscuts any fields of the international legal order and entails a three-step analysis: suitability, necessity and proportionality *stricto sensu*; the flexible part, contrariwise, allows the judge to give to the principle a concrete content which usually changes depending on the normative field where it is resorted to and, *a fortiori*, on the different assessment of each of the aforementioned parameters. This is equally true as far as international investment law is concerned, which means once again that context matters. Seen from this angle, the balancing process that proportionality involves always takes into account certain circumstances that mainly rest on the business risk taken by the investor on the one hand and the kind of prejudice the investment may suffer on the other hand. Arguably, proportionality as an FET element has gone so far as to embody a general principle specific to international investment law.

5.2 Proportionality as a General Principle of International Law

Proportionality, in the same vein as due process of law and legitimate expectations, represents one of the core elements helping define FET. It serves as a benchmark by means of which the arbitrator reviews a State or public interest *vis-à-vis* an investor's rights, thereby accommodating such competing prerogatives.[1] Moving on from this premise, and bearing in mind the approach followed in the foregoing chapters, the terms of the question do not change; it must be established whether proportionality embodies a norm of general international law and, as such, may ultimately be subsumed under FET.

With the exception of a few scholars, who are sceptical regarding the possibility of relying on general international law[2] or derive the legitimacy of proportionality

---

[1] It is worth noting that proportionality, besides being a criterion that courts take into account in reviewing legislative or administrative measures, is *a fortiori* a canon of conduct for both the legislator and the administration themselves. On the twofold function of proportionality, *see* Villamena 2008. More in general, on proportionality, *see* recently Cognetti 2011.

[2] This opinion may be credited to Higgins 1994, p. 236, who prefers regarding proportionality as a concept to ease the appropriate application of norms of international law in particular cases: 'Whether proportionality is yet a general principle of law is doubtful. [O]ne is left with a sense of subjectivity in the decision-making of the Court as to whether burdens imposed are or are not out of proportion to the object sought. [The principle of proportionality is meant] to oil the wheels of decision-making.' Further scholars who express the same scepticism include Krugmann 2004, p. 124 and Alvarez 2014, p. 221.

from natural law,[3] legal doctrine usually solves the question in the affirmative. Nonetheless, it strongly disagrees on the specific kind of source that would be relevant in this context. For some writers, proportionality should be regarded as a general principle of law recognized by civilized nations in the traditional meaning of this concept, viz. originating from most representative national legal systems all over the world.[4] Other commentators suggest the existence of a crosscutting customary norm with respect to the different substantive areas of international law.[5] Others rely on a combination of these sources of international law, arguing that 'the core of the principle of [proportionality] is customary and perhaps also a general principle of law.'[6] Finally, the opinion has been put forward whereby proportionality would fit in the corpus of *general principles of international law* with its own foundations in the international legal order. The latter opinion, which was first advanced by Friedhelm Krüger-Sprengel[7] and Jost Delbrück,[8] and is increasingly followed by contemporary legal writers (for example Enzo Cannizzaro,[9] Riccardo

---

[3] *See*, e.g., Reisman and Stevick 1998, p. 129: '[The] Natural Law criteria of necessity and proportionality are indispensable, for they help us to consider and then fashion and appraise legal instruments in terms of social goals, costs and alternative consequences.'

[4] *See* Gardam 1999, p. 161; Mitchell 2007, pp. 985–1008; Stone Sweet and Mathews 2008, p. 74; Stone Sweet and Della Cananea 2014, p. 938; Bücheler 2015, pp. 28 et seq.

[5] Cohen and Shany 2007; Martin 2014.

[6] Meron 1989, p. 65.

[7] Krüger-Sprengel 1979, p. 194, according to whom proportionality 'est un principe général dont il faut tenir compte dans l'interprétation des règles pertinentes du droit international.'

[8] Delbrück 1997, p. 1144: 'Apart from the embodiment of the principle of proportionality in various international treaties, whether the principle can be said to underlie the whole of the international legal order as a general principle of law (ICJ Statute, Article 38(*c*) or as a general principle of international law might be open to discussion. The way in which the principle has developed from domestic law into international law could support the former view but the widespread acceptance of the principle in various areas of international law and its fundamental importance for the international law-applying process suggests that proportionality can already be characterized as a general principle of international law. This view should be accepted as it adequately reflects the relevance of a basic principle such as proportionality, not least for the proper administration of international law which has become more and more sophisticated and will continue to do so'.

[9] Cannizzaro 2000. Apparently, Cannizzaro's argument does not rely on the category of general principles of international law. In his view, proportionality 'represents a *structural principle of international law*, a principle which may be deduced from the observation of the formal structure of the legal situations to which it applies. It is common experience that each legal order includes general principles which may be deduced from the analysis of positive rules that articulate their content by application to concrete situations' (emphasis added). Still, one gets the impression that the alleged category of *structural principles of international law*, as described by this author, ends up overlapping with the category of general principles of international law *tout court*. The way they come into existence, i.e. the fact that both categories of principles have their own foundations in the international legal order, makes it difficult to identify any substantive difference. In other words, this is the classical case where apparently different words may have the same meaning.

Pisillo Mazzeschi[10] and Emily Crawford),[11] ends up being the most convincing; and not only because all the main rules of international law (like those on international responsibility,[12] maritime delimitation[13] and human rights)[14] involve proportionality. From this angle, indeed, no real difference may be found between the argument under consideration and that claiming the existence of a custom. Plausibly, the main reason supporting such a conclusion can be explained in the following terms.

Resorting to general principles—it is worth repeating—makes it possible to overcome all the difficulties closely related to the alleged existence of a custom, and which mainly rest on the lack of a consistent practice in the matter.[15] In effect, when dealing with the principle of proportionality, an apparent paradox emerges insofar as the normative content of the principle is simultaneously 'fixed' and 'flexible'. The *fixed part* of proportionality enhances its typical function as a general principle of law, i.e. to prescribe a direction that the judge is expected to follow in the exercise of his duties. This is possible thanks to the well-known three-step structure of the principle, the application of which entails the assessment of a threefold parameter: suitability, necessity and proportionality *stricto sensu*. On the other hand, the *flexible part* of proportionality allows the judge to give to the principle a concrete content that usually changes depending on the normative field where it is invoked and, *a fortiori*, the different assessment of each of the aforementioned parameters.[16] Put differently, proportionality echoes the classic way a general

---

[10] Pisillo Mazzeschi 2002, p. 1035 (reviewing Cannizzaro 2000).

[11] Crawford 2011, p. 1: 'Proportionality is a principle found in a number of different areas of both international and domestic law, including the law of armed conflict, the law of treaties, the law regarding the use of force, maritime delimitation law, and human rights law. As such, it has a number of different permutations according to the specific area in which it operates. However, as a general principle [...], proportionality means that a State's acts must be a rational and reasonable exercise of means towards achieving a permissible goal, without unduly encroaching on protected rights of either the individual or another State.'

[12] We essentially refer to proportionality as one of the main preconditions for countermeasures as well as for self-defence to be legitimate.

[13] In *North Sea Continental Shelf cases*, Judgment of 20 February 1969, para 154, the ICJ stated that one of the key factors underpinning its decision was 'the element of a reasonable degree of proportionality, which a delimitation carried out in accordance with equitable principles ought to bring about between the extent of the continental shelf areas appertaining to the coastal State and the length of its coast.'

[14] For example, the ECtHR, since its establishment, has always applied considerations of proportionality in assessing restrictions of fundamental rights. *See infra* Sect. 5.5.

[15] Cannizzaro 2000, p. 450.

[16] What has been observed in the text may represent a useful counter-argument in response to the doubts raised by Higgins on the nature of proportionality as a general principle of law. According to Higgins '[i]n international law the principle in maritime law is entirely different from the principle in other areas. In the other areas, there are common elements to the invocation of the principle, but many doubts surround it still—whether, as in the laws of war, it exists as a separate principle at all; and whether, in human-rights law, it has a meaningful separate existence from the notion of necessity.' Indeed, in this author's view, the fact that the principle ends up having a

principle of international law should work: first, *by way of induction*, the judge infers the principle from pre-existing rules (of both conventional and customary nature); second, *by way of deduction* and therefore on the basis of the principle which has been identified, that same judge lays down the rule applicable to a given case. This is anything but surprising. As has been observed several times in the previous chapters, if one assumes that general principles may be seen as guiding criteria, applying a principle primarily means giving to it a concrete content.

On these assumptions, the present chapter discusses the principle of proportionality, having regard to its *function* and *scope* as an FET element. The practice existing in the matter is still fairly scant; nonetheless, there is increasing convergence in the way arbitral tribunals apply the principle.

5.3 Proportionality and Its Three-Step Normative Structure: Suitability, Necessity and Proportionality *Stricto Sensu*

Proportionality, in the form developed by continental European legal thinking, consists of three different elements which need to be ascertained cumulatively.[17] The first step lies in the assessment of suitability, that is to say (i) whether the purpose underlying a certain measure (intended to limit a particular interest) may be regarded as proper; and (ii) in case of positive assessment, to what extent the measure itself is suitable to achieve that purpose.[18] In other words, 'a causal relationship between the measure and its object' must be ascertained.[19] On the other hand, it is open to discussion if the measure under consideration could be evaluated at the moment it was enacted, i.e. from an *ex ante* perspective, or when the measure is analysed by the court, i.e. from an *ex post* perspective. Arguably this is a matter of pure discretion, but it does not necessarily imply any substantive differences.[20]

(Footnote 16 continued)

different content depending on the concerned area of international law shows exactly the opposite, i.e. the nature of proportionality as a general principle.

[17] Jans 2000, p. 240.

[18] As has been rightly observed '[s]trictly speaking, proportionality involves a four-step analysis since the first prong comprises two different questions. First, is the goal pursued by the legislator or the executive a legitimate one? Second, is the State measure a suitable means to attain this goal?' (Bücheler 2015, p. 37, at footnote 43). An analysis of this kind, for example, is relied on by Barak 2012, p. 131. However, insofar as the suitability test necessarily presupposes the ascertainment of a proper purpose, the terms of the question do not change. This is the reason why, according to the conventional understanding of the proportionality principle, it consists of three tests (Bücheler 2015, p. 37).

[19] Jans 2000, p. 240.

[20] Andenas and Zleptnig 2007, p. 387.

The necessity test (also called 'the least intrusive alternative')[21] raises the different question of whether, among all the potential alternative measures (which are deemed equally effective in reaching the pursued aim), the State has chosen the least intrusive, namely harming citizens or the public interest as little as possible.

Once the measure has been deemed legitimate and necessary, its proportionality *stricto sensu* demands to be assessed. This test involves a veritable balance between the different interests at stake. In brief, one must establish to what extent the restriction of a certain interest is actually justified because of the importance of the aim underlying the State action: '[t]he more intense the restriction of a particular interest, the more important the justification for the countervailing objective needs to be.'[22] It follows that while the first two steps concern the evaluation of the means chosen with a view to achieving a certain objective, this third step involves assessing the objective itself, or rather the 'weight' that the objective (*rectius* the degree of its fulfilment) is able to assume in a given case. Anyway, it is clear that there exists an almost 'symbiotic' relation among the several steps falling under the control of proportionality,

> a *continuum*, in which the weighting elements are not confined to the last, possible step, but impact on the entire process. The inquiry into the compatibility [...] between rights and principles or objectives of general interest, does not consist of simply carrying out the three steps surrounding the proportionality test (first the evaluation of means, then the evaluation of the weight of interests involved): rather, it has a necessarily holistic character; it is the search for an insightful balance between the means available, the degree of satisfaction of a right or principle, and the level of injury suffered by another right or principle.[23]

5.4 Proportionality and Domestic Courts

The three-step structure of proportionality has emerged almost synchronically into domestic and international legal orders. And this by means of a process which can be defined as of mutual interference. Such a circumstance, while suggesting proportionality be regarded as a principle of international law (with its own foundations in the international legal order), makes it appropriate to establish its scope into domestic legal systems as well. In this connection, as rightly observed by an ICSID tribunal, 'the most developed body of jurisprudence is in Europe. It is very well-established law in a number of European countries that there is a principle of

[21] Jans 2000, p. 240.

[22] Andenas and Zlepting, *supra* note 20.

[23] Pino 2010, p. 207 (own translation).

proportionality which requires that administrative measures must not be any more drastic than is necessary for achieving the desired end.'[24]

To start with, the practice of German courts, which according to some authors deeply influenced several domestic and international legal regimes,[25] proves significant insofar as they developed the first systematic formulation of proportionality in the form of a three-step test. Reference is made, *inter alia*, to the judgment passed by the Constitutional Court on 11 June 1958, better known as *Apothekenurteil*.[26] The case raised the question whether a Bavarian legislation, limiting the number of licenses for pharmacies, was compatible with Article 12 of the *Grundgesetz* providing for the freedom to practice one's profession.[27] Accordingly, the conflict between a fundamental constitutional freedom and a public measure aimed at achieving a legitimate purpose was to be managed. To this end, the Constitutional Court engaged in a balancing process (*Abwägung*), the adoption of which included the three aforementioned elements:

> The [purpose of] constitutional right should be to protect the freedom of the individual [while the purpose of] the regulation should be to ensure sufficient protection of societal interests. The individual's claim to freedom will have a stronger effect [...] the more his right to free choice of a profession is put into question; the protection of the public will become more urgent, the greater the disadvantages that arise from the free practicing of professions. When one seeks to maximize both [...] demands in the most effective way, then the solution can only lie in a careful balancing of the meaning of the two opposed and perhaps conflicting interests.[28]

In the same vein, one may mention the Italian legal order: both the Constitutional Court and administrative tribunals, when resorting to proportionality as a judicial criterion, usually make use of the three-step analysis. Suffice it to recall a judgment rendered in 2000 by the *Consiglio di Stato* (the Italian Supreme Administrative Court) (Section VI, No. 1885). In this case, the proportionality of a Decree of the President of Council of Ministers (25 February 1999) was discussed, where it fixed at 2% the maximum limit for public participation in the social capital of *Sea*

---

[24] *Occidental Petroleum Corp., Occidental Exploration and Production Company v. Ecuador*, ICSID Case No. ARB/06/11, Award of 5 October 2012, para 403.

[25] Barak 2012, pp. 178–183. Georg Nolte 2010, p. 246, doubts 'whether this development [...] was due to some inherent quality of the concept of proportionality as a product of the German legal system'; plausibly, this is nothing but the result of human rights instruments (such as the Universal Declaration of Human Rights, the European Convention of Human Rights and Fundamental Freedoms, and the International Covenant on Civil and Political Rights), the universality of which 'requires some uniformity concerning the method of the determination of rights.'

[26] 7 BVerfGE 377.

[27] In particular, para 1 of this Article states as follows: 'All Germans shall have the right freely to choose their occupation or profession, their place of work and their place of training. The practice of an occupation or profession may be regulated by or pursuant to a law.'

[28] 7 BVerfGE 377, at 404–405. This translation has been provided by Stone Sweet and Mathews 2008, pp. 107–108. Later on, proportionality was regarded as part of the notion of *Rechtsstaat* (*see supra* Chap. 2, Sect. 2.6) going so far as to become a general principle of the legal order.

Aereoporti S.p.a. of Rome. In the words of the *Consiglio di Stato* the principle of proportionality was described as follows:

> [N]ational and Community administrative authorities cannot impose, neither with legislative, nor with administrative acts, obligations and restrictions on the freedom of citizens protected under Community law to a greater extent (i.e. disproportionately) than is strictly necessary in the public interest for the achievement of the objective that the authority is required to accomplish, so that the measure adopted is *suitable* (i.e. adequate with respect to the objective to be pursued) and *necessary* (meaning that no other equally effective instrument, but less [...] intruding, is available).[29]

On this basis, while the setting of a limit for public participation was deemed legitimate, with regard to proportionality in the strict sense it was argued that 'the extent of this limit escapes judicial control inasmuch as it constitutes a choice of economic policy'.[30]

Also outside civil law countries and Europe more generally, proportionality ends up being applied along similar lines. From this angle, the decision of the Canadian Supreme Court in *Regina v. Oakes*[31] (which was rendered shortly after the entry into force of the Canadian Charter of Rights and Freedoms of 1982) is particularly illustrative. In this case the Court was called upon to decide on the compatibility between a criminal law provision (of the Narcotics Control Act), whereby whoever is found in possession of drugs is automatically presumed to be a drug dealer (unless the contrary is proved), and the presumption of innocence as protected by Section 11 of the Canadian Charter. With a view to establishing a violation of this section, the decision resorted to proportionality in its three-phase structure:

> Although the nature of the proportionality test will vary depending on the circumstances, in each case courts will be required to balance the interests of society with those of individuals and groups. There are, in my view, three important components of a proportionality test. First, the measures adopted must be carefully designed to achieve the objective in question. They must not be arbitrary, unfair or based on irrational considerations. In short, they must be rationally connected to the objective. Second, the means, even if rationally connected to the objective in this first sense, should impair 'as little as possible' the right or freedom in question. Third, there must be a proportionality between the effects of the measures which are responsible for limiting the Charter right or freedom, and the objective which has been identified as a 'sufficient importance'.[32]

A similar wording may be found in a decision rendered by the Constitutional Court of South Africa in a case concerning the compatibility of the death penalty with the constitutional right not to be subjected to inhuman and degrading treatment. Once again, in order to solve the question, proportionality in its 'three-step' structure was relied on:

---

[29] Point 10 of the motivation (own translation).

[30] Idem.

[31] *R. v. Oakes*, [1986] 1 S.C.R., at 103.

[32] Idem, at 139. Bücheler 2015, p. 44, rightly observes that '[t]he similarities between the Canadian and the German proportionality test are obvious: both contain a three-step approach that differentiates between suitability, necessity, and proportionality in the strict sense.'

> In the balancing process, the relevant considerations will include the nature of the right that is limited, and its importance to an open and democratic society based on freedom and equality; the purpose for which the right is limited and the importance of that purpose to such a society; the extent of the limitation, its efficacy, and particularly where the limitation has to be necessary, whether the desired ends could reasonably be achieved through other means less damaging to the rights in question.[33]

Last, but not least, the US domestic system deserves a particular consideration. Even though it is generally admitted that in this context the principle of proportionality (as well as its three-step structure) is not firmly rooted such as in the domestic jurisdictions discussed above, there exist several constitutional law concepts having a similar function, the normative structure of which is very akin to the proportionality analysis. One example is the so-called 'dormant commerce clause' doctrine, i.e. a doctrine allowing for a true balancing test between legitimate State objectives and the burdens placed upon commerce.[34] Hence, Gebhard Bücheler is right when he concludes that the jurisprudence of the US Supreme Court provides no reason to deny proportionality's belonging to general international law.[35]

5.5 Proportionality and International Courts

Proportionality, understood as a three-step test, has been resorted to in international case law as well. The practice of the CJEU is relevant to this effect. In EU Law—as may be already inferred from the above-mentioned judgment of the Italian *Consiglio di Stato*, proportionality falls under the category of general principles with implications similar to those it entails within domestic systems: in order to be lawful, a State or public measure limiting individuals' interests or rights must be compatible with the threefold parameter of suitability, necessity and proportionality *stricto sensu*. In the words of the Luxembourg Court's decision in *Fedesa*,

> [...] the principle of proportionality is one of the general principles of Community law. By virtue of that principle, the lawfulness of the prohibition of an economic activity is subject to the economic condition that the prohibitory measures are appropriate and necessary in order to achieve the objectives legitimately pursued by the legislation in question; when there is a choice between several appropriate measures recourse must be had to the least onerous, and the disadvantages cause must not be disproportionate to the aims pursued.[36]

---

[33] *State v. Makwanyane and Another*, 1995 (3) SA 391, 436 (CC).

[34] *See*, *inter alia*, Mathis 2008.

[35] Bücheler 2015, p. 61.

[36] CJEU, Judgment of 13 November 1990, point 13. In this respect, the opinion of Advocate General Van Gerven delivered on 11 June 1991 (*Society for the Protection of Unborn Children Ireland*) is revealing. Having regard to the possible consistency between the prohibition of the distribution of information and the principle of proportionality, he states as follows: 'I consider that the following points should be considered on the basis of the principle of proportionality. First, does the prohibition on the provision of information which is at issue pursue a legitimate aim of public interest which fulfils a imperative social need? Secondly, is that aim being realized using

Alongside the general principle of proportionality, one should also recall the eponymous principle set forth by Article 5, para 4, of the TUE: 'Under the principle of proportionality, the content and form of Union action shall not exceed what is necessary to achieve the objectives of the Treaties'. The difference between the two principles under consideration lies in the fact that while the former, as already said, is a means by which to protect individuals against EU institutions and national authorities, the latter pertains to the relationship between EU competences and those of Member States for which it represents a specific guarantee. Further, as it has been observed, with regard to both principles, the normative structure is always the same; accordingly the principle enshrined in Article 5, para 4, TEU may be regarded as a specific concretization of 'the general principle with the same denomination'.[37]

The Strasbourg Court is another international judicial body that frequently makes use of proportionality, especially as an element to establish the legality of derogations under Article 15 of the ECHR; the legality of State interference with the right to property under Article 1 of the First Additional Protocol to the ECHR; or with those conventional rights[38] in respect of which the so-called 'national margin of appreciation' may be applied. In all these cases, proportionality always comes into consideration according to its typical threefold structure. For example, with regard to the 'margin of appreciation' doctrine, it commonly refers to the space for manoeuvre that the Strasbourg Court is willing to grant national authorities when fulfilling their obligations under the European Convention on Human Rights, should some specific circumstances occur; that is to say, those circumstances making it possible to evaluate whether the national restriction of a conventional right proves lawful.[39] And indeed: the restriction must be provided by the law, as well as necessary (in order to preserve the public order and/or guarantee others' rights) and proportionate to the aim pursued (which is presumed to be legitimate).[40]

Lastly, proportionality has gained much importance within the WTO, especially thanks to the presence of rules within which the principle has been tacitly subsumed and actually serves as a canon of conduct for member States. Special reference is made to Article XX of the GATT on *General Exceptions*. As is known, this

(Footnote 36 continued)

means which are necessary (and acceptable) in a democratic society in order to achieve that aim? Thirdly, are the means employed in proportion to the aim pursued and is the fundamental right concerned, in this case freedom of expression, impinged upon as a result?' (para 35).

[37] Daniele 2010, p. 378. (own translation) In this regard, *see* also Ciciriello 1999.

[38] Reference is especially made to the right to respect for private and family life (Article 8 ECHR); the freedom of thought, conscience and religion (Article 9); the freedom of expression (Article 10); and the freedom of assembly and association (Article 11). Paragraph two of all these provisions contains a limitation clause that follows the pattern described in the text.

[39] *See* Sapienza 1991; Nigro 2008; Palombino 2010.

[40] In other words, as has been observed by Cannizzaro 2000, p. 70, while the margin of appreciation doctrine serves to identify the space for manoeuvre that a State enjoys in determining the purposes of its actions, proportionality serves to assess the legitimacy of the means relied on to carry out these actions. The same opinion may be ascribed to Padelletti 2003, p. 233. More generally, on the function of the proportionality analysis in European law, *see* Harbo 2015.

provision gives the contracting countries the possibility to adopt measures restricting trade wherever necessary to achieve legitimate purposes, such as the protection of public morals and health or the compliance with laws or regulation including those relating to customs enforcement or protection of patents and trademarks. It is also required that such measures do not constitute a means of arbitrary and unjustifiable discrimination between countries where the same conditions prevail, nor a disguised restriction on international trade. Now, it is evident that proportionality, intended as a canon of conduct, often turns into a 'judgment test' that the Dispute Settlement Body (DSB) is called upon to apply, should a State contest the validity of a measure adopted pursuant to Article XX. In this regard, several authors argue that the DSB has not yet developed a coherent and uniform pattern of the proportionality test. For Axel Desmedt, for example,

> there is no basis yet for the recognition in WTO law if an unwritten and overarching proportionality principles as known in EC law. Proportionality requirements exist only where there is a textual basis underlying such obligation. Depending on the language that is used, the scope of the proportionality principle will differ. In this sense the different formulations of the proportionality principle are, in my view, significant, leading to me to the conclusion that there is no uniform proportionality principle in WTO.[41]

However, under closer examination of case law and in line with other scholars' view, it is arguable that this pattern exists and possesses the typical threefold structure of proportionality, albeit conceived in a somewhat flexible way.[42] One may mention the decision of the Appellate Body in *Korea Beef*.[43] In this case, it was to be assessed whether a State measure which impacted on the labelling and sale of meat to the country of origin was necessary in order to protect public health. To this end, the Appellate Body relied on a proper proportionality assessment and articulated it in the threefold parameter of suitability, necessity and proportionality *stricto sensu*:

> [D]etermination of whether a measure, which is not 'indispensable', may nevertheless be 'necessary' within the contemplation of Article XX(*d*), involves in every case a process of weighing and balancing a series of factors which prominently include the contribution made by the compliance measure to the enforcement of the law or regulation at issue, the importance of the common interests or values protected by that law or regulation, and the accompanying impact of the law or regulation on imports or exports.[44]

---

[41] Desmedt 2001, pp. 478–479. The author, on the other hand, argues that 'the chapeau of Article XX could lead to the emergence of such a principle through judicial activism.'

[42] Hilf and Puth 2002; Andenas and Zlepting 2007.

[43] Report of 11 December 2000.

[44] Para 164. Proportionality is resorted to also in other fields of international law, especially that concerning the use of force. Yet, in this case, proportionality 'is not strictly used as an 'ends-means' balancing test between competing interests over a single asset but rather as a means of limiting harm against others in situations of armed conflict. [T]he right to self-defence against an armed attack is itself subject to limitations and requirements. One of these is that any act in self-defence to an armed attack must itself be "proportional" to that armed attack' (Crawford 2011, p. 3).

5.6 Proportionality as an FET Element

The fact that proportionality, at least in its minimum reach, is clear-cut and, as such, embodies a general principle of international law, answers the question pertaining to its content only partially; as has been observed, its maximum scope dramatically changes depending on the normative field where it is supposed to be applied, which means once again that context matters. From this angle, international investment law—a field within which proportionality, as an FET element, has acquired a specific content—is no exception.

The first decision expressly involving a proportionality approach is that passed in the previously discussed *Tecmed* case.[45] In this case, the use of proportionality was intended to verify whether there was an indirect expropriation capable, as such, of being compensated. As is known, an expropriation of this kind consists of State measures that cannot be *formally* qualified as measures of expropriation, but that are in practice similar to the latter either because they produce the same effects or because they seek to achieve the same result.[46] Based on these assumptions, and using the notion of proportionality as developed by the European Court of Human Rights,[47] the *Tecmed* tribunal pointed out that, in order to properly qualify the State measure challenged by the applicant, it had to assess whether a reasonable relationship of proportionality between the effects and the result of that measure did exist:

> After establishing that regulatory actions and measures will not be initially excluded from the definition of expropriatory acts, in addition to the negative financial impact of such actions or measures, the Arbitral Tribunal will consider, in order to determine if they are to be characterized as expropriatory, whether such actions or measures are proportional to the public interest presumably protected thereby and to the protection legally granted to investments, taking into account that the significance of such impact has a key role upon deciding the proportionality [...] There must be a reasonable relationship of proportionality between the charge or weight imposed to the foreign investor and the aim sought to be realized by any expropriatory measure.[48]

[45] *Tècnicas Medioambiente Tecmed S.A. v. Mexico*, ICSID Case No. ARB (AF)/00/2, Award of 29 May 2003. For a summary of the facts underlying the decision, *see* Chap. 4, Sect. 4.6.1. Henckels 2015, p. 107, observes that '[a]lthough the case is regarded by some as methodologically sound approach to proportionality analysis in the context of indirect expropriation, this book argues that the decision exemplifies a flawed methodology and an overly strict approach to the standard of review.'

[46] Mauro 2003, pp. 266 et seq.

[47] *See* paras 122 et seq. of the decision. In particular, according to the tribunal, the statements of the Strasbourg Court in this matter 'apply to the actions of the State in its capacity as administrator, not only to its capacity as law-making body.'

[48] *See* para 122.

Nonetheless, the tribunal excluded *ab origine* the existence of a causal link between the measure and the aim pursued (suitability test), and accordingly it did not engage in any further proportionality analysis,[49] for example by checking whether the measure was the least intrusive for its recipients.

The decision under scrutiny does not mention proportionality among the FET elements, but one may conclude so from the large majority of scholarship[50] (with the sole exception of one commentator)[51] as well as from the judicial practice developed in the aftermath of *Tecmed*; already in an award of 2004 (*MTD Equity*), for example, the tribunal concerned highlighted as follows:

> The parties agree that there is an obligation to treat investments fairly and equitably. The parties also agree with the statement of Judge Schwebel that 'the meaning of what is fair and equitable is defined when that standard is applied to a set of specific facts.' As defined by Judge Schwebel, 'fair and equitable treatment' is 'a broad and widely-accepted standard encompassing such fundamental standards as good faith, due process, non-discrimination, and *proportionality*.[52]

[49] Such a remark may be found in Kläger 2011, p. 242: '[A]ltough such analysis resembles some of the elements of a structured proportionality test, the tribunal did not review whether the host State actually applied the least restrictive measure in the sense of the necessity requirement. Moreover, the tribunal did not extend its particular concept of proportionality to the analysis of the fair and equitable treatment.'

[50] *See* Muchlinski 1995, p. 625 ('The concept of fair and equitable treatment is not precisely defined. It offers a general point of departure in formulating an argument that the foreign investor has not been well treated on account of discrimination or other measures being taken against its interests. It is, therefore, a concept that depends on the interpretation of specific facts for its content. At most it can be said that the concept connotes the principle of non-discrimination and proportionality in the treatment of foreign investors.'); Kläger 2011, p. 245 ('In summary, arbitral case law reveals little consistency with regard to the structure and intensity of review in the context of fair and equitable treatment. Although a number of arbitral awards employ the notion of proportionality, it seems that it is not yet fully established in arbitral jurisprudence. This is especially true if one considers a structured proportionality analysis following the steps of suitability, necessity and proportionality *stricto sensu*, being at best rudimentarily applied by arbitral tribunals. Nevertheless, arbitral tribunals seem to recognize, at least implicitly, that all steps of proportionality analysis are relevant for the finding of a breach of fair and equitable treatment. It is indeed of importance whether: a State measure is suitable to pursue a legitimate public purpose; there are less restrictive measures available; and, in a broader balancing, the interests of the investor or those of the host State ultimately prevail. Usually, however, such considerations are not discussed under the concept of proportionality, but are shrouded by other notions, referring to the reasonableness of the State measure, the legitimacy or reasonableness of the investor's expectations or the existence of a reasonable basis for a differential treatment'); Bücheler 2015, pp. 182 et seq.; Henckels 2015, pp. 70 et seq.

[51] Xiuli 2007, p. 639: '[W]e do not regard that the fair and equitable treatment principle includes the principle of proportionality.'

[52] *MTD Equity v. Chile*, ICSID Case No. ARB/01/7, Award of 25 May 2004, para 109; emphasis added.

More generally, as has been rightly observed,

> [w]hile proportionality analysis is not yet firmly established in arbitral jurisprudence related to FET, it does not go against any major tenets of this jurisprudence either. Quite the opposite, applying proportionality […] to FET provisions is compatible with existing jurisprudence and furnishes some of its most important elements with an analytical framework.[53]

5.6.1 *Business Risk and Its Impact on the Proportionality Analysis*

Going more into detail, the proportionality test intended as an FET element has served primarily to complement and specify the principle of legitimate expectations, helping determine the extent to which expectations generated by a given regulatory framework can be deemed legitimate. The case law in this matter proves significant for at least two reasons.[54]

First, it operates a proportionality test in accordance with the classic three-step pattern, namely by assessing—in a manner that is not always straightforward—suitability, necessity and proportionality *stricto sensu*. In this respect, the decision adopted by an UNCITRAL tribunal in *Glamis* is of assistance.[55] The case at hand concerned the new California Law relating to the operators of the extraction industry and aimed at limiting their activities both for environmental purposes and for the need to protect the cultural heritage of Native Americans. According to the applicant—a Canadian company active in that field (Glamis Gold Ltd.), this law would have rendered totally unproductive the investment made in the host country, disregarding in this way the legitimate expectations generated by the previous regulatory framework. In order to determine whether or not the law in question was

[53] Bücheler 2015, p. 198.

[54] Idem, pp. 199–202.

[55] *Glamis Gold Ltd v. United States*, UNCITRAL, Award of 8 June 2009. In the same terms, one may mention *Saluka Investments B.V. v. Czech Republic*, UNCITRAL, Partial Award of 17 March 2006. In this case, indeed, albeit in a somewhat non-linear fashion, it is expressly recognized that the State measure modifying the regulatory framework existing at the time of the investment, must be suitable, necessary and proportionate to the aim pursued (paras 306–307): 'The determination of a breach of Article 3.1 by the Czech Republic therefore requires a weighing of the Claimant's legitimate and reasonable expectations on the one hand and the Respondent's legitimate regulatory interests on the other […] A foreign investor protected by the Treaty may in any case properly expect that the Czech Republic implements its policies bona fide by conduct that is, as far as it affects the investors' investment, reasonably justifiable by public policies and that such conduct does not manifestly violate the requirements of consistency, transparency, even-handedness and non-discrimination. In particular, any differential treatment of a foreign investor must not be based on unreasonable distinctions and demands, and must be justified by showing that it bears a reasonable relationship to rational policies not motivated by a preference for other investments over the foreign-owned investment.'

compatible with FET, the tribunal conducted a proportionality assessment and concluded that the disputed measure was (i) suitable to achieve its purpose,[56] (ii) the least intrusive among the potentially available means,[57] and (iii) in line with the need to balance the public and private interests at stake.[58]

The second reason of interest towards this case law lies in the features of the balance operated within the control of proportionality. Indeed, whatever may be the outcome, such an operation always moves from the assumption whereby investors cannot expect that the existing regulatory framework at the time of the investment remains completely unchanged. The business risk the investor assumes also covers the possibility that the law might change and the negative effects that may arise from this change. In other words—it is worth repeating—'the conduct of the investor in relation to any undertaking of stability is also, so to speak subjectively, relevant, [which means] that BITs are not insurances policies against bad business judgments and *the investor has its own duty to investigate the host State's applicable law*.'[59] On this basis, and *a fortiori*, arbitral tribunals have always refused to check the proportionality *stricto sensu* of State measures taken in response to a financial, political or social crisis and considered legitimate and necessary. Indeed, as it has been observed by the *BP Group Plc* tribunal, since such measures involve choices of 'political economy', they are excluded from any judicial control regarding their 'reasonableness or effectiveness'.[60]

5.6.2 The 'Minimum Threshold of Prejudice' Requirement and Its Impact on the Necessity Test

An additional relevant factor in assessing the proportionality of a State measure is the prejudice that measure can cause to a given investment. This is an *objective* factor which, as such, is completely irrespective of the investor's expectations and

---

[56] In this regard, the tribunal makes the point clear that the contested measure 'was rationally related to its stated purpose and reasonably drafted to address its objectives. It is the Claimant's burden to prove a manifest lack of reasons for the legislation, and the tribunal holds that it has not met this burden' (para 803); in its view, indeed, 'the government has a sufficient good faith belief that there was a reasonable connection between the harm and the proposed remedy' (para 805).

[57] On this point, the tribunal observes that 'the adoption of the proposed regulation requiring backfilling and site recontouring of open fit surface mine excavations for metallic minerals [was] necessary for the immediate preservation of the public general welfare': para 181.

[58] In this respect, the tribunal expressly recognizes that 'governments must compromise between the interests of competing parties and, if they were bound to please every constituent and address every harm with each piece of legislation, they would be bound and useless': para 804. *See* also *Charanne B.V. and Construction Investments S.A.R.L. v. Spain*, Arbitration Institute of the Stockholm Chamber of Commerce, Award of 21 January 2016, para 517.

[59] *Total S.A. v. Argentina*, ICSID Case No ARB/04/1, Decision on Liability of 27 December 2010, para 124 (emphasis added).

[60] *BP Group Plc v. Argentina*, UNCITRAL, Award of 24 December 2007, para 344:

refers to the possibility of identifying a 'minimum threshold of prejudice', i.e. a prejudice that is serious enough to trigger the State's responsibility under the FET standard. Arguably, what may be considered by the judge for this threshold to be ascertained is the overall market value of the investment. A conclusion of this kind is of course corroborated by the decision in *Middle East Cement Shipping* and the necessity test carried out therein.[61]

In this case, as discussed earlier,[62] and perhaps in conformity with Egyptian law, the seizure and auctioning of a ship had been notified on-board (despite the fact that the ship was without crew at that moment), reported to the chief of local police, and featured in a newspaper article. In order to find an FET violation, the tribunal tacitly engaged in a proper proportionality-type analysis, noting that both measures, even if legitimate under domestic law, did not pass the necessity test; actually, considering the investor's nationality as well as the serious prejudice those acts had the potential to cause also in view of the market value of the investment, a direct notification to the person affected (as also allowed by Egyptian Law itself) was of course required:

> [A] matter as important as the seizure and auctioning of a ship of the Claimant should have been notified by a direct communication for which the law No. 308 provided under the 1st paragraph of Art. 7, irrespective of whether there was a legal duty or practice to do so by registered mail with return receipt requested as argued by Claimant [...]. The tribunal find that the procedure in fact applied here does not fulfill the requirements of Art. 2.2 and 4 of the BIT. [63]

5.6.3 *The 'Minimum Threshold of Prejudice' Requirement and Its Impact on Proportionality* Stricto Sensu

The 'minimum threshold of prejudice' requirement may have an impact not only on the necessity test but also on proportionality *stricto sensu*. From this angle, the decision rendered in the already mentioned *Azurix* case appears relevant.[64]

Here, by the same token as in *Tecmed*, the proportionality test has been applied not in relation to FET, but with a view to establishing whether an expropriation was lawful. By expressly referring to the case law of the European Court of Human Rights,[65] the tribunal clarified that (i) an expropriation measure is lawful insofar as there exists a reasonable relation of proportionality between the means employed

[61] *Middle East Cement Shipping and Handing Co.S.A. v. Egypt*, ICSID Case No. ARB/99/6, Award of 12 April 2002.

[62] *See* Chap. 3, Sect. 3.5.2.

[63] *See* para 143.

[64] *Azurix v. Argentina*, ICSID Case No. ARB/01/12, Award of 14 July 2006.

[65] The decision to be relied on is that passed in *James et al. v. United Kingdom*, Judgment of 21 February 1986.

and the aim sought to be realised; (ii) such a relation 'will not be found if the person concerned bears an individual and excessive burden'; and finally (iii) in assessing the economic prejudice 'there may be legitimate reasons for requiring nationals to bear a greater burden in the public interest than non-nationals'.[66] In other words, when the host State adopts a measure of expropriation for public utility, it cannot demand from the foreign investor a sacrifice similar to that required for citizens. These principles have also influenced the case law on FET, namely that relying on proportionality as an element of this standard. But, in addition to the criterion adopted by the ECHtR for the economic prejudice to be assessed (i.e. the investor's nationality), the overall market value of the investment also demands consideration. Emblematic in this regard is the decision in the *EDF* case.[67]

At the heart of the dispute was the Romanian policy against corruption. In line with this policy, and by means of a legislative measure, the host State revoked the licences for the management of airport duty-free shops, including those owned by the applicant, and this latter claimed an FET violation as a consequence. The tribunal concerned, quoting approvingly the *Azurix* decision,[68] clarified that State measures affecting a foreign investment are consistent with FET only where there is a reasonable relation of proportionality between the means employed and the aim sought to be realized, and where the investor involved is not excessively damaged. On this assumption, the State measure was found to be legitimate: in the tribunal's view, that measure affected all operators of airport duty-free shops and its impact on the value of the investment made by the applicant was relatively scarce.[69]

In the same perspective one may mention the decision in *Occidental Petroleum Corp., Occidental Exploration and Production Company*,[70] even though, in this case, the tribunal pronounced in favour of the investor. In detail, it was to establish whether Ecuador's termination of the investor's contract could be regarded as a proportionate response to the investor's breach of that contract. To this end, what is first pinpointed in the decision is the existence of

---

[66] Para 311.

[67] *EDF v. Romania*, ICSID Case No. ARB/05/13, Award of 8 October 2009.

[68] *Supra* note 64, para 311.

[69] Idem, para 294: 'In view of the foregoing considerations, Claimant's allegation that the enactment of GEO 104 was 'discriminative' and 'clearly designed as a pretext to take away Claimant's right to do business' is unsustainable. As a measure of a general nature taken in accordance with Romanian law, GEO 104 equally applied to the other airport duty-free operators in Romania. Such operators were all affected by the loss of their duty-free licenses, including those present at airports where Claimant did not operate, as shown by the evidence produced by Respondent. Following expiry on March 27, 2002, of its rights to commercial spaces at the Otopeni Airport, Claimant's right to do business was limited by GEO 104 to the conduct of duty-free operations on 49 m^2 of space at Constanta Airport until June 8, 2005.'

[70] *Occidental Petroleum Corp., Occidental Exploration and Production Company v. Ecuador*, ICSID Case No. ARB/06/11, Award of 5 October 2012. For a comment on this case, *see* Martin 2014; Henckels 2015, pp. 83–86; Bücheler 2015, pp. 202–208.

> a growing body of arbitral law, particularly in the context of ICSID arbitrations, which holds that the principle of proportionality is applicable to potential breaches of bilateral investment treaty obligations. In the present case, the Treaty provides at Article II.3(a) that investments shall at all times be accorded fair and equitable treatment […] The obligation for fair and equitable treatment has on several occasions been interpreted to import an obligation of proportionality.[71]

Bearing this in mind and arguing that 'the overriding principle of proportionality requires that any […] administrative goal must be balanced against the Claimant's own interests and against the true nature and effect of the conduct being censured',[72] the tribunal regarded the Ecuador's measure as contrary to the principle and awarded damages of $ 1.77 billion to Occidental. In its view:

> the price paid by the Claimants – *total loss of an investment worth many hundreds of millions of dollars* – was out of proportion to the wrongdoing alleged against OEPC, and similarly out of proportion to the importance and effectiveness of the 'deterrence message' which the Respondent might have wished to send to the wider oil and gas community.[73]

The decision in question, and its solidification of proportionality within the FET context, has been considered of paramount importance inasmuch as it suggests that 'arbitrators have broad scope to rule on proportionality of measures as a general principle applicable to all State obligations [including FET] under an investment treaty, a conclusion that no other investment tribunal has thus far reached.'[74] At the same time, however, more than one caution would be required.

> Future Tribunals […] must further develop the standard to provide host countries more protection because interpretation of the principle of proportionality thus far has tipped the balance to provide investors much greater protection than host countries. Additionally, in cases of breach of the proportionality principle, Tribunals will have difficulty awarding damages because they will need to consider how the investor's own bad act led to the disproportionate response and reduce the award by that amount. Finally, because the tribunal's decision has shown a preference for investors over host countries, developing countries that depend on foreign investment will be vary of ICSID arbitration and bilateral investment treaties.[75]

In our view, a criticism like this is not altogether convincing. An overall assessment of the practice in matter of proportionality clearly shows the tribunals' attitude to apply it only under some strict circumstances. This is not to say that the amount of damages is always determined in the right way; not by coincidence, precisely in *Occidental Petroleum*, that amount was dramatically reduced in 2015 by an annulment committee.[76]

---

[71] Paragraph 404.

[72] Paragraph 450.

[73] Idem (emphasis added).

[74] Henckels 2015, p. 86.

[75] Martin 2014, pp. 67–68. The same argument has been advanced by Henckels 2015, pp. 85–86.

[76] *Occidental Petroleum Corp., Occidental Exploration and Production Company v. Ecuador*, ICSID Case No. ARB/06/11, Decision on Annulment of the Award of 2 November 2015, paras 585–586.

5.7 Conclusion

The considerations made thus far with regard to proportionality show that also this principle, in the same vein as due process of law and expectations, ends up assuming a specific content that is adequate to the context of international investment law and that, as such, falls under FET. Actually, the balance of interests which proportionality entails cannot ignore certain circumstances, i.e. (i) the ordinary business risk assumed by the investor (who is supposed to know the host State's applicable law) and (ii) the extent of the prejudice a State measure may cause to that investment; in this last regard, a 'minimum threshold' is required, viz. a prejudice which is serious enough to deserve protection.

References

Alvarez JE (2014) 'Beware: Boundary Crossings' – A Critical Appraisal of Public Law Approaches to International Investment Law. Journal of World Trade and Investment 17:171–228

Andenas M, Zleptnig S (2007) Proportionality: WTO Law: in Comparative Perspective. Texas International Law Journal 42: 371–427

Barak A (2012) Proportionality. Constitutional Rights and their Limitations. Cambridge University Press, Cambridge

Bücheler G (2015) Proportionality in Investor-State Arbitration. Oxford University Press, Oxford

Cannizzaro E (2000) Il principio della proporzionalità nell'ordinamento internazionale. Giuffré, Milan

Ciciriello MC (1999) Il principio di proporzionalità nell'ordinamento comunitario. Editoriale Scientifica, Naples

Cognetti S (2011) Principio di proporzionalità. Profili di teoria generale e di analisi sistematica. Giappichelli, Turin

Cohen A, Shany Y (2007) A Development of Modest Proportions. The Application of the Principle of Proportionality in the Targeted Killings Case. Journal of International Criminal Justice 5:310–321

Crawford E (2011) Proportionality. Max Planck Encyclopedia of Public International Law, Online Edition. Available at http://opil.ouplaw.com

Daniele L (2010) Diritto dell'Unione europea. Sistema istituzionale - Ordinamento - Tutela giurisdizionale – Competenze. Giuffrè, Milan

Delbrück J (1997) Proportionality. In: Bernhardt R (ed) The Encyclopedia of International Law, vol. III. Elsevier, Amsterdam, pp. 1140–1144

Desmedt A (2001) Proportionality in WTO Law. Journal of International Economic Law 4:441–480

Gardam J (1999) Proportionality as a Restraint on the Use of Force. Australian Yearbook of International Law 20:162–173

Harbo T-I (2015) The Function of the Proportionality Analysis in European Law. Nijhoff, Leiden

Henckels C (2015) Proportionality and Deference in Investor-State Arbitration. Balancing Investment Protection and Regulatory Autonomy. Cambridge University Press, Cambridge

Higgins R (1994) Problems and Process: International Law and How We Use It. Clarendon Press, Oxford

Hilf M, Puth S (2002) The Principle of Proportionality on its Way into WTO/GATT Law. In: Von Bogdandy A, Movroidis PC, Mény Y (eds) European Integration and International

Co-ordination: Studies in Transnational Economic Law in Honour of Claus-Dieter Ehlermann. Kluwer Law International, The Hague, pp. 199–218
Jans JH (2000) Proportionality Revisited. Legal Issue of Economic Integration 27:239–265
Kläger R (2011) 'Fair and Equitable' Treatment in International Investment Law. Cambridge University Press, Cambridge
Krüger-Sprengel F (1979) Le Concept de proportionalité dans le droit de la guerre. Revue de droit penal militaire et de droit de la guerre 19:177–204
Krugmann M (2004) Der Grundsatz der Verhältnismäßigkeit im Völkerrecht. Duncker & Humblot, Berlin
Martin AM (2014) Proportionality: An Addition to the International Centre for the Settlement of Investment Disputes' Fair and Equitable Treatment Standard. Boston College International & Comparative Law Review 37:58–71
Mathis JH (2008) Balancing and Proportionality in US Commerce Clause Cases. Legal Issues of Economic Integration 35:273–282
Mauro MR (2003) Gli accordi bilaterali sulla promozione e la protezione degli investimenti. Giappichelli, Turin
Meron T (1989) Human Rights and Humanitarian Norms as Customary Law. Clarendon Press, Oxford
Mitchell AD (2007) Proportionality and Remedies in WTO Disputes. European Journal of International Law 17:985–1008
Muchlinski P (1995) Multinational Enterprises and the Law. Blackwell, Oxford
Nigro R (2008) Il margine di apprezzamento e la giurisprudenza della Corte europea dei diritti dell'uomo. Diritti umani e diritto internazionale 2:71–105
Nolte G (2010) Thin or Thick? The Principle of Proportionality and International Humanitarian Law. Law & Ethics of Human Rights 4:244–255
Padelletti ML (2003) La tutela della proprietà nella Convenzione europea dei diritti dell'uomo. Giuffré, Milan
Palombino FM (2010) Laicità della Stato ed esposizione del crocifisso nella sentenza della Corte europea dei diritti dell'uomo nel caso *Lautsi*. Rivista di diritto internazionale 93:134–139
Pino G (2010) Diritti e interpretazione. Il ragionamento giuridico nello Stato costituzionale. Il Mulino, Bologna
Pisillo Mazzeschi R (2002) Book review (reviewing Cannizzaro E (2000) Il principio della proporzionalità nell'ordinamento internazionale). European Journal of International Law 13:1031–1036
Reisman M, Stevick D (1998) The Applicability of International Law Standards to United Nations Economic Sanctions Programmes. European Journal of International Law 9:86–141
Sapienza R (1991) Sul margine di apprezzamento statale nel sistema della Convenzione europea dei diritti dell'uomo. Rivista di diritto internazionale 74:571–614
Stone Sweet A, Della Cananea G (2014) Proportionality, General Principles of Law, and Investor State Arbitration: a Response to José Alvarez. NYU Journal of International Law and Politics 46: 911–54
Stone Sweet A, Mathews J (2008) Proportionality Balancing and Global Constitutionalism. Faculty Scholarship Series. Paper 1296. http://digitalcommons.law.yale.edu/fss_papers/1296
Villamena S (2008) Contributo in tema di proporzionalità amministrativa. Ordinamento comunitario, italiano e inglese. Giuffrè, Milan
Xiuli H (2007) The Application of the Principle of Proportionality in *Tecmed v. Mexico*. Chinese Journal of International Law 6:635–652

Chapter 6
FET and the Driving Role of Case Law

Contents

Abstract This chapter explores the driving role of case law in the shaping of FET. It is argued that the approach followed in investor-State arbitration is the 'taking into account' approach, which means that the arbitrator is obliged to consider previous decisions, but may disregard them where reasons of substantive justice, or the mere need to foster a proper development of the law, suggest doing so.

Keywords Precedent · Definition · Bindingness · Persuasiveness · 'Taking into account' approach · Consistency

6.1 Introduction

The approach followed in investor-State arbitration as to the role of case law transcends the traditional dichotomy between binding and persuasive precedent. Rather, it echoes the so-called 'taking into account' approach, which means that the arbitrator is obliged to consider previous decisions, but may disregard them where reasons of substantive justice, or the mere need to foster a proper development of the law, suggest doing so. In these terms, one is facing a technique that is somewhat

F.M. Palombino, *Fair and Equitable Treatment and the Fabric of General Principles*, https://doi.org/10.1007/978-94-6265-210-1_6

different from that consisting of overruling prior decisions, because its very foundation proves dissimilar: the duty it presupposes is *procedural* in nature, insofar as what the judge is required to do is not to follow a precedent, but to take it into account. This is not only a terminological question but the acceptance of the perspective whereby (i) it is more important to have a right decision than a decision consistent with previous cases and (ii) the rule of precedent is by now sufficiently flexible to accommodate this need. Notably, the approach here scrutinized, while being fairly well-established in both national and international practice, proves particularly fitting with regard to an open-texture standard such as FET.

6.2 'Taking into Account' Approach and Domestic Jurisdictions

The manner by which FET has been shaped in international investment law, namely a consistent jurisprudence that has made its content increasingly stable, raises the issue regarding the role of precedent more generally. As is well known, precedent is a judicial decision susceptible to serve as a rule in future similar or analogous cases.[1] Bearing in mind the investor-State arbitration context and in particular the absence therein of a jurisdictional hierarchical system, the kind of precedent deserving attention is what is sometimes referred to as 'horizontal precedent'. Thus meaning that the question here is not the extent to which lower courts are obliged to follow judgments of their respective higher courts ('vertical precedent'), but rather a court's approach to its own decisions: 'a court should be consistent with itself over time, in order to let the citizens rely upon a credible forecast that the court will not change its own perspective day by day.'[2]

Yet the force of precedent understood in these terms is supposed to change radically depending on the national legal system under consideration: its authority would be *binding* in common law countries and *persuasive* in civil law countries. This line of thought may be ascribed, for example, to Jason Haynes. In his words, precedent would be the 'rule rather than exception in domestic judicial proceedings across most of the Commonwealth world today, though it has been expressly rejected in civil law countries.'[3] Still, such an approach has lost much of its importance. Indeed, the Anglo-Saxon and continental traditions increasingly converge on this subject matter, insofar as common law jurisdictions have abandoned a rigid view of precedent; and almost synchronically, civil law jurisdictions have embraced a less reductive idea of it, sometimes going so far as to admit that precedents, at least *de facto*, constitute a veritable source of law. The following considerations corroborate this argument.

---

[1] Taruffo 2007a, p. 13.

[2] Taruffo 2007b.

[3] Haynes 2014, p. 450.

In England, at least until the second half of the twentieth century, the rule of precedent did not tolerate any exception. At that time, indeed, not only were the decisions of the higher courts regarded as binding on the lower courts, but the House of Lords itself (which has been replaced by the Supreme Court since 1 October 2009) was bound to follow all of its own previous decisions, even if this created injustice; the only way to contest a precedent consisted of recommending its amendment to Parliament. Yet the rigidity of such a rule was strongly reduced when this Court, with a Practice Statement issued under the power of self-regulation recognized to common law courts, decided to escape from the constraints of *stare decisis*. The Practice Statement, which was introduced by Lord Gardiner on 26 July 1966, states as follows:

> Their Lordships regard the use of precedent as an indispensable foundation upon which to decide what is the law and its application to individual cases. It provides at least some degree of certainty upon which individuals can rely in the conduct of their affairs, as well as a basis for orderly development of legal rules. Their Lordships nevertheless recognise that too rigid adherence to precedent may lead to injustice in a particular case and also unduly restrict the proper development of the law. They propose, therefore, to modify their present practice and, while treating former decisions of this House as normally binding, to depart from a previous decision when it appears right to do so. In this connection they will bear in mind the danger of disturbing retrospectively the basis on which contracts, settlements of property and fiscal arrangements have been entered into and also the especial need for certainty as to the criminal law.[4]

In other words, previous decisions must be considered in the solution of a given case, but may be disregarded where 'it appears right to do so.'[5]

In *Payne v. Tennessee*, the US Supreme Court reasoned along similar lines:

> *Stare decisis* is the preferred course, because it promotes the evenhanded, predictable and consistent development of legal principles, fosters reliance on judicial decisions, and contributes to the actual and perceived integrity of the judicial process. Adhering to precedent is usually the wise policy, because, in most matters, it is more important that the applicable rule of law be settled than it be settled right. Nevertheless, when governing decisions are unworkable or are broadly reasoned, this Court has never felt constrained to follow precedent.[6]

Arguably, in the US, *stare decisis* is seen more as a principle of policy (whereby similar issues should be decided in a similar way), rather than an 'inexorable command' or 'a mechanical formula of adherence to the latest decision':[7] the judge acknowledges the benefits linked to the consideration of a precedent in terms of predictability; but should some reasons that justify a different solution occur, the previous decision may be modified, mitigated as well as even disregarded.[8]

---

[4] House of Lords, Practice Statement (Judicial Precedent) [1966] 1WLR 1234.

[5] Regarding the role of precedent in England, the existing body of literature is large. *See*, also for the literature cited therein, Whittaker 2007.

[6] *Payne v. Tennessee*, 501 U.S. 808, 827–8, 111 S.Ct. 2597, 2609.

[7] Idem.

[8] Idem. On the doctrine of precedent in the US, *see* Sellers 2007.

On the other hand, within continental countries the judge is no longer perceived as a mere 'executor of the law', which means that his jurisprudence increasingly transcends the limits set by the law itself. More than one reason explains a circumstance of this kind. First, in several civil law systems, court decisions enjoy formal recognition as a source of law. One may mention, for example, Article 1 of the Swiss Civil Code ('Application of the Law') which states as follows: '1. The law applies according to its wording or interpretation to all legal questions for which it contains a provision. 2. In the absence of a provision, the court shall decide in accordance with customary law and, in the absence of customary law, *in accordance with the rule that it would make as legislator*. 3. In doing so, *the court shall follow established doctrine and case law*.'[9] Needless to say, nothing hinders the judge from disregarding previous decisions, should it be right to do so. Second, even where precedent does not embody a formal source of law, the duty to take it into account (as well as the possibility of departing from it) has been tacitly or expressly recognized. This is the case of the Spanish Civil Code; its Article 1, para 6, expressly states that '[c]ase law shall complement the legal system by means of the doctrine repeatedly upheld by the Supreme Court in its interpretation and application of statutes, customs and general legal principles.'[10] In the same vein, one may consider the Italian legal system, where a series of legislative amendments to the Code of Civil Procedure has strengthened the internal consistency of the case law produced by the Supreme Court.[11] Last but not least, the French experience is significant insofar as 'there is a strong tendency on the part of the French courts [...] to follow precedents, especially those of the higher courts [...] The Court of Cassation can, of course, always overrule its own prior decisions. But it is equally certain that it will not do so without weighty reasons.'[12]

Now, notwithstanding the formal differences existing among common law and civil law countries, the way horizontal precedent ends up operating is basically the same and echoes what one may define 'taking into account' approach. This approach transcends the traditional dichotomy between binding and persuasive precedent and entails a *mid-level degree of bindingness*[13] that can be described in this fashion: the judge feels obliged to consider prior decisions, but may disregard them where there are sound reasons for doing so and provided that the arguments justifying such a disregarding be made explicit in the *rationes decidendi*.

[9] Emphasis added.

[10] *See* García Cantero 2007.

[11] *See* Cipriani 2009.

[12] David and De Vries 1958, p. 113.

[13] This expression must be credited to MacCormick and Summers 1997, p. 545. On the 'taking into account' approach, *see* also Krug 2006.

6.3 'Taking into Account' Approach and International Jurisdictions

As well as domestic jurisdictions, international courts and tribunals rely on the 'taking into account' approach when facing the question of horizontal precedent. To start with, the experience of the Caribbean Court of Justice (CCJ), an international court established by the Caribbean Community (CARICOM) with a view to adjudicating on breaches of the 2001 Revised Treaty of Chaguaramas (RTC), is of much assistance. This is because the court's adherence on precedent is not due to a judicial strategy, but rather to a treaty-mandate: Article 221 of the RTC (entitled 'Judgment of the Court to Constitute Stare Decisis') provides that '[j]udgments of the Court shall constitute legally binding precedents for parties in proceedings before the Court unless such judgments have been revised in accordance with Article 219.' Still, the way this provision is applied remains flexible and may be assimilated to the 'taking into account' approach. Suffice it to consider the view of Duke Pollard, former Justice of the Court:

> [Article 221] constitutes [...] an important innovation in traditional international law [...] By requiring the CCJ to apply the doctrine of *stare decisis* in arriving at judgments, however, competent decision-makers of CARICOM were concerned to ensure certainty in the applicable norms, stability of expectations on the part of economic actors and predictability of outcomes for investment decisions by investors. It is contemplated that the doctrine of *stare decisis* would be applied flexibly. In effect, competent decision-makers sought to ensure that the Court would promote dynamic stability in the applicable law and not espouse the petrification of relevant norms.[14]

Even in the absence of a provision like that scrutinized, international courts and tribunals end up resorting to a *de facto* horizontal precedent anyway. It is in this connection that the practice of the ICJ must be assessed. As is well known, Article 59 of the ICJ Statute states that '[t]he decision of the Court has no binding force except between the parties and in respect of that particular case.' On the other hand, however, Article 38, para 1(d), of the same Statute recognizes that the Court may apply judicial decisions as subsidiary means for the determination of the rule of law. These decisions include those of the ICJ itself, an argument which is clearly corroborated by the dissenting opinion appended by Judge Red to the decision in *Anglo-Iranian Oil Co.*[15] In his words, the expression 'judicial decisions' certainly includes the jurisprudence of the ICJ, that is to say 'the principles applied by the Court on the basis of its decisions.' Moving on from these premises, the question exists as to what role horizontal precedent plays in the ICJ system.

According to Antonio Cassese, even though the doctrine of *stare decisis* remains extraneous to the ICJ system, it is equally true that 'given the rudimentary character of international law, and the lack of both a central law-making body and a central judicial institution endowed with compulsory jurisdiction, [the Court's decisions]

---

[14] Pollard 2004, p. 97. In this regard, from a more general perspective, *see* Haynes 2014.

[15] *Anglo-Iranian Oil Co. case (Jurisdiction)*, Judgment of 22 July 1952, p. 93.

are bound to have crucial importance in establishing the existence of customary rules, or in defining their scope and content, or in promoting the evolution of new concepts.'[16] Philip Cahier, on the contrary, enhances the ICJ judicial activism going so far as to recognize the Court's power to act as a veritable legislator.[17] Finally, the dominant opinion must be considered, whereby the ICJ is inclined to follow its prior decision, but disregards them where reasons of substantive justice or the need to foster a proper development of the law makes it right to do so. In this last regard, one may mention Mohamed Shahabuddeen and his renowned book 'Precedent in the World Court'.[18] The view is offered therein, whereby

> [a] decision of the Court [...], which is relevant, cannot be ignored; the Court *has to take account of it* [...] In that sense, it seems permissible to say that it regards its decisions as authoritative. There are no less authoritative than are decisions of the House of Lords. The House also has a power to depart; in contrast with the Court, it has openly and repeatedly exercised the power; nevertheless, until and unless the power is exercised, a previous decision is regarded as authoritative. A similar position suggests itself in the case of the Court. With submission, the view is offered that *there is an acceptable sense in which, subject to a power to depart, decisions of the Court may be regarded as authoritative.*[19]

In this author's view, both the first and the second line of thought must be rejected: the first because it appraises the previous ICJ case law from too reductive a perspective, the second because it vests the Court with a power which the Court

[16] Cassese 2005, pp. 194–195.

[17] Cahier 1996.

[18] Shahabuddeen 1996.

[19] Idem, p. 239. (emphasis added) In the same vein one may consider Rosenne 2006, p. 1555: 'Corresponding to this is the care evinced by the Court not formally to overrule earlier decisions, but rather, where necessary, to try to explain away, usually on the ground of some factual particularity, an earlier decision which it feels unable to follow. The attitudes adopted in later decisions towards the 1959 decision in the *Aerial Incident* of 27 July 1955 illustrate this process, and the relativity of the requirement of consistency of jurisprudence.' Last, the remarks drawn by judge Tanaka in the separate opinion appended to *Barcelona Traction Light and Power Limited* (*Preliminary Objections*), Judgment of 24 July 1964, are of importance: 'I am well aware that some consideration should be given to the existence of precedents in regard to a case which the Court is called upon to decide. Respect for precedents and maintenance of the continuity of jurisprudence are without the slightest doubt highly desirable from the viewpoint of the certainty of law which is equally required in international law and municipal law. The same kind of cases must be decided in the same way and possibly by the same reasoning. This limitation is inherent in the judicial activities as distinct from purely academic activities. On the other hand, the requirement of the consistency of jurisprudence is never absolute. It cannot be maintained at the sacrifice of the requirements of justice and reason. The Court should not hesitate to overrule the precedents and should not be too occupied with the authority of its past decisions. The formal authority of the Court's decision must not be maintained to the detriment of its substantive authority. Therefore, it is quite inevitable that, from the point of view of the conclusion or reasoning, the minority in one case should become the majority in another case of the same kind within a comparatively short space of time.'

itself has always declared it does not possess.[20] Contrariwise, the opinion advanced by Mohamed Shahabuddeen, which clearly echoes the 'taking into account' approach, is the most adherent to the ICJ practice. The decision in *Land and Maritime Boundary between Cameroon and Nigeria*[21] is quite revealing in that respect. Its para 28 states:

> It is true that, in accordance with art. 59, the Court's judgments bind only the parties to and in respect of a particular case. There can be no question of holding Nigeria to decisions reached by the Court in previous cases. The real question is whether in this case, there is cause not to follow.

Likewise one must consider the 2015 decision in *Croatia v. Serbia.*[22] In effect, at para 125, the Court

> recalls that, in its Judgment of 26 February 2007 in the *Bosnia and Herzegovina v. Serbia and Montenegro* case, it considered certain issues similar to those before it in the present case. It will *take into account* that Judgment to the extent necessary for its legal reasoning here. This will not, however, preclude it, where necessary, from elaborating upon this jurisprudence, in light of the arguments of the Parties in the present case.[23]

Horizontal precedent understood in the above terms is resorted to also by the numerous specialized international courts and tribunals that are active in the international realm. First of all, this is true of international criminal tribunals. In *Aleksovski*, the Appeals Chamber of the International Criminal Tribunal for the former Yugoslavia (ICTY) expressed the following opinion:

> 107. [A] proper construction of the Statute, taking due account of its text and purpose, yields the conclusion that in the interests of certainty and predictability, the Appeals Chamber should follow its previous decisions, but should be free to depart from them for cogent reasons in the interests of justice.
>
> 108. Instances of situations where cogent reasons in the interest of justice require a departure from a previous decision include cases where the previous decision has been decided on the basis of a wrong legal principle or cases where previous decision has been given *per incuriam*, that is a judicial decision that has been 'wrongly decided, usually because the judge were ill-informed about the applicable law.[24]

In addition, the same principle has been provided for in the Statute of the ICC. Its Article 21, para 2, recognizes that the Court 'may apply principles and rules of law as interpreted in its previous decisions.'[25]

---

[20] One may mention the decision in *Fisheries Jurisdiction (United Kingdom v. Iceland) (Merits)*, Judgment of 25 July 1974. Its para 53 states that the Court 'as a court of law [...] cannot render judgment *sub specie legis ferendae* or anticipate the law before the legislator has laid it down.'

[21] *Land and Maritime Boundary between Cameroon and Nigeria (Cameroon v. Nigeria) (Preliminary Objections)*, Judgment of 11 June 1998.

[22] *Application of the Convention on the Prevention and Punishment of the Crime of Genocide (Croatia v. Serbia)*, Judgment of 3 February 2015.

[23] Emphasis added.

[24] *Prosecutor v. Aleksovski*, IT-95-14/1-A, Appeals Chamber, Judgment of 24 March 2000.

[25] In this regard, *see*, *inter alia*, Harris 2001; Shahabuddeen 1999, pp. 899 et seq.

The WTO judicial system is another international forum where horizontal precedent (intended along the lines of the 'taking into account' approach) is usually relied on. The most significant decision in this regard is that passed by the Appellate Body in *US—Stainless Steel.*[26] In this case, the question under scrutiny was dealt with as follows:

> Dispute settlement practice demonstrates that WTO Members attach significance to reasoning provided in previous panel and Appellate Body reports. Adopted panel and Appellate Body reports are often cited by parties in support of legal arguments in dispute settlement proceedings, and are relied upon by panels and the Appellate Body in subsequent disputes. In addition, when enacting or modifying laws and national regulations pertaining to international trade matters, WTO Members take into account the legal interpretation of the covered agreements developed in adopted panel and Appellate Body reports. Thus, the legal interpretation embodied in adopted panel and Appellate Body reports becomes part and parcel of the *acquis* of the WTO dispute settlement system. Ensuring 'security and predictability' in the dispute settlement system, as contemplated in Article 3.2 of the DSU [Dispute Settlement Understanding], implies that, absent cogent reasons, an adjudicatory body will resolve the same legal question in the same way in a subsequent case.[27]

Lastly, at European level, the practice of both the ECHtR and the CJUE are illustrative. With regard to the ECHtR, it is worth remembering that Article 46 of the European Convention, while providing that ECHtR judgments are binding on the parties, does not recognize formally any principle of precedent. As a matter of practice, however, the Court itself has always regarded its own decisions as the final authority on the interpretation of the Convention. In *Cossey* it was observed:

> It is true that [...] the Court is not bound by its previous judgments [...] However, it usually follows and applies its own precedents, such a course being in the interests of legal certainty and the orderly development of the Convention case-law. Nevertheless, this would not prevent the Court from departing from an earlier decision if it was persuaded that there were cogent reasons for doing so. Such a departure might, for example, be warranted in order to ensure that the interpretation of the Convention reflects societal changes and remains in line with present-day conditions.[28]

Turning to the CJEU and bearing in mind the wording of Article 288 of the Treaty on the Functioning of the European Union (TFEU), in this case too the principle is well established, whereby the Court does not apply a doctrine of *de jure* horizontal precedent. Such a circumstance may be explained 'by the drafters' desire

---

[26] WT/DS344/AB/R, Report of 30 April 2008

[27] Paragraph 160.

[28] *Cossey v. United Kingdom*, Decision of 27 September 1990, para 35. The same *cogent reasons* justifying a departure from previous case law are mentioned in *Stafford v. United Kingdom*, Judgment of 28 May 2002, paras 67–68: '[I]t is of crucial importance that the Convention is interpreted and applied in a manner which renders its rights practical and effective [...] A failure by the Court to maintain a dynamic and evolutive approach would risk rendering it a bar to reform or improvement.' In academic writing, *see* Wildhaber 2000, p. 1545: '[T]he existing case-law and the doctrine of precedent should be observed, except for compelling, serious and objective reasons.'

to progressively develop a new and autonomous legal order of the European Union without placing unnecessary restrictions on the CJEU's jurisdiction.'[29] Nevertheless, it is common ground that the Court 'should, as a matter of practice, follow its previous case law except where there are strong reasons for not doing so.'[30]

6.4 'Taking into Account' Approach and Investor-State Arbitration

The 'taking into account' approach has ended up penetrating investor-State arbitration as well.[31] Arguably, from the angle of this form of arbitration, the question of horizontal precedent should not arise at all: first, all ICSID tribunals are established with regard to a given case only and are not required, in principle, to act consistently with each other; second, their decisions are confidential and may be made public only with the consent of the parties. Nonetheless, these two circumstances are unsusceptible to prevent the rule of precedent from being relevant. On the one hand, these tribunals work under the auspices of the same 'international investment dispute institution that is permanent in terms of its infrastructure and secretariat [...]: ICSID [precisely]'.[32] On the other hand, the real problem behind the emergence of a doctrine of precedent is not how many decisions are in the public domain, but rather the quality of the argumentations founding them.[33] That said, in order to deal with the matter, the starting point is of course represented by the provisions of the Washington Convention referring to the effects of the awards.

Article 53, para 1, of the Convention states that awards rendered under it are 'binding on the parties and shall not be subject to any appeal or to any other remedy except those provided for in this Convention.' Moving on from this premise, and bearing in mind both the wording of some decisions[34] and the absence of any

---

[29] Haynes 2014, p. 518.

[30] *Merck et al v. Primecrown Ltd et al.*, Judgment of 5 December 1996.

[31] For some insightful remarks in this regard, *see* Zarra 2016, pp. 25 et seq.

[32] Diehl 2012, p. 183.

[33] Paulsson 2010, p. 710: 'In other words, the interesting inquiry is not whether precedents are norms in and of themselves (in the international field the debate may be cut short by answering with one word: 'no') but how they may contribute to the development of norms–generation as well as refinement.'

[34] One may mention, for example, *SGC v. Philippines*, ICSID Case No. ARB/02/6, Decision on Jurisdiction of 24 January 2004, para 97: 'The ICSID Convention provides only that awards rendered under it are 'binding on the parties' (Article 53(1)), a provision which might be regarded as directed to the *res judicata* effect of awards rather than their impact as precedents in later cases. In the tribunal's view, although different tribunals constituted under the ICSID system should in general seek to act consistently with each other, in the end it must be for each tribunal to exercise its competence in accordance with the applicable law, which will by definition be different for each BIT and each Respondent State. Moreover there is no doctrine of precedent in international law, if

indication in the preparatory works of the Convention, several commentators exclude the possibility of applying the rule of precedent to investor-State arbitration, making clear that previous decisions are to be viewed neither retrospectively or prospectively.[35] In the last few years, however, the question at stake has developed along two main phases.

The first phase is tied to the increasing use, since 2004, of the notion of *jurisprudence constante*, i.e. a long line of cases that apply a certain rule of law in a similar way and that, for their persuasiveness, may be considered as precedents in later cases. One may mention the awards in *SGS*[36] and *AES*[37] where the contribution of the ICSID case law to a 'common legal opinion' was recognized, as well as the attitude of this 'opinion' to resolve some of the most difficult legal issues

(Footnote 34 continued)

by precedent is meant a rule of the binding effect of a single decision. There is no hierarchy of international tribunals, and even if there were, there is no good reason for allowing the first tribunal in time to resolve issues for all later tribunals.' Likewise, the decision in *Joy Mining Machinery Limited v. Arab Republic of Egypt* (ICSID Case No. ARB/03/11, Award of 6 August 2004, para 80) is of interest: 'this tribunal is not called upon to sit in judgment on the views of other tribunals. It is only called to decide this dispute in light of its specific facts and the law.' Most recently, the same position has been taken in *Garanti Koza LLP v. Turkmenistan*, ICSID Case No. ARB/11/20, Award of 19 December 2016, para 149 ('The tribunal cites to the decisions of other tribunals in other investment treaty cases where such decisions help to explain a point, to clarify a concept of international law, or to illustrate how similar issues have been resolved in other cases, but the tribunal is not in any way bound by such decisions.'), but, as will be clarified hereinafter, in current judicial practice this rests an isolated position.

35 *See*, for example, Schreuer 2008, p. 1190: '[Article 53 (1) of the ICSID Convention] may be read as excluding the applicability of the principle of binding precedent to successive ICSID cases. Nothing in the Convention's *travaux préparatoires* suggests the doctrine of *stare decisis* should be applied to ICSID arbitration'.

36 *SGS v. Philippines*, ICSID Case No ARB/02/6, Decision on Jurisdiction of 29 January 2004, para 97: 'The ICSID Convention provides only that awards rendered under it are 'binding on the parties' (Article 53(1)), a provision which might be regarded as directed to the *res judicata* effect of awards rather than their impact as precedents in later cases. In the tribunal's view, although different tribunals constituted under the ICSID system should in general seek to act consistently with each other, in the end it must be for each tribunal to exercise its competence in accordance with the applicable law, which will by definition be different for each BIT and each respondent State. Moreover there is no doctrine of precedent in international law, if by precedent is meant a rule of the binding effect of a single decision. There is no hierarchy of international tribunals, and even if there were, there is no good reason for allowing the first tribunal in time to resolve issues for all later tribunals. It must be initially for the control mechanisms provided for under the BIT and the ICSID Convention, and in the longer term for the development of a common legal opinion or *jurisprudence constante*, to resolve the difficult legal questions discussed by the *SGS v. Pakistan* tribunal and also in the present decision.'

37 *AES v. Argentina*, ICSID Case No ARB/02/17, Decision on Jurisdiction of 17 June 2005, para 33: 'From a more general point of view, one can hardly deny that the institutional dimension of the control mechanisms provided for under the ICSID Convention might well be a factor, in the longer term, for contributing to the development of a common legal opinion or *jurisprudence constante*, to resolve some difficult legal issues discussed in many cases, inasmuch as these issues share the same substantial features.'

handled in many cases. Despite the absence of any further explanations in the decisions in question, Gabrielle Kaufmann-Kohler argues that such a jurisprudence should be interpreted in the sense that where a consistent line of decisions exists, arbitral tribunals would be under a veritable duty to follow it.[38]

Still, the impression one gets is that the 'taking into account' approach has established itself over the years (phase II). First of all, reference is made to those decisions whereby, despite the absence in the Convention of Washington of a formal obligation of *stare decisis*, it is a reasonable assumption that 'international arbitral tribunals, notably those established within the ICSID system, will generally take account of the precedents established by other arbitration organs.'[39] This kind of reasoning has been further specified in a series of decisions. The *Suez/AWG* tribunal, for example, made the point clear that

> considerations of basic justice would lead tribunals to be guided by the basic judicial principle that 'like cases should be decided alike', unless a strong reason exists to distinguish the current case from previous ones [...] *Thus, absent cogent reasons to the contrary, a tribunal should always consider heavily solutions established in a series of consistent cases.*[40]

In other words, also in the presence of a consistent line of decisions, what the judge is required to do is only to consider, rather than to follow, it.

[38] Kaufmann-Kohler 2006, p. 377: 'This would actually be a *stare decisis* doctrine applied not to a single decision, but to a line of cases, or a *jurisprudence constante.*' A similar argument was advanced by Thomas Wälde in the separate opinion appended to *International Thunderbird Gaming Corporation v. Mexico*, UNCITRAL (NAFTA) Arbitration Proceedings, Award, 26 January 2006: 'While individual arbitral awards by themselves do not as yet constitute a binding precedent, a consistent line of reasoning developing a principle and a particular interpretation of specific treaty obligations should be respected; if an authoritative jurisprudence evolves, it will acquire the character of customary international law and must be respected. A deviation from well and firmly established jurisprudence requires an extensively reasoned justification. This approach will help to avoid the wide divergences that characterises some investment arbitral awards—not subject to a common and unifying appeals' authority. Otherwise, there is the risk of discrediting the health of the system of international investment arbitration which has been set up as one of the major new tools in improving good governance in the global economy.'

[39] *El Paso Energy International Co. v. Argentina*, ICSID Case No. ARB/03/15, Decision on Jurisdiction of 27 April 2006, para 39.

[40] *Suez et al.* and *AWG Group v. Argentina*, ICSID Case No. ARB/03/19, Decision on Liability of 30 July 2010, para 189 (emphasis added). In the same vein, *see Saipem S.p.a. v. Bangladesh*, ICSID Case No. ARB/05/07, Decision on Jurisdiction and Recommendation on Provisional Measure of 21 March 2007, para 67, and most recently *Renée Rose Levy and Gremcitel S.A. v. Republic of Peru*, ICSID Case No. ARB/11/17, Award of 9 January 2015, para 76, and *Churchill Mining PLC and Planet Mining Pty Ltd v. Indonesia*, ICSID Case No. ARB/12/14 and 12/40, Award of 6 December 2016, para 253.

6.4.1 'Taking into Account' Approach and FET

Unquestionably, most decisions discussing the question of precedent in international investment law do so through the lens of FET. Hence, it is not a coincidence that the 'taking into account' approach is precisely that used by arbitral tribunals with a view to shaping all the main elements falling under this standard, viz. due process of law, legitimate expectations, and proportionality. One may consider, for example, legitimate expectations, the protection of which is regarded as the most important function of FET. In this regard, and once again, the *Suez/AWG* decision provides assistance: the tribunal observed that in interpreting such a vague and flexible standard as FET, it had 'the benefit of decisions by prior tribunals that have struggled strenuously, knowledgeably, and sometimes painfully, to interpret the words 'fair and equitable' in a wide variety of factual situations and investment relationships.'[41] On this assumption, the original case law approach to expectation by legislation was taken into account, but replaced with the so-called 'by induction' model. And indeed: sound reasons existed that suggested doing so.[42]

Some commentators do not welcome arbitral tribunals' reliance on previous decisions for the FET content to be tackled; in their view, an approach of this kind would be incompatible 'with the framework of international law-making which requires demonstrating the content of legal norms from the evidence of the agreements between States.'[43] A similar argument, on the other hand, has been advanced with regard to investment arbitration more generally; from this angle, cementing judicial practice into a doctrine of precedent is supposed to be potentially harmful in terms of transparency, since it ends up 'concealing the extent of disagreement among adjudicators or [...] masking the motivating reasons for decisions.'[44] But in our view this is a price worth paying, especially due to the flexibility of the approach followed by arbitral tribunals in this matter: 'a recognized goal of international investment law is to establish a predictable, stable legal framework for investments, a factor that justifies tribunals in giving due regard to previous decisions on similar issues'.[45] This is even more so in the case where FET, i.e. the *Grundnorm* of international investment law, is concerned.

---

[41] *Supra* note 40, para 189.

[42] Idem, para 226. On the role played by case law in the shaping of FET, *see* McLachlan 2008, p. 375.

[43] This is the opinion of Orakhelashvili 2008, 104: 'The use of previous decisions, which on their part fall short of identifying the intrinsic content of 'fair and equitable treatment', to deal with the 'fair and equitable treatment' standard with no defined content, as if it had is in fact an attempt to compensate for the absence of evidence of such defined content.'

[44] Ten Cate 2013, 423. *See* also Schultz 2014.

[45] *Supra* note 41, para 189.

6.4.2 'Taking into Account' Approach and Annulment Committees Decisions

What has been observed thus far is equally true in the case where an annulment committee, established pursuant to Article 52 of the Washington Convention,[46] is called upon to exercise its jurisdiction. Of course, these committees' decisions, while being vested with a particular authority which depends on their composition,[47] serve the limited role to assess the legitimacy of a given award and not its correctness: 'the ICSID Convention is alien to the idea of creating a hierarchical system of 'appellate' control over the arbitral tribunals.'[48] In this light, the *MCI* annulment committee took the position whereby

> [t]he annulment mechanism is not designed to bring about consistency in the interpretation and application of international investment law. The responsibility for ensuring consistency in the jurisprudence and for building a coherent body of law rests primarily with the investment tribunals. They are assisted in their task by the development of a common legal opinion and the progressive emergence of '*une jurisprudence constante*.'[49]

Notwithstanding this, the same committee considered it appropriate

> *to take [previous] decisions into consideration*, because their reasoning and conclusions may provide guidance to the committee in settling similar issues arising in these annulment proceedings and help to ensure consistency and legal certainty of the ICSID annulment mechanism, thereby contributing to ensuring trust in the ICSID dispute settlement system and predictability for governments and investors.[50]

---

[46] This Article states as follows: '1. Either party may request annulment of the award by an application in writing addressed to the Secretary-General on one or more of the following grounds: (a) that the tribunal was not properly constituted; (b) that the tribunal has manifestly exceeded its powers; (c) that there was corruption on the part of a member of the tribunal; (d) that there has been a serious departure from a fundamental rule of procedure; or (e) that the award has failed to state the reasons on which it is based.'

[47] Paragraph 3 of Article 52 establishes: 'On receipt of the request the Chairman shall forthwith appoint from the Panel of Arbitrators an *ad hoc* committee of three persons. None of the members of the committee shall have been a member of the tribunal which rendered the award, shall be of the same nationality as any such member, shall be a national of the State party to the dispute or of the State whose national is a party to the dispute, shall have been designated to the Panel of Arbitrators by either of those States, or shall have acted as a conciliator in the same dispute. The committee shall have the authority to annul the award or any part thereof on any of the grounds set forth in para (1).'

[48] De Brabandere 2012, p. 278.

[49] *MCI Power Group L.C. and New Turbine Inc. v. Ecuador*, ICSID Case No. ARB/03/6, Decision on Annulment of 19 October 2009, para 24.

[50] Idem, para 25.

A similar argument may be found in *Enron*,[51] *Impregilo*[52] and *Kiliç*[53] as well as in academic writing,[54] and corroborates the idea whereby, at least on the horizontal level (i.e. in the relationship between annulment committees), a previous committee's decision demands a careful consideration, but may be disregarded where there are sound reasons to do so.

6.4.3 The Interference Between ICSID and UNCITRAL Case Law

A last question needs to be assessed and regards the terms in which ICSID and UNCITRAL case law interact with each other; this is because also UNCITRAL tribunals have contributed to the shaping of the FET content.

As a rule, a question like this should fall under the issue of 'external precedent': a court relies on the decisions of tribunals operating under a different legal order or regime with a view to determining the scope of a certain rule of law. This is a hypothesis which occurs in the relationship between national courts of different countries as well as different international courts,[55] and describes what academic writing has long indicated with the term of art '*cross-fertilization*'.[56] Yet the judicial practice analysed thus far makes the point clear that ICSID and UNCITRAL tribunals feel part of the same dispute settlement system and act

[51] *Enron Creditors Recovery Corp. Ponderosa Assets L.P. v. Argentina*, ICSID Case No. ARB/01/3, Decision on the Application for Annulment of the Argentine Republic of 30 July 2010, para 66: '[I]n relation to matters which fall within the competence of an *ad hoc* committee to decide, it is in the committee's view to be expected that the *ad hoc* committee will have regard to relevant previous ICSID awards and decisions, including other annulment decisions, as well as to other relevant persuasive authorities.'

[52] *Impregilo S.P.A. v. Argentina*, ICSID Case No. ARB/07/17, Decision of the *Ad Hoc* committee on the Application for Annulment of 24 January 2014, para 2: 'The committee [...] *may take into account* the reasoning and findings of other committees on annulment' (emphasis added).

[53] *Kiliç İnşaat İthalat İhracat Sanayi Ve Ticaret Anonim Şirketi v. Turkmenistan*, ICSID Case No. ARB/10/1, Decision on Annulment of 14 July 2015, para 49: 'While the present committee is not bound to use the same criteria as previous committees, it will *consider and take into account* for its own decisions reasoning used by previous committees regarding the relevant issues' (emphasis added).

[54] Sacerdoti (2011, pp. 18–19), for example, points out that these committees 'have no formal authority for setting precedent for different future disputes, their authority being limited to annul the ward submitted to them for the specific ground listed in Article 52. However, in respect of the interpretation of [the] grounds for annulment, an issue which is always raised before them and which only these committees are competent to decide upon, consistent jurisprudence should be expected.'

[55] As observed by Guillaume 2011, p. 19 '[n]umerous examples could be given of cases in which various judges and arbitrators have to apply the same law in a specific sector. In such cases, they of course have no obligation to follow decisions adopted by other judges or arbitrators.'

[56] In this regard, *see* Palombino 2008, pp. 10 et seq., footnotes.

accordingly. In other words, where an ICSID (or UNCITRAL) tribunal resorts to an UNCITRAL (or ICSID) decision, it does so regarding that decision as an internal precedent. On the other hand, it is not uncommon that a dispute be administered by an ICSID tribunal, but under the UNCITRAL rules.[57]

Perhaps the notion of 'external precedent' may be used with regard to the decisions passed, for example, by the ICJ[58] or the ECHtR, and that are relied on in investor-State arbitration by way of example: an example the only function of which, in the words of Michele Taruffo, is to show that a given rule of law has been applied in a certain way in a certain case; hence, the 'example' limits itself to informing the judge, but does not require that subsequent decisions take it into account.[59] Both the *Mondev*[60] and *Tecmed*[61] decisions, and their reliance on the ECHtR case law in matters of immunity and proportionality, clearly illustrate the above dynamic.

6.5 Conclusion

To conclude, the FET content has been shaped by means of a jurisprudence that has rendered its essential elements stable. The way precedent operates in investor-State arbitration echoes what has been called 'taking into account' approach, which means that the arbitrator is obliged to consider previous decisions, but may disregard them where there are sound reasons to do so. Of course an approach of this kind risks compromising the 'transparency' of the decisions' reasoning. But this is a

---

[57] See Chap. 1, footnote 54.

[58] From this perspective, the remarks drawn by Hirsch 2014, pp. 161 et seq., appear somewhat curious: '*On the vertical level*, investment tribunals are formally not subject to the authority of the ICJ [...] In reality, however, investment tribunals behave quite similarly to tribunals operating in hierarchical systems and mostly subject to the de facto authority of the ICJ. Investment tribunals frequently cite decisions of the ICJ as authoritative statements of existing international legal rules [...] The exceptionally influential role of the ICJ is also noticeable in empirical studies revealing that investments tribunals often cite decisions of the ICJ as a proof of the existence of international customary law.' Yet, also from a *de facto* perspective, the relationship between ICJ and investment tribunals has nothing to do with the rule of vertical precedent, a rule which necessarily presupposes a hierarchical structure between tribunals; accordingly, reliance on the Taruffo's category of 'example' proves much more suitable to explain the phenomenon under consideration. With regard to the relevance of ICJ case law in investment arbitration, *see* Pellet 2013.

[59] Taruffo 2007a, p. 32. Quite the opposite, Guillaume 2011, pp. 5, 19, points out that also in this case judges are required to consider previous 'decisions—either to follow or distinguish them—while justifying their choice.'

[60] *Mondev International Ltd. v. United States*, ICSID Case No. ARB (AF)/99/2, Award of 11 October 2002, paras 141 et seq.

[61] *Técnicas Medioambiente Tecmed S.A. c. Mexico*, ICSID Case No. ARB (AF)/00/2, Award of 29 May 2003, paras 122 et seq.

risk worth taking in order to guarantee a predictable legal framework for investments: a framework within which FET has played and continues to play a crucial role.

References

Cahier P (1996) Le rôle du juge dans l'élaboration du droit international. In: Makarczyk J (ed) Theory of International Law at the Threshold of the 21st Century: Essays in Honour of Krzystof Skubiszecki. Kluwer Law International, The Hague, pp. 353–365

Cassese A (2005) International Law, 2nd edn. Oxford University Press, Oxford

Cipriani F (2009) La riforma del giudizio di Cassazione. Cedam, Padua

David R, de Vries HP (1958) The French Legal System: An Introduction to Civil Law. Oceana, New York

De Brabandere E (2012) Arbitral Decisions as a Source of International Investment Law. In: Gazzini T, De Brabandere E (eds) International Investment Law. The Sources of Rights and Obligations. Nijhoff, Leiden, pp. 245–288

Diehl A (2012) The Core Standard of International Investment Protection. Fair and Equitable Treatment. Kluwer Law International, Alphen aan den Rijn

García Cantero G (2007) Le précédent et la loi. In: Hondius E (ed) Precedent and the Law. Bruylant, Brussels, pp. 189–207

Guillaume G (2011) The Use of Precedent by International Judges and Arbitrators. Journal of International Dispute Settlement 2:5–23

Harris C (2001) Precedent in the Practice of the ICTY. In: May R et al (eds) Essays on ICTY Procedure and Evidence in Honour of Gabrielle Kirk McDonald. Kluwer Law International, The Hague, pp. 341–356

Haynes J (2014) The Emergence of a Doctrine of *De Jure Horizontal Stare Decisis* at the Caribbean Court of Justice: Fragmentation or Pluralism of International Law? Journal of International Dispute Settlement 5:498–530

Hirsch M (2014) The Sociology of International Law. In: Douglas Z, Pauwelyn J, Viñuales JE (eds) The Foundations of International Investment Law: Bringing Theory into Practice. Oxford University Press, Oxford, pp. 143–167

Kaufmann-Kohler G (2006) Arbitral Precedent: Dream, Necessity or Excuse? Arbitration International 23:357–378

Krug P (2006) Internalizing European Court of Human Rights Interpretations: Russia's Courts of General Jurisdiction and New Directions in Civil Defamation Law. Brooklyn Journal of International Law 32:1–65

MacCormick DN, Summers RS (1997) Further General Reflections and Conclusions. In: MacCormick DN, Summers RS (eds) Interpreting Precedents: A Comparative Study. Ashgate, Dartmouth, pp. 531–545

McLachlan QC C (2008) Investment Treaties and General International Law. International and Comparative Law Quarterly 57:361–401

Orakhelashvili A (2008) The Normative Basis of 'Fair and Equitable Treatment': General International Law on Foreign Investment? Archiv des Völkerrechts 46:74–105

Palombino FM (2008) Gli effetti della sentenza internazionale nei giudizi interni. Editoriale Scientifica, Naples

Paulsson J (2010) The Role of Precedent in Investment Arbitration. In: Yannaca-Small K (ed) Arbitration under International Investment Agreements. A Guide to Key Issues. Oxford University Press, Oxford, pp. 699–718

Pellet A (2013) The Case Law of the ICJ in Investment Arbitration. ICSID Review 28:223–240

Pollard D (2004) The Caribbean Court of Justice: Closing the Circle of Independence. The Caribbean Law Publishing Company Ltd, Kingston
Rosenne S (2006) The Law and Practice of the International Court. Nijhoff, Leiden
Sacerdoti G (2011) Precedent in the Settlement of International Economic Disputes: The WTO and Investment Arbitration Models. Bocconi Legal Studies Research Paper No. 1931560. Available at http://ssrn.com/abstract=1931560
Schreurer C (2008) A Doctrine of Precedent? In: Muchlinski P, Ortino F, Schreurer C (eds) The Oxford Handbook of International Investment Law. Oxford University Press, Oxford, pp. 1188–1206
Schultz T (2014) Against Consistency in Investment Arbitration. In: Douglas Z, Pauwelyn J, Viñuales JE (eds) The Foundations of International Investment Law: Bringing Theory into Practice. Oxford University Press, Oxford, pp. 297–316
Sellers MNS (2007) The Doctrine of Precedent in the United States of America. In: Hondius E (ed) Precedent and the Law. Bruylant, Brussels, pp. 111–135
Shahabuddeen M (1996) Precedent in the World Court. Cambridge University Press, Cambridge
Shahabuddeen M (1999) Consistency in the Case Law of the ICTY. In: Venturini G, Bariatti S (eds) Liber Fausto Pocar, vol. I. Giuffrè, Milan, pp. 899–911
Taruffo M (2007a) Precedente e giurisprudenza. Editoriale Scientifica, Naples
Taruffo M (2007b) Precedents in Italy. In: Hondius E (ed) Precedent and the Law. Bruylant, Brussels, pp. 177–188
Ten Cate IM (2013) The Costs of Consistency: Precedent in Investment Treaty Arbitration. Columbia Journal of Transnational Law 51:418–478
Whittaker S (2007) Precedent in English Law: A View from the Citadel. In: Hondius E (ed) Precedent and the Law. Bruylant, Brussels, pp. 27–73
Wildhaber L (2000) Precedent in the European Court of Human Rights. In: Mahoney P, Matscher F, Petzold H (eds) Protecting Human Rights: the European Perspective: Studies in Memory of Rolv Ryssdal. Carl Heymann, Cologne, pp. 1529–154
Zarra G (2016) Parallel Proceedings in Investment Arbitration. Giappichelli/Eleven, Turin/The Hague

Chapter 7
Conclusion

Contents

Abstract This chapter discusses the main results of the inquiry, reiterating both the normative basis and the content (in terms of its minimum reach) of FET. Moreover, some concise and final thoughts are given to the relevance of FET within the never-ending debate over the fragmentation of international law as a result of the existence of self-contained regimes.

Keywords *Grundnorm* · Definition · Fragmentation · Self-contained regime · Symbiosis · General international law

No doubt the obligation of the host State to accord fair and equitable treatment to foreign investments embodies the *Grundnorm* of international investment law, but its open-texture nature does not help tackle its normative basis, nor its content. The investigation carried out thus far has tried to shed new light on both of them. As to the FET normative basis, the view has been offered in this book whereby the standard under consideration has penetrated into the fabric of general international law, but by means of a source somewhat neglected in legal doctrine. This is the category of general principles peculiar to a certain field of international law, i.e. those principles that have their own foundations in the international legal order itself, but which, through the mediation of the judge, end up being shaped according to the features typical of a specific normative field (Chap. 2). An argument of this kind has proved convenient from more than one angle. First, it makes it possible to overcome any difficulties closely related to the alleged existence of a custom or a general principle common to domestic systems, and which mainly depend on the lack of the traditional requirements necessary to this end. Second, it

F.M. Palombino, *Fair and Equitable Treatment and the Fabric of General Principles*, https://doi.org/10.1007/978-94-6265-210-1_7

is the argument that provides most insight into the current FET content, the minimal and essential elements of which include (i) due process of law (Chap. 3), (ii) legitimate expectations (Chap. 4), and (iii) proportionality (Chap. 5).

Going further into detail, it seems clear enough that all the main FET elements have been forged through the lens of the same 'unifying' factor: the need to balance the State power to regulate in the public interest and the investor's concern about having his investment protected other than from prejudice which is part of normal business risk. Bearing this in mind, due process has been seen in terms of denial of justice and fairness in administrative proceedings. *In terms of denial of justice*, what counts for the State responsibility to be ascertained is not the absence of a decent system of justice, but rather a judicial misinterpretation or misapplication of national law which proves 'manifestly unjust'; whoever decides to invest part of his capital in a foreign country does so in the wake of the whole regulatory framework existing in that country, therefore having regard not only to the rules that make the investment convenient, but also to those governing the judicial system and which may be relevant when a dispute between the investor and the host State arises. *In terms of fairness in administrative proceedings*, due process requires the host State to ensure the investor's participation in these proceedings, should the challenged measure cause a serious economic loss.

Legitimate expectations, as an additional FET element, are generated by three types of State conduct: contractual commitment, unilateral promise, and legislation. The first form of legitimate expectations occurs when the breach of a contract by the host State is combined with a reference to other elements, for example the fact that the State changes the course of conduct in the fulfillment of its contractual commitments. Expectations by unilateral promise demand safeguarding, under the requirement that promise be given intentionally by an administrative authority which is entitled to do so. Finally, expectations by legislation postulates the occurrence of a qualified conduct of the legislator, that is to say a normative act put in place with the specific aim of inducing foreign investments and on which the foreign investor relied in making his investment (the so-called 'expectation by induction').

Proportionality consists of a normative content which proves both 'fixed' and 'flexible'. Its fixed part crosscuts any fields of the international legal order and entails a three-step analysis: suitability, necessity and proportionality *stricto sensu*; the flexible part, contrariwise, allows the judge to give to the principle a concrete content which usually changes depending on the substantive field where it is resorted to and, *a fortiori*, the different assessment of each of the aforementioned parameters. This is equally true as far as international investment law is concerned, which means, once again, that context matters. From this angle, the balancing process that proportionality involves as an FET element always takes into account certain circumstances which mainly rest on the business risk taken by the investor on the one hand and the kind of prejudice the investment may suffer on the other hand.

With respect to each of the elements discussed above, this book has also pointed out the driving role played by case law (Chap. 6). It has been argued that the approach followed in investor-State arbitration for the FET content to be pinpointed transcends the traditional dichotomy between binding and persuasive precedent. Rather, it echoes the so-called 'taking into account' approach, which means that the arbitrator is obliged to consider previous decisions, but may disregard them where there are sound reasons for doing so. In these terms, one is facing a technique that is somewhat different from that consisting of overruling prior decisions, because its very foundation proves dissimilar: the duty it presupposes is *procedural* in nature, insofar as what the judge is required to do is not to follow a precedent, but to take it into account. This is not only a terminological question but the acceptance of the perspective whereby (i) it is more important to have a right decision than a decision consistent with previous cases and (ii) the rule of precedent is by now sufficiently flexible to accommodate this need.

To conclude, and even though an in-depth analysis of this subject lies outside the scope of the present book, some concise and final thoughts may be given to the relevance of FET within the never-ending debate over the fragmentation of international law as a result of the existence of self-contained regimes.

As is well known, the topic is so controversial as to have been an object of study for the ILC.[1] Yet a significant terminological confusion still exists. And the fact that the very concept of self-contained regime may be understood in different ways is evidence of this. More squarely, if considered from a narrow perspective, the term denotes 'a special set of secondary rules under the law of State responsibility that claims primacy to the general rules concerning consequences of a violation.'[2] Alternatively, in a sense which may be called 'intermediate', self-contained regimes are supposed to consist of 'interrelated wholes of primary and secondary rules [...] that cover some particular problem differently from the way it would be covered under general law.' Seen in this way, 'self-containedness fuses with international law's contractual bias: where a matter is regulated by a treaty, there is normally no reason to have recourse to other sources.'[3] Lastly, in the broadest sense, the notion here scrutinized alludes to the existence of entire fields of international law being 'special' in nature, which means that 'rules of general international law are assumed

[1] *See* ILC, Fifty-eight session, *Fragmentation of International Law: Difficulties Arising from the Diversification and Expansion of International Law*, Report of the Study Group of the International Law Commission finalized by Martti Koskenniemi, A/CN.4/L.682, 13 April 2006. Paragraph 8 of the Report (at 11) refers to investment law in the following terms: 'The fragmentation of the international social world has attained legal significance especially as it has been accompanied by the emergence of specialized and (relatively) autonomous rules or rules-complexes, legal institutions and spheres of legal practice. What one appeared to be governed by 'general international law' has become the field of operation for such specialist system as [...] 'investment law' [...] each possessing their own principles and institutions.' For a view that tends to underestimate the question of fragmentation in international law, *see* Conforti 2007.

[2] Idem, p. 68.

[3] Idem.

to be […] excluded in their administration.'[4] The last mentioned notion is that commonly used by some scholars, like Stephan Schill[5] and Jeswald W. Salacuse,[6] with a view to describing investment law. Accordingly, it is argued that both the large number of investment treaties and the case law under them would led to the creation of a veritable regime in the strongest sense.

Yet, on closer inspection, there is much evidence to support the contrary. Already in the first ICSID treaty arbitration, for example, the position was taken whereby

> a BIT is not a self-contained closed legal system limited to provide for substantive material rules of direct applicability, but it has to be envisaged within a wider juridical context in which rules from other sources are integrated though implied incorporation methods, or by direct reference to certain supplementary rules, whether of international law character or of domestic law nature.[7]

---

[4] Idem, p. 68. For a critical evaluation of these notions, *see, inter alia*, Gradoni 2009, p. 20, and Di Benedetto 2013, p. 24.

[5] Schill 2009, pp. 280–281: 'Taken together, investment treaty arbitration thus operate as part of an autopoietic, self-referential, and normatively closed system of law, that overarches the myriad number of bilateral investment treaty relations, unites them under common principles governing international investment relations and contributes to providing a legal framework for the functioning of the global economic system.'

[6] Salacuse 2010, pp. 435–436: 'The use of regime theory as a lens to examine the mass of investment treaties negotiated over the last sixty years would seem to have several potential advantages. First, it offers an analytical framework to understand and capture the essential, common elements of the 3000 legally separate and distinct treaties and to understand the systemic nature of what States have created through the treaty making process. Second, it may enable observers and scholars to better understand the dynamics of the relationships established by these treaties among States and between States and foreign investors […] Third, regime theory may make more visible the political nature and dimensions of these treaties, for political issues are often at the hearth of investment relationships between States and are also deeply imbedded in investor-State disputes, regardless of their applicable legal superstructures […] And finally, one might also suggest that while lawyers and arbitrators do not normally use the term 'regime' in referring to investment treaties, they implicitly treat investment treaties as constituting a regime in that they regularly refer to prior decisions applying one treaty in order to interpret a wholly separate treaty. Regime analysis may make explicit what has heretofore been implicit.'

[7] *Asian Agricultural Products Ltd v. Sri Lanka*, ICSID Case No. ARB/87/3, Award of 21 June 1990, para 21. The same opinion has been expressed more generally by Judge Greenwood in the Declaration appended to the *Diallo* case (*Republic of Guinea v. Congo*) (*Compensation*) Judgment of 19 June 2012. Para 8 of the Declaration states as follows: 'International law is not a series of fragmented specialist and self-contained bodies of law, each of which functions in isolation from the others; it is a single, unified system of law and each international court can, and should, draw on the jurisprudence of other international courts and tribunals, even though it is not bound necessarily to come to the same conclusions.' On the concept of unity in international law, *see* Prost 2012.

Over the years this approach has been constantly followed by arbitral tribunals;[8] suffice it to consider the widespread use of general international law for the existence of a wrongful act to be ascertained.[9]

Bearing this in mind, Campbell McLachlan QC regards the relationship between the substantive standards protected in BITs and general international law as symbiotic: 'the content of the treaty obligation may be informed by general international law. In turn, the promulgation of the treaty obligation, and its application by arbitral tribunals, may inform the progressive development of general international law.'[10] An assumption like this may firstly be coupled with the theory that perceives international investment law as a subsystem of international law with its own peculiarities, but operating nonetheless within the realm of general international law;[11] secondly, it is, of course, shareable in the present book's perspective for a reason which is not hard to grasp.

FET has been shaped by arbitral tribunals, moving on from general principles of international law[12] and giving to them a content considered the most fitting in respect of international investment law; as a result, it has created a sort of bridge between the international legal order, which through this standard implants its own principles into international investment law, and this latter, the *specificity* of which is guaranteed by the way those principles end up being applied by the judge. In a nutshell, FET, while embodying at this point in time a principle specific to international investment law, *a fortiori* is nothing but a source *tout court* of a unified international legal order.

References

Conforti B (2007) Unité et fragmentation du droit international: 'Glissez, mortels, n'appuyez pas!' Revue générale de droit international public 111:5–18

Di Benedetto S (2013) International Investment Law and the Environment. Edward Elgar, Cheltenham

---

[8] One good example is *Phonix Action v. Czech Republic*, ICSID Case No. ARB/06/5, Award of 15 April 2009, para 78. '[T]he ICSID Convention's jurisdictional requirement cannot be read in isolation from public international law, and its general principles. To take an extreme example, nobody suggests that ICSID protection should be granted to investments made in violation of the most fundamental rules of protection of human rights, like investments made in pursuance of torture or genocide or in support of slavery or trafficking of human organs.'

[9] *See*, for example, Di Benedetto 2013, pp. 158 et seq.

[10] McLachlan 2008, p. 364.

[11] Some insightful observations in this regard may be found in Savarese 2012, p. 230 and Di Benedetto 2013, p. 22. More generally, on the topic under consideration here and also for the literature cited therein, *see* Sourgens 2014.

[12] In the words of McLachlan 2008, p. 374, 'the *term* ['FET'] is undoubtedly the product of the bilateral investment treaty process, adopting consciously new language to what had gone before. But its *function* has, from the start, been linked to the pre-existing general international law.'

Gradoni L (2009) *Regime Failure* nel diritto internazionale. Cedam, Padua
McLachlan QC C (2008) Investment Treaties and General International Law. International and Comparative Law Quarterly 57:361–401
Prost M (2012) The Concept of Unity in Public International Law. Hart, Oxford
Salacuse JW (2010) The Emerging Global Regime for Investment. Harvard International Law Journal 51:427–473
Savarese E (2012) La nozione di giurisdizione nel sistema ICSID. Editoriale Scientifica, Naples
Schill S (2009) The Multilateralization of International Investment Law. Cambridge University Press, Cambridge
Sourgens FG (2014) Law's Laboratory: Developing International Law on Investment Protection as Common Law. Northwestern Journal of International Law & Business 34:181–247

Table of Cases

Permanent Court of International Justice

Oscar Chinn (*United Kingdom v. Belgium*), Judgment of 12 December 1934

International Court of Justice

Corfu Channel (*Great Britain v. Albania*), Judgment of 9 April 1949
Anglo-Iranian Oil Co (*United Kingdom v. Iran*) (*Jurisdiction*), Judgment of 22 July 1952
Nationals of the United States of America in Morocco (*France v. United States*), Judgment of 27 August 1952
Barcelona Traction (*Belgium v. Spain*) (*Preliminary Objections*), Judgment of 24 July 1964
North Sea Continental Shelf (*Germany v. Denmark*; *Germany v. Netherlands*) Judgment of 20 February 1969
Barcelona Traction (*Belgium v. Spain*), Judgment of 5 February 1970
Fisheries Jurisdiction (*United Kingdom v. Iceland*) (*Merits*), Judgment of 25 July 1974
Nuclear Tests (*Australia v. France*), Judgment of 20 December 1974
Nuclear Tests (*New Zealand v. France*), Judgment of 20 December 1974
Continental Shelf (*Tunisia v. Libya*) (*Merits*), Judgment of 24 February 1982
Military and Paramilitary Activities in and against Nicaragua (*Nicaragua v. United States*), Judgment of 27 June 1986
Frontier Dispute (*Burkina Faso v. Mali*), Judgment of 22 December 1986
ELSI Sicula (United States v. Italy), Judgment of 20 July 1989
Oil Platforms (*Iran v. United Sates*), Judgment of 12 December 1996
Land and Maritime Boundary between Cameroon and Nigeria (Cameroon v. Nigeria) (*Preliminary Objections*), Judgment of 11 June 1998

F.M. Palombino, *Fair and Equitable Treatment and the Fabric of General Principles*, https://doi.org/10.1007/978-94-6265-210-1

Application of the Convention on the Prevention and the Punishment of the Crime of Genocide (*Bosnia and Herzegovina v. Serbia and Montenegro*), Judgment of 26 February 2007
Diallo (*Guinea v. Congo*) (*Preliminary Objections*), Judgment of 24 May 2007
Diallo (*Guinea v. Congo*) (*Compensation*), Judgment of 19 June 2012
Jurisdictional Immunities of the State (Germany v. Italy: Greece intervening), Judgment of 3 February 2012
Application of the Convention on the Prevention and Punishment of the Crime of Genocide (*Croatia v. Serbia*), Judgment of 3 February 2015

International Tribunal for the Law of the Sea

Juno Trader (*San Vincent and the Grenadines v.Guinea-Bissau*), Judgment of 18 December 2004

International Labour Organization Administrative Tribunal

Judgment of 27 June 1989, No. 962.

WTO Judicial Organs—Appellate Body

Korea Beef, Report of 11 December 2000
US—Stainless Steel, Report of 30 April 2008

Court of Justice of the European Union

Algera et al. v. Common Assembly, Judgment of 12 July 1957
Transocean Marin Paint Association v. Commission, Judgment of 23 October 1974
Les Verts v. Parliament, Judgment of 23 April 1986
The Queen v. Minister of Agriculture, Fisheries and Food and Secretary of State for Health, ex parte Fedesa, Judgment of 13 November 1990
Merck et al. v. Primecrown Ltd et al., Judgment of 5 December 1996
David Charles Hayes and Jeannette Karen Hayes v. Kronenberger GmbH, Judgment of 20 March 1997

Court of First Instance of the European Union

Lisrestal et al. v. Commission, Judgment of 6 December 1994
Opel Austria v. Council, Judgment of 22 January 1997

European Court of Human Rights

James et al. v. United Kingdom, Judgment of 21 February 1986
Cossey v. United Kingdom, Decision of 27 September 1990
Stafford v. United Kingdom, Judgment of 28 May 2002

International Criminal Tribunal for the Former Yugoslavia

Prosecutor v. Erdemović,IT-96-21, Appeals Chamber, Judgment of 7 October 1997
Prosecutor v. Aleksovski,IT-95-14/1-A, Appeals Chamber, Judgment of 24 March 2000

United States-Mexico General Claims Commission

Neer v. Mexico, Award of 15 October 1926
Roberts v. Mexico, Award of 2 November 1926

Iran-US Claims Tribunal

Shahin Shaine Ebrahimi et al. v. Iran, Final Award of 12 October 1994

ICSID and ICSID Additional Facilities

Amco I v. Indonesia, ICSID Case No. ARB/81/1, Award of 20 November 1984

Klöckner v. Cameron, ICSID Case No. ARB/81/2, Decision on Annulment of 31 May 1985

Amco Asia Corp, Pan American Development Ltd and PT Amco Indonesia v. Indonesia, ICSID, Award of 31 May 1990

Asian Agricultural Products Ltd v. Sri Lanka, ICSID Case No. ARB/87/3, Award of 21 June 1990

Amco II v. Indonesia, ICSID Case No. ARB/81/1, Award in the Resubmitted Case of 5 June 1990

Robert Azinian v. Mexico, ICSID Case No. ARB(AF)/97/2, Award of 1 November 1999

Metalclad Corporation v. Mexico, ICSID Case No. ARB(AF)/97/11, Award of 30 August 2000

Wena Hotels LTD v. Egypt, ICSID Case No. ARB/98/4, Award of 8 December 2000

Genin et al. v. Estonia, ICSID Case No. ARB/99/2, Award of 25 June 2001

Middle East Cement Shipping and Handling Co.S.A. v. Egypt, ICSID Case No. ARB/99/6, Award of 12 April 2002

Mondev International ltd v. United States, ICSID Case No. ARB(AF)/99/2, Award of 11 October 2002

Técnicas Medioambiente Tecmed S.A. v. Mexico, ICSID Case No. ARB (AF)/00/2, Award of 29 May 2003

Loewen v. United States, ICSID Case No. ARB/98/3, Award of 26 June 2003

Generation Ukraine, Inc v. Ukraine, ICSID Case No. ARB/00/9, Award of 16 September 2003

SGS v. Philippines, ICSID Case No. ARB/02/6, Decision on Jurisdiction of 29 January 2004

Waste Management, Inc. v. Mexico, ICSID Case No. ARB(AF)/00/3, Award of 30 April 2004

MTD Equity v. Chile, ICSID Case No. ARB/01/7, Award of 25 May 2004

Joy Mining Machinery Limited v. Egypt, ICSID Case No. ARB/03/11, Award of 6 August 2004

Noble Ventures. Inc. v. Romania, ICSID Case No. ARB/01/11, Award of 29 March 2005

Camuzzi International S.A. v. Argentina, ICSID Case No. ARB/03/2, Decision on Objections to Jurisdiction of 11 May 2005

CMS Gas Transmission Company v. Argentina, ICSID Case No. ARB/01/8, Award of 12 May 2005

AES v. Argentina, ICSID Case No. ARB/02/17, Decision on Jurisdiction of 17 June 2005

El Paso Energy International Co. v. Argentina, ICSID Case No. ARB/03/15, Decision on Jurisdiction of 27 April 2006

Azurix v. Argentina, ICSID Case No. ARB/01/12, Award of 14 July 2006
Inceysa v. El Salvador, ICSID Case No. ARB/03/26, Award of 2 August 2006
LG&E Energy Corporation v. Argentina, ICSID Case No. ARB/02/1, Award of 3 October 2006
Saipem S.p.a. v. Bangladesh, ICSID Case No. ARB/05/07, Decision on Jurisdiction and Recommendation on Provisional Measure of 21 March 2007
Enron v. Argentina, ICSID Case No. ARB/01/3, Award of 21 May 2007
Parkerings-Compagniet AS v. Lithuania, ICSID Case No. ARB/05/8, Award of 11 September 2007
Sempra Energy International v. Argentina, ICSID Case No. ARB/02/16, Award of 18 September 2007
Victor Pey Casado et al. v. Chile, ICSID Case No. ARB/98/2, Award of 8 May 2008
Rumeli Telekom A.S. et al. v. Kazakhstan, ICSID Case No. ARB/05/16, Award of 29 July 2008
Duke v. Ecuador, ICSID Case No. ARB/04/19, Award of 18 August 2008
Jan de Nul v. Egypt, ICSID Case No. ARB/03/13, Award of 6 November 2008
PSEG v. Turkey, ICSID Case No. ARB/02/04, Award of 19 January 2009
Phonix Action v. Czech Republic, ICSID Case No. ARB/06/5, Award of 15 April 2009
Waguih Elie George Siag and Clorinda Vecchi v. Egypt, ICSID Case No. ARB/05/15, Award of 1 June 2009
Bayindir Insaat Turizim Ticaret ve Sanayi A v. Pakistan, ICSID Case No. ARB/03/29, Award of 27 August 2009
EDF v. Romania, ICSID Case No. ARB/05/13, Award of 8 October 2009
MCI Power Group L.C. and New Turbine Inc. v. Ecuador, ICSID Case No. ARB/03/6, Decision on Annulment of 19 October 2009
Joseph Charles Lemire v. Argentina, ICSID Case No. ARB/06/18, Decision on Jurisdiction and Liability of 14 January 2010
ATA Construction, Industrial and Trading Company v. Jordan, ICSID Case No. ARB/08/02, Award of 18 May 2010
Hamester v. Ghana, ICSID Case No. ARB/07/24, Award of 18 June 2010
Enron Creditors Recovery Corp. Ponderosa Assets L.P. v. Argentina, ICSID Case No. ARB/01/3, Decision on the Application for Annulment of Argentina of 30 July 2010
Suez et al. and *AWG Group v. Argentina*, ICSID Case No. ARB/03/19, Decision on Liability of 30 July 2010
Total S.A. v. Argentina, ICSID Case No. ARB/04/1, Decision on Liability of 27 December 2010
El Paso Energy International Company v. Argentina, ICSID Case No. ARB/03/15, Award of 31 October 2011
Occidental Petroleum Corp., Occidental Exploration and Production Company v. Ecuador, ICSID Case No. ARB/06/11, Award of 5 October 2012

Deutsche Bank AG v. Sri Lanka, ICSID Case No. ARB/09/2, Award of 31 October 2012

Electrabel S.A. v. Hungary, ICSID No. ARB/07/19, Decision on Jurisdiction, Applicable Law and Liability of 30 November 2012

SAUR International S.A. v. Argentina, ICSID Case No. ARB/04/4, Decision on Jurisdiction and Liability of 6 June 2012

Toto Costruzioni SpA v. Lebanon, ICSID Case No. ARB/07/12, Award of 7 June 2012

Iberdrola v. Guatemala, ICSID Case No. ARB/09/15, Award of 17 August 2012

Franck Charles Arif v. Moldova, ICSID Case No. ARB/11/23, Award of 8 April 2013

The Rompetrol Group N.V. v. Romania, ICSID Case No. ARB/06/3, Award of 6 May 2013

Ioana Micula at al. v. Romania, ICSID Case No. ARB/05/20, Final Award of 11 December 2013

Impregilo S.P.A. v. Argentina, ICSID Case No. ARB/07/17, Decision of the *Ad Hoc* Committee on the Application for Annulment of 24 January 2014

Perenco Ecuador Limited v. Ecuador, ICSID Case No. ARB/08/6, Decision on Remanding Issues of Jurisdiction and Liability of 12 September 2014

Gold Reserve Inc. v. Venezuela, ICSID Case No. ARB(AF)/09/1, Award of 22 September 2014

Dan Cake (Portugal) S.A. v. Hungary, ICSID Case No. ARB/12/9, Decision on Jurisdiction and Liability of 24 August 2015

Flughafen Zürich A.G. and Gestión e Ingeniería IDC S.A. v. Venezuela, ICSID Case No. ARB/10/19, Award of 18 November 2014

OI European Group B.V. v. Venezuela, ICSID Case No. ARB/11/25, Award of 10 March 2015

Renée Rose Levy and Gremcitel S.A. v. Peru, ICSID Case No. ARB/11/17, Award of 9 January 2015

Kiliç İnşaat İthalat İhracat Sanayi Ve Ticaret Anonim Şirketi v. Turkmenistan, ICSID Case No. ARB/10/1, Decision on Annulment of 14 July 2015

Ampal-American Israel Corp et al. v. Egypt, ICSID Case No. ARB/12/11, Decision on Jurisdiction of 1 February 2016

Crystallex International Corporation v. Venezuela, ICSID Case No. ARB(AF)/ 11/2, Award of 4 April 2016

Philip Morris et al. v. Uruguay, ICSID Case No. ARB/10/7, Award of 8 July 2016

Rusoro v. Venezuela, ICSID Case No. ARB(AF)/12/5, Award of 22 August 2016

Churchill Mining PLC and Planet Mining Pty Ltd v. Indonesia, ICSID Case No. ARB/12/14 and 12/40, Award of 6 December 2016

Urbaser S.A. et al. v. Argentina, ICSID Case No. ARB/07/26, Award of 8 December 2016

Garanti Koza LLP v. Turkmenistan, ICSID Case No. ARB/11/20, Award of 19 December 2016

UNCITRAL Tribunals

S.D. Myers Inc v. Canada, UNCITRAL (NAFTA), Partial Award of 13 November 2000
Pope and Talbot v. Canada, UNCITRAL (NAFTA), Award on the Merits on Phase 2 of 10 April 2001
Lauder v. Czech Republic, UNCITRAL, Final Award of 3 September 2001
CME Czech Republic B.V. v. Czech Republic, UNCITRAL, Partial Award of 13 September 2001
International Thunderbird Gaming Corporation v. Mexico, UNCITRAL (NAFTA) Arbitration Proceedings, Award of 26 January 2006
Saluka Investments BV v. Czech Republic, UNCITRAL, Partial Award of 17 March 2006
BP Group Plc v. Argentina, UNCITRAL, Award of 24 December 2007
Glamis Gold Ltd. v. United States, UNCITRAL (NAFTA), Award of 8 June 2009
Merrill &Ring Forestry L. P. v. Canada, UNCITRAL (NAFTA), Award of 31 March 2010
Frontier Petroleum Services Ltd v. Czech Republic, UNCITRAL, Final Award of 12 November 2010
Grand River Enterprises Six Nations, Ltd. et al. v. United States, Award of 12 January 2011
Bilcon of Delaware et al v. Canada, UNCITRAL (NAFTA), PCA Case No. 2009-04, Award on Jurisdiction and Liability of 17 March 2015
Flemingo DutyFree v. Poland, UNCITRAL, Award of 12 August 2016
Al-Warraq v. Indonesia, UNCITRAL, Final Award of 15 December 2014

Arbitration Institute of the Stockholm Chamber of Commerce

Petrobart v. Kyrgyzstan, Award of 29 March 2005
Charanne B.V. and Construction Investments S.A.R.L. v. Spain, Award of 21 January 2016

London Court of International Arbitration

Occidental Exploration and Protection Company v. Ecuador, UNCITRAL, Award of 1 July 2004

Other Investor-State Arbitrations

Cotesworth and Powell (Great Britain v. Colombia), Award of 5 November 1875
Robert E. Brown (U.S.) v. Great Britain, Award of 23 November 1923
Texaco v. Libya, Ad Hoc Award of 19 January 1977
Eureko v. Poland, Partial Award of 19 August 2005

Domestic Courts

Canadian Supreme Court, *Regina v. Oakes*, [1986] 1 S.C.R.
Constitutional Court of South Africa, *State v. Makanyane and Another*, 1995 (3) SA 391, 436 (CC)
German Constitutional Court, *Apothekenurteil,* J7 BVerfGE 377, Judgment of 11 June 1958
German Constitutional Court, *Vattenfall*, 1 BvR2821/11, Judgment of 6 December 2016
Italian Supreme Court (United Sections), Judgment of 11 November 1991, No. 12014
Italian Supreme Administrative Tribunal (Section VI), Judgment of 1 April 2000, No. 1885
Italian Constitutional Court, Judgment of 19 November 2012, No. 264
Italian Supreme Court, Judgment of 19 October 2015, No. 21085
UK House of Lords, *Ridge v. Boldwin* [1964] AC 40
US Supreme Court, 397 U.S. 254 (1970)
US Supreme Court, *Payne v. Tennessee*, 501 U.S. 808, 111 S.Ct. 2597 (1991)
US Supreme Court, *Landgraf v. USI Film Products*, 511 U.S. 244, 265–66 (1994)
Wisconsin Supreme Court, *Hoffman v. Red Owl Store* (26 Wis. 2d 683, 133 N.W. 2d 267) (1965)

Bibliography

Abs H, Shawcross H (1960) The Proposed Convention to Protect Foreign Investment: A Round Table: Comment on the Draft Convention by its Authors. Journal of Public Law 9: 115–118

Acconci P (2004) The Requirement of Continuous Nationality and Customary International Rules on Foreign Investments. Italian Yearbook of International law 14:225–236

Alvarez JE (2014) Beware: Boundary Crossings. New York University Public Law & Legal Theory Research Paper Series, Working Paper No. 14–51. Available at http://papers.ssrn.com/sol3/papers.cfm?abstract_id=2498182

Alvik I (2011) Contracting with Sovereignty. State Contracts and International Arbitration. Hart, Oxford

Andenas M, Zleptnig S (2007) Proportionality: WTO Law: in Comparative Perspective. Texas International Law Journal 42:371–427

Anzilotti D (1906) La responsabilité international des États: la raison des dommages soufferts par des étrangers. Revue générale de droit international public 13:5–29

Anzilotti D (1964) Corso di diritto internazionale, vol. I, 4th edn. Cedam, Padua

Atik J (1994–1995) Fairness and Managed Foreign Direct Investment. Columbia Journal of Transnational Law 32: 1–42

Balladore Pallieri G (1962) Diritto internazionale pubblico. Giuffrè, Milan

Barak A (2012) Proportionality. Constitutional Rights and their Limitations. Cambridge University Press, Cambridge

Barak-Erez D (2005) The Doctrine of Legitimate Expectations and the Distinctions between the Reliance and Expectation Interests. European Public Law 11 (4):583–602

Barile P (1983) Lezioni di diritto internazionale, 2nd edn. Cedam, Padua

Bartels LL (2010) *The WTO Enabling Clause*. In Remiche B, Fabri HR (eds) Le commerce international entre bi- et multilatéralisme. Larcier, Paris, pp. 261–277

Battini S (2008) Le due anime del diritto amministrativo globale. In: Il diritto amministrativo oltre i confini. Omaggio degli allievi a Sabino Cassese. Giuffré, Milan, pp. 1–22

Berge GT, Widdershoven R (1998) The Principle of Legitimate Expectations in Dutch Constitutional and Administrative Law. In: Hondius EH (ed) Netherlands Report to the Fifteenth International Congress of Comparative Law. Intersentia, Antwerp, pp 421–452

Bernasconi-Osterwalder N (2016) Giving Arbitrators carte blanche - Fair and Equitable Treatment in Investment Treaties. In: Lim CL (ed) Alternative Visions of the International Law on Foreign Investment. Essays in Honour of Muthucumaraswamy Sornarajah. Cambridge University Press, Cambridge, 324–346

Bifulco R (2001) Articolo 41. In: Bifulco R, Cartabia M, Celotto A (eds) L'Europa dei diritti. Commento alla Carta dei diritti fondamentali dell'Unione europea. Il Mulino, Bologna, pp. 284–293

Bobbio N (1994) Contributo ad un dizionario giuridico. Giappichelli, Turin

Bonnichta J (2015) Substantive Protection under Investments Treaties. A Legal and Economic Analysis. Cambridge University Press, Cambridge

F.M. Palombino, *Fair and Equitable Treatment and the Fabric of General Principles*, https://doi.org/10.1007/978-94-6265-210-1

Borchard E (1940) The 'Minimum Standard' of the Treatment of Aliens. Michigan Law Review 38:445–461

Bosco G (1938) Il fondamento giuridico della valore obbligatorio del diritto internazionale. Rivista di diritto pubblico 30:626–636

Bronfman M (2006) Fair and Equitable Treatment: An Evolving Standard. Max Planck Yearbook of United Nations Law 10:609–680

Brower CH (2003) Structure, Legitimacy and NAFTA's Investment Chapter. Vanderbilt Journal of Transnational Law 36: 37–94

Brown C (2009) The Protection of Legitimate Expectations As a 'General Principle of Law': Some Preliminary Thoughts. Transnational Dispute Management 6 (1):1–10

Bücheler G (2015) Proportionality in Investor-State Arbitration. Oxford University Press, Oxford

Buffoni L (2008) Il rango costituzionale del 'giusto procedimento' e l'archetipo del 'processo'. Forum dei Quaderni costituzionali 2:1–43

Byers M (1999) Custom, Powers and the Power of Rules. International Relations and Customary International Law. Cambridge University Press, Cambridge

Cahier P (1996) Le rôle du juge dans l'élaboration du droit international. In: Makarczyk J (ed) Theory of International Law at the Threshold of the 21st Century: Essays in Honour of Krzystof Skubiszecki. Kluwer Law International, The Hague, pp. 353–365

Cannizzaro E (2000) Il principio della proporzionalità nell'ordinamento internazionale. Giuffré, Milan

Cannizzaro E (2016) Diritto internazionale, 3rd edn. Giappichelli, Turin

Cantegreil J (2011) The Audacity of the Texaco/Calasiatic Award: René-Jean Dupuy and the Internationalization of Foreign Investment Law. European Journal of International Law 22:441–458

Carbone SM (1967) Promessa e affidamento nel diritto internazionale. Giuffrè, Milan

Carbone SM (1975) Promise in International Law: A Confirmation of its Binding Force. The Italian Yearbook of International Law, vol. I:166–172

Cassese A (1995) Self-Determination of Peoples. A Legal Reappraisal. Cambridge University Press, Cambridge

Cassese A (2005) International Law, 2nd edn. Oxford University Press, Oxford

Cassese S (2006) Oltre lo Stato. Laterza, Rome-Bari

Charpentier J (1963) De la non-discrimination dans les investissements. Annuaire français de droit international 9:35–63

Choi WM, Won-Mog YS (2012) Facilitating Preferential Trade Agreements Between Developed and Developing Countries: A Case for 'Enabling' the Enabling Clause. Minnesota Journal of International Law 21: 1–20

Ciciriello MC (1999) Il principio di proporzionalità nell'ordinamento comunitario. Editoriale Scientifica, Naples

Cipriani F (2009) La riforma del giudizio di Cassazione. Cedam, Padua

Ciurtin H (2015) Beyond the Norm: The Hermeneutic Function of Treaty Preambles in Investment Arbitration and International Law. Romanian Arbitration Review 36:64–80

Cognetti S (2011) Principio di proporzionalità. Profili di teoria generale e di analisi sistematica, Giappichelli Editore, Turin

Cohen A, Shany Y (2007) A Development of Modest Proportions. The Application of the Principle of Proportionality in the Targeted Killings Case. Journal of International Criminal Justice 5:310–321

Collins D (2016) An Introduction to International Investment Law. Cambridge University Press, Cambridge

Conforti B (2007) Unité et fragmentation du droit international: 'Glissez, mortels, n'appuyez pas!' Revue générale de droit international public 111:5–18

Conforti B (2015) Diritto internazionale, 10th edn. Editoriale Scientifica, Naples

Conforti B, Labella A (2012) An Introduction to International Law. Nijhoff, Leiden

Cordero Moss GC (2008) Full Protection and Security. In: Reinisch A (ed) Standards of Investment Protection. Oxford University Press, Oxford, pp. 131–150

Coviello PJJ (2004) La protección de la confianza del administrado. Abeledo Perrot, Buenos Aires

Crawford E (2011) Proportionality. Max Planck Encyclopedia of Public International Law. Online Edition. Available at http://opil.ouplaw.com

Crawford J (2012) Brownlie's Principles of Public International Law, 8th edn. Oxford University Press, Oxford

Crawford J (2013) Chance, Order, Change: The Course of International Law. Recueil des Cours 365:9–389

Crivellaro A (2001) La rilevanza dei preamboli nell'interpretazione dei contratti internazionali. Diritto del commercio internazionale 15:777–791

D'Amato A (1988) Custom and Treaty: A Response to Professor Weisburd. Vanderbildt Journal of International Law 21:459–472

D'Aspremont J (2012) International Customary Law: Story of a Paradox. In: Gazzini T, De Brabandere E (eds) International Investment Law. The Sources of Rights and Obligations. Nijhoff, Leiden

Daniele L (2010) Diritto dell'Unione europea. Sistema istituzionale - Ordinamento - Tutela giurisdizionale – Competenze. Giuffrè, Milan

David R, de Vries HP (1958) The French Legal System: An Introduction to Civil Law. Oceana Publications, New York

De Brabandere E (2012) Arbitral Decisions as a Source of International Investment Law. In: Gazzini T, De Brabandere E (eds) International Investment Law. The Sources of Rights and Obligations. Nijhoff, Leiden, 245–288

De Nova R (1956) Considerazioni sulla neutralità permanente dell'Austria. Comunicazioni e Studi 8:1–32

De Visscher C (1935) Le déni de justice en droit international. Recueil des Cours 52:365–442

Dedov D (2014) The Rule of Law and Legal State Doctrines as a Methodology of the Philosophy of Law. In: Silkenat JR, Hickey Jr JE, Barenboim PD (eds) The Legal Doctrines of the Rule of Law and the Legal State (Rechtsstaat). Springer, Heidelberg, pp. 61–70

Degan VD (1970) L'équité e le droit international. Nijhoff, The Hague

Delbrück J (19997) Proportionality. In: Bernhardt R (ed) The Encyclopedia of International Law, vol. III. Elsevier, Amsterdam, pp. 1140–1144

Della Cananea G (2009) Al di là dei confini statuali. Principi generali del diritto pubblico globale. Il Mulino, Bologna

Della Cananea G (2010) Minimum Standards of Procedural Justice in Administrative Adjudication. In: Schill S (ed) International Investment Law and Comparative Public Law. Oxford University Press, Oxford, pp. 39–74

Della Cananea G (2011) The Genesis and Structure of General Principles of Global Public Law. In: Chiti E, Mattarella BG (eds) Global Administrative Law and EU Administrative Law. Relationships, Legal Issues and Comparison. Springer, Heidelberg

De Luca A (2016) Lodo favorevole alla Spagna a conclusione del primo degli investment arbitration sorti da impianti fotovoltaici: un precedente rilevante? (Lodo 21 gennaio 2016). Diritto del commercio internazionale 30:250–275

Desmedt A (2001) Proportionality in WTO Law. Journal of International Economic Law 4:441–480

Di Benedetto S (2013) International Investment Law and the Environment. Edward Elgar, Cheltenham

Diebold NF (2011) Standards of Non-Discrimination in International Economic Law. International and Comparative Law Quarterly 60:831–865

Diehl A (2012) The Core Standard of International Investment Protection. Fair and Equitable Treatment. Wolters Kluwer, Alphen aan den Rijn

Doehring K (2004) Völkerrecht, 2nd edn. Müller, Heidelberg

Dolzer R, Schreurer C (2012) Principles of International Investment Law, 2nd edn. Oxford University Press, Oxford

Dorigo S, Pustorino P (2009) Diritto a una tutela giurisdizionale effettiva e revisione dei processi penali. Diritti umani e diritto internazionale 3:85–110

Dörr O, Schmalebach K (2012) Vienna Convention on the Law of Treaties. Springer, Heidelberg

Douglas Z (2009) The International Law of Investment Claims. Cambridge University Press, Cambridge

Douglas Z (2014) International Responsibility for Domestic Adjudication: Denial of Justice Deconstructed. International and Comparative Law Quarterly (63):867–900

Dumberry P (2013) The Fair and Equitable Treatment Standard: A Guide to NAFTA Case Law on Article 1105. Kluwer Law International, Alphen aan den Rijn

Dumberry P (2016) Has the Fair and Equitable Treatment Standard Become a Rule of Customary International Law? Journal of International Dispute Settlement 7:1–24

Dworkin R (1977) Taking Rights Seriously. Harvard University Press, Harvard

Eckart C (2012) Promises of States under International Law. Hart, Oxford

Falcón y Tella MJ (2008) Equity and Law. Nijhoff, Leiden

Fatouros A A (1962) Government Guarantees to Foreign Investors. Columbia University Press, New York

Fietta S (2005) Most Favoured Nation Treatment and Dispute Resolution under Bilateral Investment Treaties: a Turning Point? International Arbitration Law Review 4:131–138

Fietta S (2006) The "Legitimate Expectations" Principle under Article 1105 NAFTA – International Thunderbird Gaming Corporation v. The United Mexican States. The Journal of World Investment and Trade 7 (3):423–432

Fitzmaurice G (1932) The Meaning of the Term 'Denial of Justice'. British Yearbook of International Law 13:93–114

Focarelli C (2009) Denial of Justice. Max Planck Encyclopedia of Public International Law, Online Edition. Available at http://opil.ouplaw.com

Focarelli C (2015) Trattato di diritto internazionale. UTET, Turin

Forsyth CF (1985) The Provenance and Protection of Legitimate Expectations. Cambridge Law Journal 47 (2):238–260

Francioni F (2007) Equity in International Law. Max Planck Encyclopedia of Public International Law, Online Edition. Available at http://opil.ouplaw.com

Francioni F (2009) Access to Justice, Denial of Justice and International Investment Law. European Journal of International Law 20:729–747

Franck TM (1995) Fairness in International Law and Institutions. Oxford University Press, Oxford

Gaffney JP (1999) Due Process in the World Trade Organization: The Need for Procedural Justice in the Dispute Settlement System. American University International Law Review 14: 1173–1221

Gaja G (2008) General Principles of Law. Max Planck Encyclopedia of Public International Law, Online Edition. Available at http://opil.ouplaw.com

García Cantero G (2007) Le précédent et la loi. In: Hondius E (ed) Precedent and the Law. Bruylant, Brussels, 189–207

Garcìa-Amador F V, Sohn L B, Baxter R R (1974) Recent Codification of the Law of State Responsibility for Injuries to Aliens. Oceana, Dobbs Ferry

Gardam J (1999) Proportionality as a Restraint on the Use of Force. Australian Yearbook of International Law 20:162–173

Gazzini T (2009) General Principles of Law in the Field of Foreign Investments. Journal of World Investment & Trade 10:103–119

Gigante M (2008) Mutamenti nella regolazione dei rapporti giuridici e legittimo affidamento. Tra diritto comunitario e diritto interno. Giuffrè, Milan

Giuliano M (1978) La cooperazione degli Stati e il commercio internazionale. Giuffrè, Milan

Gosalbo-Bono R (2010) The Significance of the Rule of Law and Its Implications for the European Union and the United States. University of Pittsburgh Law Review 72:229–360

Gradoni L (2009) *Regime Failure* nel diritto internazionale. Cedam, Padua
Grellert V (1964) Zusicherung im Beamtenrecht. Uhlig, Bonn
Guastini R (2011) Principi di diritto. Digesto delle discipline privatistiche, Sezione civile, Aggiornamento. Utet, Turin, pp. 645–653
Guillaume G (2011) The Use of Precedent by International Judges and Arbitrators. Journal of International Dispute Settlement 2:5–23
Hachez N (2013) What Elements of the Rule of Law Can Be Put to Use at International Level. Revue Belge du droit international 47:307–324
Hanessian G, Duggal K (2015) The Final 2015 Indian Model BIT: Is This the Change the World Wishes to See? ICSID Review 32:216–226
Happ R (2016) Why Investment Arbitration Contributes to the Rule of Law: Without Knowing Where We Came from We Cannot Know Where We are Heading. European Investment Law and Arbitration Review 1:278–287
Harbo T-I (2015) The Function of the Proportionality Analysis in European Law. Nijhoff, Leiden
Harris C (2001) Precedent in the Practice of the ICTY. In: May R et al. (eds) Essays on ICTY Procedure and Evidence in Honour of Gabrielle Kirk McDonald. Kluwer Law International, The Hague, 341–356
Hatshek J (1923) Völkerrecht als System rechtlich bedeutsamer Staatsakte. Deichert, Leipzig
Haynes J (2014) The Emergence of a Doctrine of *De Jure Horizontal Stare Decisis* at the Caribbean Court of Justice: Fragmentation or Pluralism of International Law? Journal of International Dispute Settlement 5:498–530
Heiskanen V (2008) Arbitrary and Unreasonable Measures. In: Reinisch A (ed) Standards of Investment Protection. Oxford University Press, Oxford, pp. 87–110
Henckels C (2015) Proportionality and Deference in Investor-State Arbitration. Balancing Investment Protection and Regulatory Autonomy. Cambridge University Press, Cambridge
Higgins R (1994) Problems and Process: International Law and How We Use It. Clarendon Press, Oxford
Hilf M, Puth S (2002) The Principle of Proportionality on its Way into WTO/GATT Law. In: Von Bogdandy A, Movroidis PC, Mény Y (eds) European Integration and International Co-ordination: Studies in Transnational Economic Law in Honour of Claus-Dieter Ehlermann. Kluwer Law International, The Hague, pp. 199–218
Hirsch M (2011) Between Fair and Equitable Treatment and Stabilization Clause: Stable Legal Environment and Regulatory Change in International Investment Law. The Journal of World Investment & Trade 12:783–806
Hirsch M (2014) The Sociology of International Law. In: Douglas Z, Pauwelyn J, Viñuales JE (eds) The Foundations of International Investment Law: Bringing Theory into Practice. Oxford University Press, Oxford, pp. 143–167
Hovell D (2016) Due Process in the United Nations. American Journal of International Law 110:1–48
Iovane M (2008) La participation de la société civile à l'élaboration et à l'application du droit international de l'environnement. Revue générale de droit international public 112:465–519
Jacob M, Schill S (2015) Fair and Equitable Treatment: Content, Practice, Method. In: Bungenberg M, Griebel J, Hobe S, Reinisch A (eds) International Investment Law. Beck/Hart/Nomos, Munich/Oxford/Baden-Baden, pp. 700–763
Janis MW (1983) The Ambiguity of Equity in International Law. Brooklyn Journal of International Law, 9: 7–34
Jans JH (2000) Proportionality Revisited. Legal Issue of Economic Integration (27):239–265
Juillard P (1994) L'évolution des sources du droit des investissements. Recueil des Cours 250: 9–216
Kahn P (1968) The Law Applicable to Foreign Investments: The Contribution of the World Bank Convention on the Settlement of Investment Disputes. Indiana Law Journal 44:1–32
Kaufmann-Kohler G (2006) Arbitral Precedent: Dream, Necessity or Excuse? Arbitration International 23:357–378

Kiestra LR (2014) The Impact of the European Convention on Human Rights on Private International Law. TMC Asser Press, The Hague

Kishoiyian B (1993) The Utility of Bilateral Investment Treaties in the Formulation of Customary International law. Northwestern Journal of International Law & Business 14:327–375

Kläger R (2011) 'Fair and Equitable' Treatment in International Investment Law. Cambridge University Press, Cambridge

Kohona PTB (1987) Investment Protection Agreements: An Australian Perspective. Journal of World Trade Law 21:79–103

Kolb R (2006) Principles as Sources of International Law (With Special Reference to Good Faith). Netherlands International Law Review 53 (1):1–36

Kotuby Jr CT (2013) General Principles of Law, International Due Process, and the Modern Role of Private International Law. Duke Journal of Comparative & International Law 23:411–443

Krieger H, Nolte G (2016) The International Rule of Law – Rise or Decline? Points of Departure. KFG Working Papers Series, No 1. Available at SSRN: https://ssrn.com/abstract=2866940

Krueger D (2003) The Combat Zone: Mondev International Ltd v. United States and the Backlash against NAFTA Chapter 11. Boston University International Law Journal 21:399–426

Krug P (2006) Internalizing European Court of Human Rights Interpretations: Russia's Courts of General Jurisdiction and New Directions in Civil Defamation Law. Brooklyn Journal of International Law 32:1–65

Krüger-Sprengel F (1979) Le Concept de proportionalité dans le droit de la guerre. Revue de droit penal militaire et de droit de la guerre 19:177–204

Krugmann M (2004) Der Grundsatz der Verhältnismäßigkeit im Völkerrecht. Duncker & Humblot, Berlin

Lanfranchi F (1968) Il trattamento dello straniero nelle clausole relative allo stabilimento degli accordi bilaterali in vigore tra l'Italia e gli altri Stati. Rivista di diritto internazionale privato e processuale 4:331–350

Leben C (1999) L'évolution du droit international des investissements. In: Dupuy PM, Leben C (eds) Un accord multilateral sur l'investissement: d'un forum de négociation à l'autre? Pedone, Paris, 7–32

Levy T (1995) NAFTA's Provision for Compensation in the Event of Expropriation: A Reassessment of the «Prompt, Adequate and Effective» Standard. Stanford Journal of International Law 31: 423–453

MacCormick DN, Summers RS (1997) Further General Reflections and Conclusions. In: MacCormick, Summers RS (eds) Interpreting Precedents: A Comparative Study. Ashgate, Dartmouth, pp. 531–545

Mani VS (1980) International Adjudication: Procedural Aspects. Nijhoff, The Hague

Mann FA (1981) British Treaties for the Promotion and Protection of Investments. British Yearbook of International Law 52:241–254

Mann FA (1982) The Legal Aspects of Money, 4th edn. Oxford University Press, Oxford

Martin AM (2014) Proportionality: An Addition to the International Centre for the Settlement of Investment Disputes' Fair and Equitable Treatment Standard. Boston College International & Comparative Law Review 37:58–71

Mathis JH (2008) Balancing and Proportionality in US Commerce Clause Cases. Legal Issues of Economic Integration 35:273–282

Mauro MR (2003) Gli accordi bilaterali sulla promozione e la protezione degli investimenti. Giappichelli, Turin

Mauro MR (2011) Investimenti stranieri. Enciclopedia del diritto, Annali. Giuffrè, Milan, pp. 628–665.

Mauro MR (2016) Conflitti di competenza e coordinamento tra fori nel diritto internazionale degli investimenti: *contract claims v. treaty claims*, Diritto del commercio internazionale 30: 725–761

Maynard S (2016) Legitimate Expectations and the Interpretation of the 'Legal Stability Obligation'. European Investment Law and Arbitration Review (1):99–114

McLachlan QC C (2008) Investment Treaties and General International Law. International and Comparative Law Quarterly 57:361–401
McLachlan C, Shore L, Weiniger M (2017) International Investment Arbitration, 2nd edn. Oxford University Press, Oxford
Meldrum DH (2000) Country Risk and Foreign Direct Investment. Business Economic 34:33–40
Meron T (1989) Human Rights and Humanitarian Norms as Customary Law. Clarendon Press, Oxford
Merusi F (2001) Buona fede e affidamento nel diritto pubblico. Dagli anni 'trenta' alla 'alternanza'. Giuffrè, Milan
Merusi F (2006) Affidamento. In: Cassese S (ed) Dizionario di diritto pubblico, vol. I. Giuffrè, Milan, pp. 144–147
Mistelis L (2011) General Principles of Law and Transnational Rules in International Arbitration: An English Perspective. World Arbitration and Mediation Review 5:201–229
Mitchell A D (2007) Proportionality and Remedies in WTO Disputes. European Journal of International Law 17:985–1008
Mo JS (1991) Some Aspects of the Australia-China Investment Protection Treaty. Journal of World Trade Law 25:43–80
Montt S (2012) State Liability in Investment Treaty Arbitration. Global Constitutional and Administrative Law in the BIT Generation. Hart, Oxford
Moore JB (1898) History and Digest of the International Arbitrations to Which the United States Has Been a Party, vol. II. Government Printing Office, Washington
Morelli G (1967) Nozioni di diritto internazionale, 7th edn. Cedam, Padua
Muchlinski P (1995) Multinational Enterprises and the Law. Blackwell, Oxford
Muchlinski P (2008) Policy Issues. In: Muchlinski P et al. (eds) The Oxford Handbook of International Investment Law. Oxford University Press, New York
Newman RA (ed) (1973) Equity in the World's Legal System. A Comparative Study. Bruylant, Brussels
Nigro R (2008) Il margine di apprezzamento e la giurisprudenza della Corte europea dei diritti dell'uomo. Diritti umani e diritto internazionale 2:71–105
Nolte G (2010) Thin or Thick? The Principle of Proportionality and International Humanitarian Law. Law & Ethics of Human Rights 4:244–255
OECD (2004) Fair and Equitable Treatment Standard in International Investment Law, OECD Working Papers on International Investment, 2004/03. OECD Publishing. http://dx.doi.org/10.1787/675702255435
Orakhelashvili A (2008) The Normative Basis of 'Fair and Equitable Treatment': General International Law on Foreign Investment? Archiv des Völkerrechts 46:74–105
Padelletti ML (2003) La tutela della proprietà nella Convenzione europea dei diritti dell'uomo. Giuffré, Milan
Palombino FM (2005) Should Genocide Subsume Crimes Against Humanity? Some Remarks in the Light of the *Krstić* Appeal Judgment. Journal of International Criminal Justice 3:778–789
Palombino FM (2008) Gli effetti della sentenza internazionale nei giudizi interni. Editoriale Scientifica, Naples
Palombino FM (2010) Laicità della Stato ed esposizione del crocifisso nella sentenza della Corte europea dei diritti dell'uomo nel caso *Lautsi*. Rivista di diritto internazionale 93:134–139
Palombino FM (2010) Judicial Economy and Limitation of the Scope of the Decision in International Adjudication. Leiden Journal of International Law 23:909–932
Palombino FM (2011) 'Fair and Equitable Treatment' degli investimenti stranieri e affidamento da atto normative in un recente lodo arbitrale. Diritto del Commercio internazionale 25:836–852
Paparinskis M (2013) The International Minimum Standard and Fair and Equitable Treatment. Oxford University Press, Oxford
Pardolesi P (2009) Promissory estoppel: affidamento e vincolatività della promessa. Cacucci, Bari
Paulsson J (2005) Denial of Justice. Oxford University Press, Oxford

Paulsson J (2010) The Role of Precedent in Investment Arbitration. In: Yannaca-Small K (ed) Arbitration under International Investment Agreements. A Guide to Key Issues. Oxford University Press, Oxford, pp. 699–718

Pech L (2009) The Rule of Law as a Constitutional Principle of the European Union. Jean Monnet Working Paper 04/09. Available at SSRN: https://ssrn.com/abstract=1463242

Pellet A (2013) The Case Law of the ICJ in Investment Arbitration. ICSID Review 28:223–240

Picone P, Ligustro A (2002) Diritto dell'Organizzazione mondiale del commercio. Cedam, Padua

Pino G (2010) Diritti e interpretazione. Il ragionamento giuridico nello Stato costituzionale. Il Mulino, Bologna

Pisillo Mazzeschi R (2002) Book review (reviewing Cannizzaro E (2000) Il principio della proporzionalità nell'ordinamento internazionale). European Journal of International Law 13:1031–1036

Pollard D (2004) The Caribbean Court of Justice: Closing the Circle of Independence. The Caribbean Law Publishing Company Ltd, Kingston

Potestà M (2013) Legitimate Expectations in Investment Treaty Law: Understanding the Roots and the Limits of a Controversial Concept. ICSID Review 28:88–122

Prost M (2012) The Concept of Unity in Public International Law. Hart, Oxford

Quadri R (1936) La sudditanza nel diritto internazionale. Cedam, Padua

Quadri R (1968) Diritto internazionale pubblico, 5th edn. Liguori, Naples

Rawls J (2001) Justice as Fairness: A Restatement. Harvard University Press, Cambridge

Razi GM (1963) Reflections on Equity in the Civil Law Systems. American University Law Review 13:24–44

Reisman M (2015) Canute Confronts the Tide: States versus Tribunals and the Evolution of the Minimum Standard in Customary International Law. ICSID Review 30:616–634

Reisman M, Stevick D (1998) The Applicability of International Law Standards to United Nations Economic Sanctions Programmes. European Journal of International Law 9:86–141

Reisman WM, Sloane RD (2003) Indirect Expropriation and Its Valuation in the BIT Generation. The British Yearbook of International Law 74:115–150

Rose-Ackerman S, Egidy S, Fowkes J (2014) Due Process Lawmaking. Cambridge University Press, Cambridge

Rosenne S (2006) The Law and Practice of the International Court. Nijhoff, Leiden

Rubin AP (1977) The International Legal Effects of Unilateral declarations. American Journal of International Law 71:1–30

Sacerdoti G (1997) Bilateral Treaties and Multilateral Instrument on Investment Protection. Recueil des Cours 269:251–460

Sacerdoti G (2008) The Proliferation of BITs: Conflicts of Treaties, Proceedings and Awards. In: Sauvant KP (ed) Appeals Mechanism in International Investment Disputes. Oxford University Press, Oxford, pp. 127–136

Sacerdoti G (2011) Precedent in the Settlement of International Economic Disputes: The WTO and Investment Arbitration Models. Bocconi Legal Studies Research Paper No. 1931560. Available at http://ssrn.com/abstract=1931560

Sacerdoti G (2011) Nascita, affermazione e scomparsa del Nuovo Ordine Economico Internazionale: Un bilancio trent'anni dopo. In: Ligustro A, Sacerdoti G (eds) Problemi e tendenze del diritto internazionale dell'economia. *Liber amicorum* in onore di Paolo Picone. Editoriale Scientifica, Naples, pp. 127–152

Salacuse JW (2010) The Emerging Global Regime for Investment. Harvard International Law Journal 51:427–473

Salmond JW (1924) Jurisprudence. Sweet & Maxwell, London

Santulli C (2015) Le traitement juste et equitable: stipulation particuliere ou principe generale de bonne conduit? Revue Générale de Droit International Public 119:69–85

Sapienza R (1991) Sul margine di apprezzamento statale nel sistema della Convenzione europea dei diritti dell'uomo. Rivista di diritto internazionale 74:571–614

Savarese E (2011) Treaty-Based Investment Arbitration and the MFN Clause: The Possible Common Denominator between Jurisdiction and Admissibility. Italian Yearbook of International Law 21:241–257
Savarese E (2012) La nozione di giurisdizione nel sistema ICSID. Editoriale Scientifica, Naples
Schachter O (1984) Compensation for Expropriation. American Journal of International Law 78:121–130
Schernbeck A (2013) Der Fair and Equitable Treatment Standard in Internationalen Investitionsschutzabkommen. Nomos, Baden-Baden
Schill S (2009) The Multilateralization of International Investment Law. Cambridge University Press, Cambridge
Schill S (2010) Fair and Equitable Treatment, the Rule of Law, and Comparative Public Law. In: Schill S (ed) International Investment Law and Comparative Public Law. Oxford University Press, Oxford, pp. 151–182
Schill S (2012) General Principles of Law and International Investment Law. In: Gazzini T, De Brabandere E (eds) International Investment Law. The Sources of Rights and Obligations. Nijhoff, Leiden, pp. 133–181
Schreuer C (1996) Decisions Ex Aequo et Bono Under the ICSID Convention. ICSID Review 11: 3–63
Schreuer C (2005) Fair and Equitable Treatment in Arbitral Practice. Journal of World Investment and Trade 6:357–386
Schreuer C (2007) Fair and Equitable Treatment (FET): Interactions with other Standards. Transnational Dispute Management 5. Available at www.transnational-dispute-management.com
Schreuer C (2007) Fair and Equitable Treatment in Investment Treaty Law. In: Ortino F, Liberty L, Sheppard A, Warner H (eds) Investment Treaty Law - Current Issues II. British Institute of International and Comparative Law, London, pp. 92–96
Schreuer C (2008) A Doctrine of Precedent? In: Muchlinski P, Ortino F, Schreuer C (eds) The Oxford Handbook of International Investment Law. Oxford University Press, Oxford, pp. 1188–1206
Schreuer C (2008) Introduction: Interrelationship of Standards. In: Reinisch A (ed) Standard of Investment Protection. Oxford University Press, Oxford, 1–7
Schreuer C (2010) Full Protection and Security. Journal of International Dispute Settlement 1:353–369
Schreuer C (2014) Victor Pey Casado and President Allende Foundation v Republic of Chile. ICSID Review 2014 29:321–327
Schreuer C, Malintoppi L, Reinisch A, Sinclair A (2009) The ICSID Convention: A Commentary, 2nd edn. Oxford University Press, Oxford
Schultz T (2014) Against Consistency in Investment Arbitration. In: Douglas Z, Pauwelyn J, Viñuales JE (eds) The Foundations of International Investment Law: Bringing Theory into Practice. Oxford University Press, Oxford, pp. 297–316
Schwarzenberger G (1960) The Abs-Shawcross Draft Convention on Investment Abroad: A Critical Commentary. Journal of Public Law 9:147–171
Sellers MNS (2007) The Doctrine of Precedent in the United States of America. In: Hondius E (ed) Precedent and the Law. Bruylant, Brussels, pp. 111–135
Sereni AP (1962) Diritto internazionale, vol. III. Giuffrè, Milan
Sereni AP (1956) Studi di diritto comparato. Giuffrè, Milan
Shahabuddeen M (1996) Precedent in the World Court, Cambridge University Press, Cambridge
Shahabuddeen M (1999) Consistency in the Case Law of the ICTY. In: Venturini G, Bariatti S (eds) Liber Fausto Pocar, vol. I. Giuffrè, Milan, pp. 899–911
Shawcross HW (1961) Le problème de investissements à l'étranger en droit international. Recueil des Cours 102:365–393
Shihata IFI (1993) Legal Treatment of Foreign Investments: 'The World Bank Guidelines'. Nijhoff, Dordrecht

Snodgrass E (2006) Protecting Investors' Legitimate Expectations: Recognizing and Delimiting a General Principle. ICSID Review 21 (1): 1–58

Sornarajah M (2010) The International Law on Foreign Investment, 3rd edn. Cambridge University Press, Cambridge

Sourgens FG (2014) Law's Laboratory: Developing International Law on Investment Protection as Common Law. Northwestern Journal of International Law & Business 34:181–247

Stamberger JL (2003) The Legality of Conditional Preferences to Developing Countries under the GATT Enabling Clause. Chicago Journal of International Law 4: 607–618

Stone Sweet A, Della Cananea G (2014) Proportionality, General Principles of Law, and Investor-State Arbitration: A Response to José Alvarez. NYU Journal of International Law and Politics 46: 911–54

Stone Sweet A, Mathews J (2008) Proportionality Balancing and Global Constitutionalism. Faculty Scholarship Series. Paper 1296. http://digitalcommons.law.yale.edu/fss_papers/1296

Story J (1846) Commentaries on Equity Jurisprudence as Administered in England and America, Vol. I, 4th edn. Maxwell, Edinburgh-Dublin

Strozzi G (1992) I 'Principi' dell'ordinamento internazionale. La Comunità internazionale 47:162–187

Strupp K (1925) Rechts- und Justizverweigerung, Rechtsverzögerung. In: Hatschek J, Strupp K (eds) Wörterbuch des Völkerrechts und der Diplomatie, Vol. II. De Gruyter, Berlin, pp. 340–341

Subedi SP (2008) International Investment Law. Reconciling Policy and Principle. Hart, Oxford

Taruffo M (2007) Precedente e giurisprudenza, Editoriale Scientifica, Naples

Taruffo M (2007) Precedents in Italy. In: Hondius E (ed) Precedent and the Law. Bruylant, Brussels, pp. 177–188

Téllez FM (2012) Conditions and Criteria for The Protection of Legitimate Expectations Under International Investment Law. ICSID Review 27:432–442

Ten Cate IM (2013) The Costs of Consistency: Precedent in Investment Treaty Arbitration. Columbia Journal of Transnational Law 51:418–478

Titi A (2014) The Right to Regulate in International Investment Law. Nomos/Dike/Hart, Baden-Baden/Zürich/St. Gallen/Oxford

Thomas JC (2002) Reflections on Article 1105 of NAFTA: History, State Practice and the Influence of Commentators. ICSID Review 17:21–101

Treves T (2005) Diritto internazionale. Problemi fondamentali. Giuffré, Milan

Treves T (2012) Customary International Law. Max Planck Encyclopedia of Public International Law, Online Edition. Available at http://opil.ouplaw.com

Tudor I (2008) The Fair and Equitable Treatment Standard in the International Law of Foreign Investment. Oxford University Press, Oxford

UNCTAD (1999) Fair and Equitable Treatment. Series on Issues in International Investment Agreements. United Nations, New York/Geneva

UNCTAD (2012) Fair and Equitable Treatment. UNCTAD Series on Issues in International Investment Agreements II. A Sequel. United Nations, New York-Geneva, 2012

Valenti M (2014) The Protection of General Interests of Host States in the Application of the Fair and Equitable Treatment Standard. In: Sacerdoti G, Acconci P, Valenti M, De Luca A (eds) General Interests of Host States in International Investment Law. Cambridge University Press, Cambridge, pp. 26–57

Vandevelde KJ (1988) The Bilateral Investment Treaty Program of the United States. Cornell International Law Journal 21: 201–276

Verdross A (1931) Les règles internationales concernant le traitement des étrangers. Recueil des Cours 37:323–412

Vicente MO (2013) Princípio da protecção da confiança como garantia dinâmica. In: Tavares da Silva S, de Fátima Ribeiro M (eds) Trajéctorias de Sustentabilida de Tributação e Investimento. Istituto Jurídico da Faculdade de Direito da Universidad de Coimbra, Coimbra, pp 153–207

Villamena S (2008) Contributo in tema di proporzionalità amministrativa. Ordinamento comunitario, italiano e inglese. Giuffrè, Milan
Vitanyi B (1982) Le positions doctrinales concernant le sens de la notion de 'principles généraux de droit reconnus par le nations civilisées'. Revue générale de droit international public 86: 46–116
Vos JA (2013) The Function of Public International Law. TMC Asser Press, The Hague
Wälde T, Kolo A (2001) Environmental Regulation, Investment Protection and Regulatory Taking in International Law. International and Comparative Law Quarterly 50 (4):811–848
Wallace D (2005) Fair and Equitable Treatment and Denial of Justice: Loewen v US and Chattin v Mexico. In: Weiler T (ed) International Investment Law and Arbitration. Cameron May, London, pp. 669–700
Walter AV (2008) The Investor's Expectations in International Investment Arbitration. In: Reinisch A, Knahr C (eds) International Investment Law in Context. Eleven International Publishing, The Hague, pp. 173–200
Wanyama E (2015) The Impact of the Calvo Doctrine on the Principles of Protection of Foreign Nationals in the Area of Investment. Nalsar International Law Journal 1: 78–96
Watts A (1994) The International Rule of Law. German Yearbook of International Law 36:15–45
Weber M (1922) Wirtschaft und Geselschaft. Mohr, Tubingen
Weeramantry JR (2012) Treaty Interpretation in Investment Arbitration. Oxford University Press, Oxford
Weiler T (2013) The Interpretation of International Investment Law. Equality, Discrimination and Minimum Standards of Treatment in Historical Context. Nijhoff, Leiden
Whiteman MM (1963–1973) Digest of International Law. Department of State Publication, Washington
Whittaker S (2007) Precedent in English Law: A View from the Citadel. In: Hondius E (ed) Precedent and the Law. Bruylant, Brussels, pp. 27–73
Wildhaber L (2000) Precedent in the European Court of Human Rights. In: Mahoney P, Matscher F, Petzold H (eds) Protecting Human Rights: The European Perspective: Studies in Memory of Rolv Ryssdal. Carl Heymann, Cologne, 1529–1545
Xiuli H (2007) The Application of the Principle of Proportionality in Tecmed v. Mexico. Chinese Journal of International Law 6:635–652
Youssef K (2012) The Present – Commercial Arbitration as a Transnational System of Justice: Universal Arbitration Between Freedom and Constraint: The Challenges of Jurisdiction in Multiparty, Multi-Contract Arbitration. In Van den Berg AJ (ed) The Next Fifty Years, Vol. 16. Kluwer Law International, Alphen aan den Rijn
Yusuf AA (1980) Differential and More Favourable Treatment. The GATT Enabling Clause. World Trade Law 14: 488–508
Zarra G (2016) Parallel Proceedings in Investment Arbitration. Giappichelli/Eleven, Turin/The Hague
Zeyl T (2011) Charting the Wrong Course: The Doctrine of Legitimate Expectations in Investment Treaty Law. Alberta Law Review 49:203–236
Ziegler AR, Baumgartner J (2015) Good Faith as a General Principle of (International Law). In: Mitchell AD, Sornarajah M and Voon T (eds) Good Faith and International Economic Law. Oxford University Press, Oxford, pp. 10–37
Zolo D (2007) The Rule of Law: A Critical Reappraisal. In: Costa P, Zolo D (eds) The Rule of Law. History, Theory and Criticism. Springer, Heidelberg, pp. 3–71

Index

F.M. Palombino, *Fair and Equitable Treatment and the Fabric of General Principles*, https://doi.org/10.1007/978-94-6265-210-1

MIX
Papier aus verantwortungsvollen Quellen
Paper from responsible sources
FSC® C105338

If you have any concerns about our products,
you can contact us on
ProductSafety@springernature.com

In case Publisher is established outside the EU,
the EU authorized representative is:
Springer Nature Customer Service Center GmbH
Europaplatz 3, 69115 Heidelberg, Germany

Printed by Libri Plureos GmbH
in Hamburg, Germany